What's Jewish about Butterflies?

36 dynamic, engaging lessons for the early childhood classroom

MAXINE SEGAL HANDELMAN
AND DEBORAH L. SCHEIN

A.R.E. Publishing, Inc.
Denver, Colorado

COVER ARTWORK

The stunning photograph of an Israeli Monarch butterfly that appears on the cover was taken by Oz Rittner, an Israeli naturalist and a breeder, collector, and photographer of butterflies and beetles. Oz also lectures on insects throughout Israel and has appeared with his live insects on Israeli television. Born in Rishon-Lezion, Israel, he is currently a graduate student of Eastern Studies and Religious Studies at Tel Aviv University. He is at work on a field guide to the beetles of Israel in collaboration with Tel Aviv University, and maintains *Oz's Insect World,* an on-line field guide to Israel's insects, butterflies, moths, and other small creatures that can be seen at http://www.nature-of-oz.com.

Published by:
A.R.E. Publishing, Inc.
Denver, Colorado
www.arepublish.com

Library of Congress Catalog Number 2004109003
ISBN 0-86705-085-3

A.R.E. Publishing, Inc. 2004

Printed in the United States of America
10 9 8 7 6 5 4 3 2 1

Dedication

Thank you, Jacob. You make the what's Jewish about my life full of joy.
— Max

To my Jeffrey, who has helped me to develop, sharpen, and understand what is Jewish about life. And in memory of my sister Marsha, who always reminded me that life is full of potential.
— D.S.

Acknowledgements

This book could not have been written without the support and suggestions of many people. We would like to thank our publisher, Steve Brodsky, for his continued support and understanding. We would also like to thank Rivka Behar, Ariella Lapidot, Cheryl Meskin, Uri Neil, Avital Plan, Frieda Robins, Lifsa Schachter, Edna Schrank, Bonnie Shapiro, Karen Shiffman, Linda Silver, Rachel Talmor, Susan Remick Topek, and Ilene Vogelstein for their review, suggestions, and advice, without which this book would not have been nearly as rich. Further, Neil, Leila, Jacob, Ariana, and Yael Handelman and Jeffrey, Benjamin, Jonah, and Hana Schein must be thanked profusely for their professional advice, supportive backrubs, and all around general cheerleading while we were writing this book. Additionally, to Yael, thank you for not being born early and for being an amazing sleeper as a newborn!

Table of Contents

Part IV: All about Me

Part V: Popular Children's Books and Authors

Introduction

Bringing What's Jewish about Butterflies? to Life or How to Use this Book

As Jewish early childhood teachers, we have many goals for the children and families we work with every day. We want our children to develop into confident, curious, adventurous learners with a strong sense of who they are, firmly grounded in a Jewish context. We want to help our families travel along their own Jewish journey, finding joy and fulfillment in the Jewish life that emerges from their child's experience in our school. When Judaism is integrated into our early childhood classrooms in a natural, daily way, we are better able to provide an environment and an educational experience which will help each child and family begin to build the foundation of a strong, positive Jewish identity.

While working for the Jewish Community Centers of Chicago, I encouraged teachers to think about "What's Jewish" with regard to everything they taught. One day, I walked into a classroom where the teachers and their three-year-old children were gathered on the rug around a box of butterflies that had recently emerged from chrysalises. The teachers saw me and said, "Okay Max, tell us, what's Jewish about butterflies?" Thus the idea for this book was born. The "What's Jewish about..." tool is designed to help teachers integrate "Jewish" into everything that happens in the classroom, no matter what the theme or unit.

The concept and format of this book were heavily influenced by the *Machon L'Morim: Bereshit* Curriculum. Its funders and developers, the Children of Harvey and Lyn Meyerhoff Philanthropic Fund, were pioneers in changing the face of Jewish early childhood education, and we are proud to be furthering this endeavor.

One of the most important ways to ensure that children are excited and invested in their own learning is by eliciting areas of learning from children and from what's going on in children's lives. Learning is engaging, and lasting, when it is relevant and vibrant, and when children can be leaders and partners in their own learning. This suggests that a teacher *not* pick up a book like *What's Jewish about Butterflies?* or any other book of themes for early childhood, and simply map out the year from what themes in the book pique her interest. Rather, in the life of the classroom, as children's interests or lives turn to look at colors, or classroom jobs, or soup, or frogs, *What's Jewish about Butterflies?* becomes a tool to enhance and enrich the topic of study at hand. Themes like the ones in this book are merely vehicles for allowing curriculum to emerge and grow with the members of the classroom. Learning that is truly relevant to children produces the richest results.

There are many tasks involved in reaching the goals we set out for our children and ourselves. Contained in this book are Jewish overlays, strategies for integrating Jewish content into thirty-six different theme units that might be part of a Jewish early childhood classroom. These overlays will help with the task of integrating Jewish content and values into the daily life of the classroom. The elements of the "What's Jewish about..." tool can be used to enhance any classroom within an emergent, developmentally appropriate framework.

The Themes

In *What's Jewish about Butterflies?* we have chosen themes and units that most often appear in the typical early childhood classroom, Jewish or otherwise. The themes are broken up into five categories: Food, Animals, The World Around, All about Me, and Popular Children's Books and Authors. This last category deserves a special note. In this category are four units, and while each unit approaches children's literature from a different angle, they all maintain a common goal. Jewish values are all around, even in secular books. When we highlight Jewish values for our children even when we are reading secular books, we enable our children to see the world through Jewish eyes. When the books of Denise Fleming can teach us about *Tikkun Olam*, or when Goldilocks can teach us about *Teshuvah*, we can then begin to see the Jewish lessons in everything around us. These four units are just examples of how to draw Jewish values out of the popular children's literature we share with our children every day. It is our hope that after using these units, teachers will be able to find "what's Jewish" about other books that they read to their children as well.

The Big Idea

What's the Big Idea? When we take a step back to look at the whole picture — building Jewish identity, not only "what am I doing in my classroom this week?" — we can see that everything we do in our classrooms, every theme we explore with our children, fits into a larger concept or idea which is foundational to creating Jewish atmosphere and building Jewish identity. Grant Wiggins and Jay McTighe, in their book, *Understanding by Design*, call these big ideas "enduring understandings." Enduring understandings are the big ideas that remain with us when all the little details disappear from our memories. Many of us approach curriculum through "activity-based teaching" — we teach different aspects of a topic by assembling a wide range of fun, hands-on, experiential activities. For example, for a unit on the senses, we might create smell jars for children to sniff, cook new things for children to taste, blindfold the children and have them lead each other around, make a chart of the children's eye colors, and paint outlines of the children's hands. In such a unit there is no real depth. Wiggins and McTighe write that with this kind of unit, "there is no enduring learning for the students to derive. The work is hands-on without being 'minds-on,' because students do not have to extract sophisticated ideas."[1] Nachama Skolnik Moskowitz, in *The Ultimate Jewish Teachers Handbook*, writes, "we must pay attention to the difference between what we think is important and what is meaningful to our students."[2] Ultimately, what is meaningful are the large concepts, patterns, and themes that weave through and support the entire curriculum. Torah, God, Israel, Jewish Time, Jewish Space, Mitzvot, and Jewish behaviors — these overarching ideas encompass all the smaller themes and activities that make up the daily fabric of our classroom lives. When a unit is built upon a well-crafted big idea, as opposed to a finite goal or objective, there is a richness of learning that is then threaded throughout all the learning activities. Big ideas lead to enduring understandings because there is purpose and lifelong insight embedded in these larger concepts, especially these big ideas of Judaism.

But sometimes it is hard to make those connections. The Big Idea section of the "What's Jewish about..." tool helps teachers see how the themes they choose to explore with their children support the whole of the Jewish life they are striving to create. For example, a big idea of exploring the senses is that every sensory experience increases our ability to appreciate the wonder of the world and God's creations all around us. Crafting a unit around this enduring understanding will lead teachers to create a unit about senses with an eye toward helping children discover how their senses connect them to the world created by God, rather than just discovering disparate facts about their senses (Eyes can see. With my nose I can tell the difference between the smell of flowers and the smell of cinnamon). If we take the time to look deep enough, we will see that any theme becomes richer, more relevant, and can lead to enduring Jewish understandings. A unit on soup can lead to great insights on how we live in Jewish time. Dinosaurs lead us to consider how God created the world.

Teachers can:
➤ Use the big idea to expand their own understanding of how their daily work builds the bigger picture.
➤ Discuss the big idea of each unit with colleagues, in order for each teacher to deepen his or her understanding of Judaism.
➤ Organize the themes they choose to explore with children around central big ideas, i.e. focus the first half of the year on themes that support the big idea of God and how God created the world.

Jewish Values

Jewish values are in action in our classrooms all the time, but most of us need help recognizing everyday events in our classroom as Jewish moments. *What's*

---

[1] Grant Wiggins and Jay McTighe, *Understanding By Design* (Alexandria, VA: Association for Supervision and Curriculum Design, 1998), 21.

[2] Nachama Skolnik Moskowitz, ed., *The Ultimate Jewish Teachers Handbook* (Denver: A.R.E. Publishing, Inc. 2003), 5.

Jewish about Butterflies? highlights some of the most common, relevant-to-early-childhood values that could be associated with each theme. Along with each value is a list of activities that bring specific values to life. While some of the activities don't seem like "Jewish" activities, a related value is indicated for each activity, demonstrating the fact that we are engaged in Jewish values almost all the time. At the end of this book is an appendix defining and elaborating on the close to fifty values that emerge from the units in this book.

Teachers can:

➤ Read the list of Jewish values for each theme, to become more aware of the Jewish aspects of what is happening in the classroom.

➤ See the Appendix for a deeper understanding of each value.

➤ Make children aware of the "Jewishness" of the things they are doing, by telling children, for example, "You know, taking care of our pet guinea pig is a Jewish thing to do."

➤ Using the examples in the list of activities and the related values, relate other activities they do to the highlighted values (i.e. having a pet in the classroom which children help care for brings to life the values of *Tza'ar Ba'alay Chayim*/ Kindness to Animals and *G'milut Chasadim*/Acts of Loving-kindness).

Israel Connection

One of the key elements of the foundation of Jewish identity that we are building in the early years is a love for and connection to the State of Israel. This is a challenging task, as the concepts related to Israel, such as "country," "distance," and different culture are not as concrete as most of the things we find developmentally appropriate for the young children we teach. In *What's Jewish about Butterflies?* we attempt to make Israel as real and relevant as possible, by highlighting aspects of Israeli life and culture that expand the theme at hand. For example, the Israel Connection section in the Butterflies unit provides web sites of butterflies that exist in Israel. The Trees unit provides information about some of the trees in Israel and a way for children to plant trees in Israel. Each Israel Connection section contains information about the unit as it relates to Israel as well as some suggestions of classroom activities that will help your children better connect to Israel.

Teachers can:

➤ Explore the web sites and resources provided in the Israel Connection section in order to become more familiar with how the theme at hand relates to Israel.

➤ Engage the children in the suggested activities, so that Israel becomes a familiar concept to children, woven into everything that happens in the classroom throughout the year.

➤ Jump at any opportunity to visit Israel. The best way to instill in young children a love for Israel is to share Israel from firsthand experience.

Hebrew Vocabulary

The Hebrew language is an integral part of Jewish culture. Hebrew connects us to Israel, to the Torah, to other Jewish texts, and to Jews around the world. Weaving Hebrew into every day helps children become comfortable with Hebrew as a matter-of-fact part of their lives, and excited about the skill of knowing another language. Learning a second language also helps build new connections in children's brains, boosting a child's brainpower, vocabulary and self-esteem.

What's Jewish about Butterflies? provides enough Hebrew resources to establish an entry point for any teacher. While it is beyond the scope of this book to provide the resources necessary to learn or teach Hebrew as a second language, current research provides us with some guidelines for using the resources that are provided here in the best way. Hebrew is a language, with structure and rhythm, not just a collection of vocabulary words. Young children are exposed to so many new words every day, that individual Hebrew words sprinkled into the general classroom environment might be absorbed simply as new words, not Hebrew words. This leads to moments like a child asking, "How do you say 'Shabbat' in Hebrew?" To help children become accustomed to the structure of Hebrew, whenever possible, children should be introduced to natural chunks of Hebrew rather than individual words ("*Atah rotzeh tapuach*?" rather than "Would you like a *tapuach* [apple]?") Current research also warns against linguistic transfer, or blending of Hebrew and English in the same sentence. This can cause confusion in understanding the structure and rhythm of both languages. It is better to use complete phrases in Hebrew. Fortunately, often two words in Hebrew are all that's needed to get the idea across ("*Sheket, b'vakasha!*" means "Be quiet, please."). Children should be introduced to Hebrew in natural, fun ways that mimic the way children learn their first language, using strategies such as repetition and social interactions like at snack time and through music. Several Hebrew immersion programs exist, which illustrate methods for introducing Hebrew to children. A program called *Im Kol haGoof* ("With the Whole Body") has been developed by Lifsa Schachter of the Siegal College of Judaic Studies in Cleveland, and Frieda Robins of the Melton Research Center for Jewish Education at the Jewish Theological Seminary recently launched a program called *Ma'alah,* training Hebrew speaking Jewish early childhood educators at preschools across the continent. (For more information, contact Lifsa Schachter at lschachter@siegalcollege.edu, or Frieda Robins at frrobins@jtsa.edu.)

Given these guidelines, what are the best ways to use the Hebrew lists of words and phrases in each unit of *What's Jewish about Butterflies?* Every teacher comes to the classroom with a different level of Hebrew ability. While it may be possible for some teachers to easily integrate whole phrases and songs in Hebrew, other teachers may find it a challenge to learn two or three new Hebrew words for each unit. Every teacher should strive to incorporate as much Hebrew as she or he can, focusing on repetition and integrating the Hebrew into the natural rhythms of the

אַתָּה רוֹצֶה תַּפּוּחַ?

classroom. Phrases such as *boker tov* (good morning) or *z'man l'sa-der* (time to clean up) are simple ways to integrate Hebrew language into the everyday rhythm of the classroom. If a teacher incorporates a few Hebrew nouns and phrases into every unit, children gain crucial exposure and mastery, and we begin to lay the foundation for a lifelong engagement with the Hebrew language. Certainly, teachers with strong Hebrew skills should use these to a larger extent in their classrooms, going beyond a few nouns and phrases to utilizing songs, books, and simple conversations in Hebrew with children on a daily basis. Every teacher should make an effort to continually increase his or her own Hebrew skills.

Every vocabulary word and phrase in *What's Jewish about Butterflies?* has been provided both in Hebrew and in transliteration (Hebrew words spelled out phonetically in English letters). The sounds and inflections of Hebrew are quite different from English, so teachers should take time to familiarize themselves with the Guide to Hebrew Pronunciation found on page 259 of this book. The accenting of syllables is also important in Hebrew pronunciation, so we have shown in bold print the syllable to be accented. With a little practice, you'll be speaking Hebrew like an Israeli in no time!

Teachers can:

➤ Pick two or three phrases to "own," to try and use all the time, instead of the English equivalent.
➤ Look for opportunities to integrate Hebrew into games, songs, books, and daily routines.
➤ Help children use Hebrew in their interactions with each other, such as greeting each other "*shalom*" or "*boker tov.*"

Songs and Poems

Music is a natural teaching tool with young children. Many of the concepts we explore with young children are best reinforced through the repetition and rhythm of songs, poems, finger plays, and chants.

In *What's Jewish about Butterflies?* you will find several "piggy back" songs (new words to familiar melodies such as "Row, Row, Row Your Boat") written to include Jewish concepts and values. Many original poems have been included in *What's Jewish about Butterflies?* as well as many songs from the growing body of North American English and Hebrew Jewish children's music.

Israeli culture holds dear its basic collection of children's music and stories. The book and recording of *100 Shirim Rishonim* (100 First Songs) can be found, tattered and well used, in just about every Israeli household where there were ever children. While new Israeli children's music is being produced all the time, simple Hebrew songs covering just about every theme from this classic lexicon of music trip off the tongue of any Israeli. Many of those songs are in this book. We invite you to bring Hebrew and Israeli culture into your classroom by singing and dancing to these songs with your children. You may also choose to use these songs by singing one or two lines (or the chorus) in Hebrew, with the rest of the song translated.

Current literature on language acquisition cautions against linguistic transfer, the blending of two languages in the same sentence. Linguistic transfer causes confusion. In *What's Jewish about Butterflies*, you will find only a few examples of "Hebrish" songs — Hebrew and English mixed together in the same sentence. (In the spider chapter, for example, you will find a simple Hebrew translation of the Itsy-Bitsy Spider rather than the Hebrish version "The Itsy-Bitsy Akavish.") Using complete Hebrew sentences helps children learn the structure of Hebrew and not just individual vocabulary words.

In the bibliography at the end of this book, there is a list of general Jewish recordings for children that go far beyond music for the holidays. Be sure to have many of these selections in your classroom. More music resources are suggested with each unit. We have made every attempt to include print and/or recorded resources for all the songs we list in this book, so teachers can easily access the music.

Teachers can:

➤ Work with children to weave Jewish concepts and values into familiar tunes by substituting Jewish concepts (i.e. "There's a dinosaur knocking at my door and he wants to have Shabbat with me")

➤ Seek out Israeli music sources when provided, and sing and play these songs with children.

➤ Dance to related Israeli music, even if you do not know the "real" dance steps. Moving around, and in and out of, a circle to the music works well too.

➤ Make up original poems with children integrating Jewish concepts and the theme at hand.

Blessings

Rabbi David Wolpe teaches about being a "normal mystic," someone who constantly sees the closeness of God reflected in the world around him or her. We can help children become normal mystics, and begin to build the foundation of their own relationship with God, by acknowledging God-like or awe-inspiring moments as they happen. One way to do this is by saying a blessing. In *What's Jewish about Butterflies?* you will find traditional blessings written in Hebrew, English, and transliteration. In many units, you will also find suggestions for a *bracha sheh b'lev*, a prayer of the heart. This acknowledges that while we may not always have Hebrew words or blessings ready at our fingertips, it is often possible, and desirable, to acknowledge an awe-filled moment by making a connection to God.

Teachers can:

➤ Become more aware of awe-inspiring moments (a flowering tree, freeing butterflies, etc.) by stopping to take notice.

➤ Bring these moments to the children's attention ("Look at that tree! Let's stop and smell the flowers" "Be very quiet so we don't scare the butterflies. Let's see where they fly as they start a new life.")

➤ Say a blessing appropriate to the moment, or say a *bracha sheh b'lev* such as, "Thank you, God, for this beautiful tree."

➤ With older children, use blessings as a way to discuss why we give thanks to God for these special moments and sights.

Story

Judaism is a religion and culture based on stories. There is a Jewish story for every aspect of life and every theme under the sun. When we share a Jewish story with our children, we are sharing the foundation of being Jewish. Stories help illustrate Jewish values in action, both in Midrashic stories and close-to-home scenarios. Discussion questions and suggestions at the end of each story help teachers revisit some of the salient points with children, and will hopefully serve to open up larger discussions.

Teachers can:
➤ Read the story to the children, and then invite the children to draw pictures to go along with the story.
➤ Tell the story using felt board pieces or puppets.
➤ Invite the children to act out the story, and perhaps to create props to go along with their reenactment.
➤ Send the story home to the families so parents can share the story and see what is Jewish about everything we do in our classrooms.
➤ With the children, seek out the Jewish values in the story.
➤ Explore the discussion questions with children, adapting for different ages and using the questions to facilitate broader discussions.

Resources

At the end of each section is a list of resources. This section may contain helpful Web sites (although there are Web site suggestions throughout each unit as well), adult resource books, music resources, Jewish children's books relevant to the topic, and occasional secular children's books that especially highlight Jewish values or concepts which emerge from the theme.

Teachers can:
➤ Use the resources to do further research into what's Jewish about the theme, either in books or online.
➤ Add Jewish books and music to the theme to make the Jewish connections concrete and apparent.

We hope you enjoy using *What's Jewish about Butterflies?* and would love to hear your feedback. Please write to us at info@arepublish.com and let us know which elements were the most helpful and what you could use more of. We would also love your suggestions for themes or units that you would like to see in possible future volumes of *What's Jewish about...?*

Maxine Segal Handelman and Deborah Schein
March 2004

Part I: Food

1. What's Jewish about Apples?

Many children enjoy eating apples and almost all children love applesauce. Apples come in a variety of colors, with a variety of names, such as Golden Delicious, Jonathan, Gala, and McIntosh. They can be used in a variety of ways — sliced, cooked into applesauce, made into cakes and breads, or wrapped in caramel. But what is Jewish about apples?

The Big Idea

On the third day of creation, the Torah tells us, God created trees bearing fruit, including apple trees. Most children learn early on that apples are good to eat and come from trees. Apple trees bloom in spring with beautiful blossoms that turn into summer apples and are picked in the fall. Jewish people eat apples dipped in honey for Rosh Hashanah to signify a sweet, good year. During winter, apples can be made into applesauce, which is traditionally eaten with Chanukah *latkes*. Apples join with nuts and wine on Pesach to make *charoset*. Because the apple is linked to so many Jewish celebrations, it helps mark Jewish time. When we cut open an apple to find the seeds, we remember that fruit trees and their seeds were part of God's original plan of creation. Each time we eat an apple, we are reminded of the miracle of creation.

Jewish Values

Sometimes, the activities we are involved in with children are Jewish moments, even if it's not readily apparent. Jewish values lead to Jewish behaviors. Appreciating the growth of an apple tree and enjoying its fruit are moments filled with Jewish values, including:

Bal Tashchit	Do not Destroy	בַּל תַּשְׁחִית
Brit	Partnership with God	בְּרִית
Hazan et Hakol	Feeding Everyone	הַזָּן אֶת הַכֹּל
Hoda'ah	Appreciation	הוֹדָאָה
"Jewish Time"	Making the Ordinary Sacred	
Kehillah	Community	קְהִלָּה

When children eat apples, cook with apples, and learn about the cycle of an apple tree, they are literally embodying Jewish values. Children's explorations are richest when the children are partners in their own learning. To engage children in these Jewish values and to deepen their learning, take time to investigate what children already know about apples. Observe children's play and analyze their comments. Seek out the children's questions and interests. Based on the children's questions, you might:

➤ Plant apple seeds, care for them, and watch them grow. Discuss with children the part they play in growing apple seeds, and the part God plays. *(Brit)*

➤ Recite the proper blessing before eating an apple or applesauce. *(Kehillah,* "Jewish Time," *Hoda'ah)*

➤ Study apples — their names, differences, and similarities. Have a taste test to determine which varieties children like and dislike. *(Hoda'ah)*

➤ Make applesauce from apples that are beginning to age. Invite another class to join you for a special snack. Try the recipe below. *(Bal Tashchit, Hazan et Hakol)*

Applesauce
Thanks to Arlene Segal

Ingredients:
12 apples
brown sugar or honey to taste
cinnamon to taste
nutmeg to taste

Directions
1. Cut apples into quarters.
2. Put in a pot with a thin layer of water on bottom (so apples don't burn).
3. Add brown sugar or honey, cinnamon, nutmeg.
4. Cover and cook with very low flame. Stir frequently. Cook until apples are extremely soft and mushy.
5. Strain and enjoy!

Israel Connection

Today, apple trees grow all over the world, including Israel and North America. Though apples are not native to the Promised Land, they have been grown there since the days of the pioneers. Israelis love to eat apples — in fact, according to Phyllis Glazer writing in the *Jerusalem Post* Internet edition of September 14, 2000, Israelis are the number one apple eaters in the world, consuming two million apples a day at the height of the season! All types of apples are now available in Israel, including Grand, Jonathan, Golden Delicious, Granny Smith, and bi-color varieties such as Pink Ladies and Brayburns. The upper Galilee and the Golan Heights, with their cool mountain climate, are the southernmost points in the northern hemisphere where apples are grown, since apples require cold weather during at least part of the growing process. In mid-August the region hosts an Apple Festival where guests can visit orchards, tour a packing house, watch apple cider being made, visit a farmer's market, and experience a variety of entertainment and culinary events. If you are traveling to Israel and love apples, be sure to call Yevulei Hagalil Packing Plant, headquarters for the Apple Festival, at (06) 690-4980. In your classroom, create your own apple festival around the time of your local apple harvest.

Hebrew Vocabulary

Here are some Hebrew words and phrases you can use as you explore apples:

Apple	Ta-**pu**-ach	תַּפּוּחַ
Tree	Eitz	עֵץ
Apple tree	Eitz Ta-**pu**-ach	עֵץ תַּפּוּחַ
Seed	**Ze**-rah	זֶרַע
Blossom	**Pe**-rach	פֶּרַח
Apple sauce	**Re**-sek ta-pu-**chim**	רֶסֶק תַּפּוּחִים
I like (m/f) to eat apples.	A-**ni** o-**hev**/o-**he**-vet le-e-**chol** ta-pu-**chim**.	אֲנִי אוֹהֵב/אוֹהֶבֶת לֶאֱכֹל תַּפּוּחִים.
Here is an apple.	Hi-**nei** ta-**pu**-ach.	הִנֵּה תַּפּוּחַ.

Songs and Poems

Tapuchim Ud'Vash (Apples and Honey)
Folk song. Found on the compact disc, "Shalom Yeladim" by Judy Caplan Ginsburg.

Tapuchim ud'Vash l'Rosh Hashanah
Tapuchim ud'Vash l'Rosh Hashanah
Shanah tovah, shanah m'tukah
Tapuchim ud'Vash l'Rosh Hashanah

Apples and honey for Rosh Hashanah
Apples and honey for Rosh Hashanah
A good new year
A sweet new year
Apples and honey for Rosh Hashanah

What is Yellow, Red or Green?

From "Apples on Holidays and Other Days" by Leah Abrams, used with permission.

What is yellow, red or green?
Big or small or in between?

Tapuach tzahov
Tapuach yarok
Tapuach adom
Yum, yum
Such a juicy, healthy nosh
Rome, Delicious, McIntosh.

Tapuach tzahov
Tapuach yarok
Tapuach adom
Yum, yum
Apple juice
Apple pie
Cake, cider
Strudel

Tapuach tzahov
Tapuach yarok
Tapuach adom
Yum, yum

Apples

From "Apples On Holidays and Other Days" by Leah Abrams. It was inspired by Ruth Musnikow's Apple Curriculum, BJE, N.Y., 1989 and is used here with permission.

Rosh Hashanah what do we eat:
Honey and apples make the year sweet.
In the Succah each on a string,
Ten little apples sway and swing
On Hanukah latkes of course,
Latkes with apples, applesauce
Now for Purim, what do we need?
Groggers with apples? Apple seeds.
Pesach we chop, chop very fine,
Walnuts and apples, raisins and wine.
On Shavuot, blintzes with cheese,
Fill them with apples if you so please.

Blessings

When we eat apples, this is the blessing we say:

בָּרוּךְ אַתָּה יְיָ אֱלֹהֵינוּ מֶלֶךְ הָעוֹלָם בּוֹרֵא פְּרִי הָעֵץ.

Ba-ruch A-tah A-do-nai E-lo-hei-nu Me-lech Ha-O-lam Bo-rei P'ri Ha-Eitz.
We praise You, our God, Creator of the universe, Who creates the fruit of the tree.

When we eat applesauce, this is the blessing we say:

בָּרוּךְ אַתָּה יְיָ אֱלֹהֵינוּ מֶלֶךְ הָעוֹלָם שֶׁהַכֹּל נִהְיֶה בִּדְבָרוֹ.

Ba-ruch A-tah A-do-nai E-lo-hei-nu Me-lech Ha-O-lam She-ha-Kol N'hi-yeh Bid-va-ro.
We praise You, our God, Creator of the universe, Who makes everything according to God's word.

Story: The Apple Tree's Discovery

By Peninnah Schram and Rachayl Eckstein Davis. © Peninnah Schram and Rachayl Eckstein Davis, used with permission.

This is one version of the story of the star inside the apple. See the "Resources" section for another version.

In a great oak forest where the trees grew tall and majestic, there was a little apple tree. It was the only apple tree in that forest and so it stood alone.

Winter came. As the snow fell to the forest floor, it covered the branches of the little apple tree. The forest was quiet and peaceful.

One night the little apple tree looked up at the sky and saw a wonderful sight. Between the branches of the trees, the little apple tree saw the stars in the sky, which appeared to be hanging on the branches of the oak trees.

"Oh God, Oh God," whispered the little apple tree, "how lucky those oak trees are to have such beautiful stars hanging on their branches. I want more than anything in the world to have stars on my branches, just like the oak trees have! Then I would feel truly special."

God looked down at the little apple tree and said gently, "Have patience! Have patience, little apple tree!"

Time passed. The snows melted and spring came to the land. Tiny white and pink apple blossoms appeared on the branches of the little apple tree. Birds came to rest on the branches. People walked by the little apple tree and admired its beautiful blossoms.

But night after night, the little apple tree looked up at the sky with the millions and millions and millions and millions of stars and cried out, "Oh God, I want more than anything in the world to have stars in my tree and in my branches and in my leaves — just like those oak trees."

And God looked down at the little apple tree and said, "You already have gifts. Isn't it enough to have shade to offer people, and fragrant blossoms, and branches for birds to rest on so they can sing you their songs?"

The apple tree sighed and answered simply, "Dear God, I don't mean to sound ungrateful, but that is not special enough! I do appreciate how much pleasure I give to others, but what I really want more than anything in the world is to have stars, not blossoms, on my branches. Then I would feel truly special!"

God smiled and answered. "Be patient, little apple tree."

The seasons changed again. Soon the apple tree was filled with many beautiful apples. People walked in the forest. Whoever saw the apple tree would reach up, pick an apple and eat it. And still, when night came to the forest, the apple tree looked at the stars in the oak trees and called out, "Oh God, I want more than **anything** in the world to have stars on my branches! Then I would feel truly special."

And God asked, "But apple tree, isn't it enough that you now have such wonderful apples to offer people? Doesn't that satisfy you? Doesn't that give you enough pleasure and make you feel special?"

Without saying a word, the apple tree answered by shaking its branches from side to side.

At that moment, God caused a wind to blow. The great oak trees began to sway and the apple tree began to shake. From the top of the apple tree an apple fell. When it hit the ground, it split open.

"Look," commanded God, "look inside yourself. What do you see?"

The little apple tree looked down and saw that right in the middle of the apple was a star. And the apple tree answered, "A star! I have a star!"

And God laughed a gentle laugh and added, "So you do have stars on your branches. They've been there all along, you just didn't know it."

Epilogue: Usually when we want to cut an apple, we cut it by holding the apple with its stem up. But in order to find its star, we must turn it on its side. If we change our direction a little bit, we too can find the spark that ignites the star inside each of us. The stars are right there within each one of us. Look carefully, look closely, and you'll find that beautiful star.

Questions and Suggestions:

➤ Where else might you find a star?

➤ Make up your own reason why God put a star in the middle of each apple.

➤ Make up your own fruit with a different surprise in the middle.

➤ How might we change ourselves just a little to find our "star"?

Resources

Books and Music

Abrams, Leah. *Apples on Holidays and Other Days.* Cedarhurst, NY: Tara Publications, 1988.
> *Includes the song "What is Yellow, Red or Green?" and the poem "Apples." Compact disc, cassette, and book available from Tara Publications, (800) TARA-400 or www.jewishmusic.com.*

Cohen, Sharon. "The Hidden Star" in Hirch, Jody, Idy Goodman, Aggie Goldenholz and Susan Roth. *Tastes of Jewish Tradition: Recipes, Activities & Stories for the Whole Family.* Milwaukee, WI: Jewish Community Center of Milwaukee, 2002.
> *In the chapter for Rosh Hashanah readers will find an alternative version of the star inside the apple story, which is adopted from folk tales by Carolyn Sherwin Baily and retold by Sharon Cohen.*

Ginsburg, Judy Caplan. *Shalom Yeladim/Hello Children.* Alexandria, LA: Judy Caplan Ginsburgh, 1993.
> *Includes the song "Tapuchim Ud'Vash." Compact disc, available from A.R.E. Publishing, Inc., (800) 346-7779 or www.arepublish.com.*

Jeunesse, Gallimard, et. al. *Fruit (A First Discovery Book).* New York: Scholastic Books, 1991.
> *Brightly painted transparent overlays to let readers experience the magic of an apple ripening.*

Robbins, Ken. *Apples.* New York: Atheneum Books for Young Readers, 2002.
> *Describes how apples are grown, harvested, and used. Also provides detailed facts about apples in history, literature, and in our daily lives.*

Schram, Peninnah, ed. *Chosen Tales: Stories Told by Jewish Storytellers.* Northvale, NJ: Jason Aronson Inc., 1995.
> *Extraordinary collection of stories told by nearly seventy gifted story tellers. Includes "The Apple Tree's Discovery."*

On the Web

Washington State Apple Commission
http://www.bestapples.com
> *An interesting site with a lot of information about apples. Includes a special "Just for Kids" section.*

Apples & More — Apple Facts
http://www.urbanext.uiuc.edu/apples/facts.html
> *Fascinating facts about apples.*

2. What's Jewish about Cookies?

No matter what the occasion, cookies provide a sweet treat. Cookies are great to bake and fun to share. So what's Jewish about cookies?

The Big Idea

Cookies create memories. Grandma passing down her secret cookie recipe, mom's kitchen filled with that sweet cookie smell when we arrived home from school, certain cookies that always held a place of honor at various gatherings and holiday times. While so many Jewish moments and celebrations revolve around food, the cookie goes to the heart of the matter. Cookies are like an edible relationship. Cookies are grandma's hug, late night giggles with girlfriends, warm times with family. God is found in significant relationships between people. When we think about all of the different relationships signified with a cookie, we are made aware of the presence of God, and of *Kedusha* (holiness).

Jewish Values

Sometimes, the activities we are involved in with children are Jewish moments, even if it's not readily apparent. Jewish values lead to Jewish behaviors. Baking, eating, and sharing cookies are moments filled with Jewish values, including:

Bikur Cholim	Visiting the Sick	בִּקּוּר חוֹלִים
Hachnasat Orchim	Hospitality/Welcoming Guests	הַכְנָסַת אוֹרְחִים
Hazan et Hakol	Feeding Everyone	הַזָּן אֶת הַכֹּל
Mishpacha	Family	מִשְׁפָּחָה
Shmirat HaGuf	Caring for the Body	שְׁמִירַת הַגוּף

When children bake, eat, and share cookies, they are literally embodying Jewish values. Children's explorations are richest when the children are partners in their own learning. To engage children in these Jewish values and to deepen their learning, take time to investigate what children already know about cookies. Observe children's play and analyze their comments. Seek out the children's questions and interests. Based on the children's questions, you might:

➤ Discuss with children how being Jewish means taking good care of our bodies. One of the ways we do that is by eating healthy foods. Cookies are something we enjoy in moderation, so that we can grow up strong. *(Shmirat HaGuf)*

➤ Invite a grandparent in to bake his or her favorite cookie recipe with the children. If s/he can tell the story of where the recipe came from, even better! *(Mishpacha)*

➤ When you bake cookies with your children, be sure to invite another class in to share them. You can read the book *The Doorbell Rang* by Pat Huchins, and award the mom and the kids in the story a *Hachnasat Orchim* award. *(Hachnasat Orchim, Hazan et Hakol)*

➤ Cookies add special sweetness and joy to birthday and Shabbat celebrations. When you sing "What do I like about Shabbat?" with your children, be sure that someone includes cookies as their favorite thing. ("Jewish Time")

➤ Jews have a special obligation to visit and care for people who are sick. Send a small basket of cookies home to a child who is sick. *(Bikur Cholim)*

Israel Connection

Gail and David Ehrlich immigrated to Israel from Queens, New York, in 1980 and live in Efrat, a settlement located between Jerusalem and Hebron. Gail (Gili), whose confectionary talents were already renowned in Efrat, was asked if she could bake cookies to be sold to a 400-strong audience during the intermission of a play. Gail accepted the theater offer, although she had only three days to bake a thousand cookies. "I was up day and night," she said.

Gili's cookies were a big hit, and on November 29th, 2001, 'Gili's Cookies' went on sale in stores in Jerusalem. Gili quit her job as a *ganenet* (pre-school teacher), David quit his film job, and they devoted themselves to cookies. They bought a five-shelf industrial oven, a forty-liter industrial mixer, and a large freezer. For many months they baked cookies in their house. In the entrance of the house there was the freezer and all the empty boxes, the dining room had the mixer, the kitchen had the industrial oven, and the den was the ingredients storeroom. By Tuesday night the floor would be covered with boxes — each Wednesday was delivery day. Eventually Gili's Cookies moved to the (unused) laundry room of nearby Kibbutz Ein Tzurim. The large wooden cubbyholes for holding the clothes of the different families became storage for packed cookies. In the new premises, they have a cookie-cutting machine, along with an eighty-liter mixer. Large sacks of flour and granola are stacked in a corner of the spacious and cheerily painted room. A dough stretcher stands on the other side, next to the fourteen-shelf oven that replaced the old five-shelf one.

Today, a small group of laborers produces 300 kilos (about 660 pounds!) of cookies a week, along with brownies and chocolate krinkles, the most popular item. You can check out the cookies at http://www.gilisgoodies.com.

In your classroom, you can set up a bakery like Gili's. What equipment will you need? You can stock your bakery with homemade Israeli cookies such as Israeli Sum Sum cookies.

Here's a simple recipe for some classic Israeli cookies:

ISRAELI SUM SUM (SESAME) COOKIES

Source: National Council of Jewish Women Cookbook

2 eggs
1/2 cup sugar
4 tablespoons olive oil
1/2 teaspoon baking soda
1/2 cup sifted flour
2 cups sesame seeds

Cream eggs, sugar, and oil together. Sift soda and flour and add. Work in the sesame seeds. Roll mixture into small balls and spread them on a greased cookie sheet. Press cookie down with your thumb. Bake in a 350-degree oven for about twenty minutes or until golden brown.

Hebrew Vocabulary

Here are some Hebrew words and phrases you can use as you bake and share cookies:

Cookie	*U-gi-yah*	עוּגִיָּה
Cookies	*U-gi-yot*	עוּגִיּוֹת
Chocolate chips	*Pei-roor sho-ko-lad*	פֵּרוּר שׁוֹקוֹלָד
Sesame	*Sum-sum*	שֻׁמְשֹׁם
Do you want a cookie (m/f)?	*A-tah ro-tzeh/*	אַתָּה רוֹצֶה/
	At ro-tzah u-gi-yah?	אַתְּ רוֹצָה עוּגִיָּה?
Very tasty!	*Ta-im m'od!*	טָעִים מְאֹד
Thank you!	*To-dah!*	תּוֹדָה

Songs and Poems

The opening words to the following classic Israeli children's song/dance do not actually mean "cake, cake, cake" (a Hebrew word similar to the word for cookie). However, dancing this circle dance with your children can create the same kind of community and relationships as sitting down and eating cookies together (for a lot fewer calories!) You can find a recording of this song on Cindy Paley's CD, *Eizeh Yom Sameach! What a Happy Day!,* or on *100 Shirim Rishonim (100 First Songs).*

Uga Uga

(Hold hands and circle together for the first four lines. At the last line, everyone sits as you sing "La-she-vet" and stands back up when you sing "La-koom.")

U-ga u-ga u-ga,
Ba-ma'a-gal na-chu-ga
Ni-sto-vev-a kol ha-yom
Ad asher nim-sa ma-kom
La-she-vet, la-kum! La-she-vet, la-kum! La-she-vet v'la-kuum!

U-ga u-ga u-ga
On the circle we go around
We will go around all day
Until we find our place
Sit down, stand up! Sit down, stand up! Sit down and stand up!

Blessings

When we eat cookies, this is the blessing we say:

בָּרוּךְ אַתָּה יְיָ אֱלֹהֵינוּ מֶלֶךְ הָעוֹלָם בּוֹרֵא מִינֵי מְזוֹנוֹת.

*Ba-**ruch** A-**tah** A-do-**nai** E-lo-**hei**-nu Me-lech Ha-O-**lam** Bo-**rei** Mi-**nei** M'zo-**not**.*
We praise You, our God, Creator of the universe, Who creates all kinds of foods.

Story: If You Give a Queen a Hamantaschen

The most famous Jewish cookie is the Hamantaschen, usually associated with the holiday of Purim. This story is great any time of the year, to serve as a preview or review of Purim, as well as being a yummy story! By Maxine Handelman, based on If You Give a Mouse a Cookie *by Laura Joffe Numeroff.*

If you give a queen a hamantaschen, she'll probably ask for some juice to go with it.

While she's drinking her juice, she'll ask you why the hamantaschen is shaped like a triangle. So you'll have to tell her about Haman and his plan to get rid of the Jewish people in Shushan.

When she hears about Haman's evil plan, she'll be frightened, so you'll have to comfort her by telling her about how Esther and Mordechai saved the day.

When she hears about brave Esther and Mordechai, she'll want to pretend to be Esther, so you'll have to bring her your dress-up clothes.

When she sees all the fancy dress-up clothes, she'll want to invite her friends to dress up with her.

When she and her friends have dressed up, they will want to act out the Purim story. You'll have to invite an audience. The play will be a huge success.

All of the applause will remind the queen that she is thirsty. She'll probably ask for a glass of juice.

And chances are if she asks for a glass of juice, she's going to want a haman-taschen to go with it.

Questions and suggestions:

➤ How is the Queen in the story doing the mitzvah of *Hachnasat Orchim*?

➤ Have your children draw illustrations for this story, and then tell the story again using their illustrations.

Resources

Books and Music

Gardosh, Daniela and Talma Alyagon. *100 Shirim Rishonim (100 First Songs)*. Tel Aviv, Israel: Kineret Publishing House, 1970.
    Includes the song, "Uga, Uga." Compact disc and songbook, available at http://www.israeliscent.com.

Goldin, Barbara Diamond. *Cakes and Miracles: A Purim Tale*. New York: Puffin Books, 1992.
    Hershel may be blind, but he can still create amazing Purim cookies.

Huchins, Pat. *The Doorbell Rang*. New York: Greenwillow Books, 1986.
    Victoria and Sam are just sitting down to a plateful of Ma's cookies when the doorbell rings, and two of their friends arrive to share the feast. How can they share cookies with everyone when the doorbell keeps ringing?

Numeroff, Laura Joffe. *If You Give a Mouse a Cookie*. New York: Laura Geringer, 1985.
    A wonderful story about a hungry — and demanding — little mouse.

Paley, Cindy. *Eizeh Yom Sameach! What a Happy Day!* Sherman Oaks, CA: Cindy Paley Aboody, n.d.
    Includes the song, "Uga, Uga Medley." Compact disc, available from Sounds Write Productions, Inc., (800) 9-SOUND-9, or http://www.soundswrite.com.

3. What's Jewish about Flour and Baking?

Baking breads and cake with flour captivates children as they learn to read recipes, measure ingredients, observe changes in ingredients, and have fun together. But what is Jewish about flour?

The Big Idea

Anyone who has grown up in a Jewish home where challah was baked knows the physical, emotional, and psychological embrace one receives when walking into a space in which challah is baking. The smell tells the body it is time to get ready for Shabbat, the day of rest, a day together with the family, a special time of the week. The taste buds get ready for the delicious taste of all the foods that will soon be eaten. The mind gets ready for prayer, study, and rest. For a child, the smell of challah foretells time with the entire family and fun with friends at synagogue. It is amazing that flour mixed with yeast and eggs can become such a strong forecaster of Jewish time!

Flour does not require yeast to help us tell Jewish time. The taste of matzah also offers Jews a sense of time, memory, and connection with family. Matzah means Pesach. With apple cake for Rosh Hashanah, a tablespoon of flour in the latkes at Chanukah, and blintzes for Shavuot, the importance of flour becomes even clearer. When we think about flour, we think about Jewish time.

Jewish Values

Sometimes, the activities we are involved in with children are Jewish moments, even if it's not readily apparent. Jewish values lead to Jewish behaviors. The Jewish values that emerge from using flour for baking can begin at a very young age and last a lifetime. These values include:

Brit	Partnership with God	בְּרִית
Hachnasat Orchim	Hospitality/Welcoming Guests	הַכְנָסַת אוֹרְחִים
Hazan et Hakol	Feeding Everyone	הַזָּן אֶת הַכֹּל
"Jewish Time"	Making the Ordinary Sacred	
Lichvod Shabbat	To Honor Shabbat	לִכְבוֹד שַׁבָּת
Mishpacha	Family	מִשְׁפָּחָה

When children bake or eat special foods made with flour, they are literally embodying Jewish values. Children's explorations are richest when the children are partners in their own learning. To engage children in these Jewish values and to deepen their learning, take time to investigate what children already know about flour. Observe the children's interactions while using flour and listen to their stories about baking. Seek out the children's questions and interests. Based on the children's questions, you might:

➤ Bake challah every week at school to create everlasting positive memories of Shabbat (see recipe below). (*Lichvod Shabbat*, "Jewish Time")

➤ Invite parents to help with baking. In this way children are exposed to many more stories and parents become a part of what goes on at school. (*Mishpacha*)

➤ Bake bread and invite another class, parents, or someone from the school or larger community to share it with you. (*Hachnasat Orchim, Hazan et Hakol*)

➤ Have children use a mortar and pestle to grind wheat seeds into flour. Ask, Where does the wheat seed come from? How does the wheat become bread? (*Brit*)

Israel Connection

In Israel, on Thursdays and Fridays, it is common to see, smell, and feel preparations for Shabbat. Flour is flying in bakeries and homes as *challot*, cakes, and cookies are being prepared for Shabbat. Here is a delicious and easy recipe for challah to use weekly with a classroom of children. The dough can be divided so that 16-20 children can prepare small *challot* to take home for their Shabbat tables.

Diane Bergen's Mother-in-Law's Challah Recipe from Colorado

Thursday

➤ In a small bowl, mix:
    2 packages of yeast — Not Fast Rising!
    1 Tbs. sugar
    1/2 cup warm water
➤ Let sit for 10 to 15 minutes
➤ In a large bowl, mix:
    1 cup sugar
    3/4 cup oil
    1 tbs. salt
    4 eggs

➤ Add 1-1/4 cup hot water to large bowl, then immediately add the yeast mixture. Gently mix together

➤ Mix in approximately 8 cups of flour — use as much as needed to make the dough not too sticky

➤ Dump onto a floured counter top and knead for 10 minutes, adding more flour if needed.

- ➤ Place dough in a very large, clean, oiled bowl
- ➤ Tightly cover bowl and place in refrigerator overnight to rise. (Be sure the bowl is quite large!)

Friday

- ➤ Take bowl of challah dough out of refrigerator and let sit for 30 minutes. Punch the dough down.
- ➤ Dump challah out onto floured counter top and divide into balls of dough (one ball for each child).
- ➤ Invite each child to knead one ball of dough for a few minutes. Children can create their own shape, or, to make a more traditional challah, divide dough into three sections, roll each section into a long snake, and then braid snakes. (Use a little flour to prevent sticking.)
- ➤ Place *challot* onto a greased cookie sheet. Allow children to paint with egg whites and sprinkle with poppy or sesame seeds (optional).
- ➤ Bake at 350 degrees for 30 minutes.

Hebrew Vocabulary

Here are some Hebrew words and phrases you can use as you explore flour:

Bread	*Le-chem*	לֶחֶם
Dough	*Ba-tzek*	בָּצֵק
Oven	*Ta-nur*	תַּנּוּר
Would you like (m/f) some Challah?	*A-tah ro-tzeh/ At ro-tzah challah?*	אַתָּה רוֹצֶה/ אַתְּ רוֹצָה חַלָה?
We are baking Challah.	*A-nach-nu o-fim challah.*	אֲנַחְנוּ אוֹפִים חַלָה.
This is flour.	*Zeh ke-mach.*	זֶה קֶמַח.
Here are eggs.	*Hi-nei bei-tzim.*	הִנֵה בֵּצִים.

Songs and Poems

I Had A Little Challah

From Ben Aronin's "Jolly Jingles for the Jewish Child," published by Behrman House, Inc., 1947. Long out of print, but may be found in some libraries or resource centers. Sung to the tune of "I Had a Little Dreidel."

I had a little challah, I made it all myself
I put it in the oven, I put it on the shelf

Now listen little challah, you mustn't go away
I need you for Shabbat, so please be sure to stay.
I didn't mean to do it, but oh it looked so nice,
I took a little nibble, I took a great big slice

And then before I knew it the pantry shelf was bare
There wasn't any challah, the challah wasn't there
 (Spoken voice:)
The one who made it, ate it!

Partnership with God
By Deborah Schein

Pop goes the seed
Deep in the ground
That the farmer planted
Tiny and round.
Up grows the wheat
Tall and straight
So the baker can use it
For bread, cookies, cakes
Thank you God, we do it together.
You give the sun, rain, and weather.
You give us brains and hands that are able
And together we put food on the table.

Blessings

When we eat things with flour, these are the blessings we say:

Blessing over bread, including challah:

בָּרוּךְ אַתָּה יְיָ אֱלֹהֵינוּ מֶלֶךְ הָעוֹלָם הַמּוֹצִיא לֶחֶם מִן הָאָרֶץ.

*Ba-**ruch** A-**tah** A-do-**nai** E-lo-**hei**-nu **Me**-lech Ha-O-**lam** Ha-**mo**-tzi **Le**-chem Min Ha-A-retz.*
We praise You, our God, Creator of the universe, Who brings forth bread from the earth.

Blessing over foods other than bread made from wheat, barley, oats or rye (Cookies, cakes, pretzels)

בָּרוּךְ אַתָּה יְיָ אֱלֹהֵינוּ מֶלֶךְ הָעוֹלָם בּוֹרֵא מִינֵי מְזוֹנוֹת.

*Ba-**ruch** A-**tah** A-do-**nai** E-lo-**hei**-nu **Me**-lech Ha-O-**lam** Bo-**rei** Mi-**nei** M'zo-**not**.*
We praise You, our God, Creator of the universe, Who creates all kinds of foods.

Story: The Little Red Hen Goes to Israel

By Deborah Schein

Every week the Little Red Hen baked bread all by herself. It was hard work, planting and sowing and threshing and baking. So one day she threw up her wings and declared, "I have had enough of all this work! I am taking my little chick and we are flying to Israel to live on a *kibbutz*."

So off they went, the Little Red Hen and her baby chick, to *Eretz Yisrael*. There they found themselves on a *kibbutz* complete with an Israeli goat named Tayish, an Israeli dog named Kelev, and an Israeli duck named Barvaz. Here on the *kibbutz* in *Eretz Yisrael*, everyone worked together to make challah. When it was time to cut the wheat, the Little Red Hen asked, "Who will help me cut the wheat?" The Little Chick said, "I will." "Oh no," said his mother, "you are much too small." Tayish, the goat, said, "I will help." And together the Little Red Hen and Tayish cut all the wheat. Next the Little Red Hen asked, "Who will help me thresh the wheat?" The Little Chick said, "I will." "Oh no," said his mother, "You are much too small." Kelev, the dog, smiled and said, "I will." Together the Little Red Hen and Kelev threshed all the wheat. Next it was time to take the threshed wheat to the mill for grinding. The Little Red Hen asked, "Who will help me carry this wheat to the mill for grinding?" The Little Chick said, "I will." "Oh no," said his mother, "You are much too small." Barvaz, the duck, quickly answered, "I will help you carry the wheat to the mill for grinding." Together the Little Red Hen and Barvaz carried off all of the wheat. Now it was time to bake the bread. Everyone gathered together to measure and mix the flour. That Friday night all the friends gathered around the Shabbat table. The Little Red Hen said, "Who will help me bless this challah?" "I will!" said the Little Chick — and he did! Everyone agreed that it was the best challah they had even eaten.

Questions and suggestions:

➤ Why was it so important for the Little Red hen to have her friends help her?

➤ Why was it the best tasting challah?

➤ Where did the wheat to bake the challah come from? Where did the seed come from?

➤ Invite the children to act out this story.

Resources

Books

Aronin, Ben. *Jolly Jingles for the Jewish Child.* New York: Behrman House, 1947.
   Includes the song, "I Had a Little Challah." Out of print, may be found in libraries or resource centers.

Davis, Abrey. *Bagels from Benny.* Tonawanda, New York: Kids Can Press, 2003.
   Benny adores helping out his Grandpa at the bagel bakery, the best in town. The young Jewish boy loves his grandfather's bagels so much, he wants to thank God for them. But how?

Epstein, Sylvia B. *How the Rosh Hashanah Challah Became Round.* New York: Gefen Publishers, 1996.
   On Rosh Hashanah the traditional braided challah is replaced with a round challah to symbolize the cycle of the new year.

Goldin, Barbara Diamond. *Cakes and Miracles: A Purim Tale.* New York: Puffin Books, 1992.
   Hershel may be blind, but he can still create amazing Purim cookies.

Kropf, Latifa Berry. *It's Challah Time!* Minneapolis, MN: Kar-Ben Publishing, 2002.
   Sharp, full-color photos show several preschool children mixing, kneading, and braiding dough for challah — and loving every minute of it.

Medoff, Francine. *The Mouse in the Matzah Factory.* Minneapolis, MN: Kar-Ben Publishing, 2003.
   A cheerful mouse follows along as wheat is taken to a mill, trucked to a city, and taken to a room to be mixed, rolled, and baked into matzah.

4. What's Jewish about Fruits and Vegetables?

We're told to eat five servings a day of fruits and vegetables. Our mothers struggled with us to eat our veggies; each of us has a favorite fruit and others we strictly avoid. But what's Jewish about fruits and vegetables?

The Big Idea

On the third day of creation, the Torah tells us, God filled the earth with vegetation: plants bearing seeds, herbs, and trees bearing fruit. We are blessed in our modern age with the opportunity to eat fruits and vegetables in all seasons, from all over the world. The fruits and vegetables we enjoy are the result of the labor of many people: those who planted, reaped, packaged, shipped, and stocked the shelves with wonderful produce for us to buy (unless you are lucky to live on a farm or in a farming community, where your family does most, if not all, of these tasks). But the existence of so many varieties of produce goes back to the seeds created by God. The healthy foods on our table are the result of a strong partnership with God, and hearken back to the very first days of creation.

Jewish Values

Sometimes, the activities we are involved in with children are Jewish moments, even if it's not readily apparent. Jewish values lead to Jewish behaviors. Eating and exploring fruits and vegetables are moments filled with Jewish values, including:

Brit	Partnership with God	בְּרִית
Hachnasat Orchim	Hospitality/Welcoming Guests	הַכְנָסַת אוֹרְחִים
Hazan et Hakol	Feeding Everyone	הַזָּן אֶת הַכֹּל
Mishpacha	Family	מִשְׁפָּחָה
Shmirat HaGuf	Caring for the Body	שְׁמִירַת הַגּוּף

When children enjoy and investigate fruits and vegetables, they are literally embodying Jewish values. Children's explorations are richest when the children are partners in their own learning. To engage children in these Jewish values and to deepen their learning, take time to investigate what children already know about fruits and vegetables. Observe children's play and analyze their comments. Seek out the children's questions and interests. Based on the children's questions, you might:

➤ Discuss with children how being Jewish means taking good care of our bodies. One of the ways we do that is by eating healthy foods. Fruits and vegetables are something that we try to eat plenty of, so that we can grow up strong. *(Shmirat HaGuf)*

➤ Invite a grandparent to make vegetable soup with the children. The book *Bone Button Borscht* by Aubrey Davis puts a Jewish spin on the classic "Stone Soup" story. *(Mishpacha, Shmirat HaGuf)*

➤ Collect your families' favorite kid-friendly recipes involving fruits and vegetables. Have the children illustrate the recipes, and send home a cookbook for everyone to enjoy. *(Mishpacha)*

➤ Have a rainbow snack — have each child bring in a fruit of a different color. Invite another class to join the color fest. *(Shmirat HaGuf, Hachnasat Orchim, Hazan et Hakol)*

➤ Investigate the seeds that come out of the fruits and vegetables you share. How did God create so many kinds of seeds? Plant a garden, and be sure to do your part in helping the seeds to grow. *(Brit)*

Israel Connection

Israelis consume more fruit and vegetables per capita than any other people in the world! This tiny country, challenged by a scarcity of arable land and water resources, produces ninety-five percent of its own food requirements. In *Machaneh Yehudah*, the *shuk* (pronounced "shook"), or open air market in Jerusalem, stalls are filled with a huge variety of fruits and vegetables. Each vendor does his best to entice shoppers to buy his wares and not his neighbor's. Set up a *shuk* or grocery store in your classroom, and let the children role-play selling and shopping. Post photos or posters of *Machaneh Yehudah* in the *shuk* the children create. (See a great picture of *Machaneh Yehudah* at http://www.golemproductions.com/alps/pics/shuk-unframed.jpg, and two more at http://members.aol.com/quordandis/edpix.html — click on numbers 16 and 17. Also, All Jewish Learning has a terrific "Good Foods" poster set with pictures of foods in the *shuk*. See "Resources" section below for further information.)

Hebrew Vocabulary

Here are some Hebrew words and phrases you can use as you eat and explore fruits and vegetables:

Fruit	*Pei-rot*	פֵּרוֹת
Vegetables	*Y'ra-kot*	יְרָקוֹת
Apple	*Ta-pu-ach*	תַּפּוּחַ

Orange	*Ta-**puz***	תַּפּוּז
Carrot	*Ge-**zer***	גֶּזֶר
Cucumber	*Me-la-fe-**fon***	מְלָפְפוֹן
Pomegranate	*Ri-**mon***	רִמּוֹן
Very tasty!	*Ta-**im** m'**od**!*	טָעִים מְאֹד

Songs and Poems

The Vegetable Song
Author unknown. Sung to the tune of "Twinkle, Twinkle Little Star."

Carrots, peas, and broccoli,
Vegetables are good for me.
For my snack and in my lunch,
Veggie sticks are great to munch.
Carrots, peas, and broccoli,
Vegetables are good for me.

Corn and beans, tomatoes too,
Vegetables are good for you.
Eat five servings every day,
Before you do, a blessing say.
Lettuce, peppers, onions too,
Thank You, God, for all you do.

The Good Food Song
Author Unknown. Sung to the tune of "Old MacDonald Had A Farm."
Use your own creativity to add other vegetables!

Vegetables are good for me,
Ee aye ee aye oh.
I say a bracha thankfully,
Ee aye ee aye oh.
With a carrot here, and a carrot there,
Here a carrot, there a carrot, everywhere a carrot, carrot.
Thank You, God, for feeding me,
Ee aye ee aye oh.

Blessings

When we eat fruits (specifically things that grow on trees), this is the blessing we say:

בָּרוּךְ אַתָּה יְיָ אֱלֹהֵינוּ מֶלֶךְ הָעוֹלָם בּוֹרֵא פְּרִי הָעֵץ.

*Ba-**ruch** A-**tah** A-do-**nai** E-lo-**hei**-nu Me-lech Ha-O-**lam** Bo-**rei** P'**ri** Ha-**Eitz**.*
We praise You, our God, Creator of the universe, Who creates the fruit of the trees.
(Interestingly enough, grapes and raisins receive this blessing, not Borei P'ri HaGafen.)

When we eat vegetables (specifically things that grow in the ground), this is the blessing we say:

בָּרוּךְ אַתָּה יְיָ אֱלֹהֵינוּ מֶלֶךְ הָעוֹלָם בּוֹרֵא פְּרִי הָאֲדָמָה.

*Ba-**ruch** A-**tah** A-do-**nai** E-lo-**hei**-nu Me-lech Ha-O-**lam** Bo-**rei** P'**ri** Ha-A-da-**mah**.*
We praise You, our God, Creator of the universe, Who creates the fruit of the earth.
Bananas are regarded as fruit of the ground, as their trunks are made from hardened leaves — therefore, the blessing over bananas is Borei P'ri Ha-A-da-mah.

Story: The Pomegranates

By Deborah Schein

Two dull red pomegranates sat on the science table for weeks. *Morah* Devorah must have brought them in sometime before Rosh Hashanah. We knew there must be a logical reason for them being there, but no one really paid much attention. Being close to the beginning of the new school year, we were all busy painting, building, playing, and most importantly, getting to know each other. Eli and Noa were the only students somewhat familiar with the fruit and called them by name. Eli called the fruit "pomegranates" and described tiny, juicy seeds. Noa, a Hebrew speaking classmate from Israel, quietly whispered "ah, *rimonim.*" All of this piqued our interest. We began to ask our teacher questions: Are these fruit from Israel? Are we going to make jelly? Will we plant the seeds? When will we look inside? Are they good to eat? When will we taste them? *Morah* Devorah answered each question with, "You will see when the time is ripe." And so we waited.

One day, just before Yom Kippur, *Morah* Devorah let out an exclamation, "Has anyone seen the pomegranates? It is time for an explanation!" No one could answer. No one knew where they could be. We searched the shelves — no pomegranates. We searched the cubbies — no pomegranates. We asked the other classrooms if they had seen our pomegranates — no luck. Finally, Noa came up and asked in her accented English, "What is wrong?" Someone translated pomegranate to *rimonim.* Noa's face lit up as she motioned us to follow her to the block area. We all followed. There on the floor was a beautiful block structure of a Torah with two *rimonim* sitting upon the *atzei chaim* (Torah scrolls).

Morah Devorah looked pleased. We all gathered around the block structure as we heard how the pomegranate has become a decoration for the Torah. According to a *midrash* (a story explaining something in the Torah) there exist 613 seeds in each pomegranate — the same as the number of *mitzvot*. Morah Devorah asked us what we knew about *mitzvot*. We knew that they were more than "good deeds." *Mitzvot* are commandments, God's rules for Jewish people to live Jewish lives full of caring, sharing, and making good choices.

Some of us were starting to realize why *Morah* Devorah had brought in the pomegranates. Tomorrow was Yom Kippur and our parents would be fasting. All Jews would be thinking about ways to be better people. We cut open the pomegranates, but started eating the seeds before we could count and check to see if there really were 613. Before we ate the pomegranate we said, "May we have as many good deeds as there are seeds in a pomegranate." As we sat sucking on the juicy seeds, we all gave thought to what we might do during the coming year to be better children, better Jews, better people of the world.

Questions and Suggestions:

➤ What might the children have decided they could do to be better children, better Jews, better people of the world? What could you do?

➤ Invite the children to draw a picture of a *rimon* and to write or dictate one important *mitzvah* they can do. Gather all the pages to create a *mitzvah* book.

➤ Learn more about pomegranates and their importance in Jewish history and art by visiting the Web sites listed in the "Resources" section below.

Resources

Books and Music

Davis, Aubrey. *Bone Button Borscht.* New York: Kids Can Press, 2002.
  A Jewish version of the classic folktale "Stone Soup."

Konigsberg, Rachel and the Children of Gan Harmony. *Something Different.* Jerusalem: Gan Harmony Productions, 1998.
  A beautiful story about Uncle Oren's citrus grove with lots of different fruit trees, and the children's reaction to a tree that's really different. To find this book, contact Gan Harmony at GanHar@netvision.net.il.

Mallett, David. *Inch by Inch: The Garden Song.* New York: HarperTrophy, 1997.
  A peppy rendition of the familiar folksong, the music to which is printed on the book's final spread.

Materials and Supplies

All Jewish Learning — (425) 385-3779 or e-mail alljewishlearning@yahoo.com
A wonderful resource of quality Judaic classroom materials, especially appropriate for early childhood.

On the Web

Pomegranate
http://www.hort.purdue.edu/newcrop/morton/pomegranate.html
A great deal of information about pomegranates, including pictures.

The Perennial Appeal of the Pomegranate
http://www.jwmag.org/articles/04Fall02/p08c.asp
Information and recipes from Jewish Woman International Magazine.

5. What's Jewish about Peanut Butter and Jelly?

Any lunchtime in an early childhood program where children bring their own lunches is sure to be host to many peanut butter and jelly sandwiches. Even with all its variations — grape or strawberry jelly, creamy or crunchy peanut butter, white bread or whole wheat — the peanut butter and jelly sandwich is a standard in comfort food. So what's Jewish about peanut butter and jelly?

The Big Idea

Peanut butter is one of America's favorite foods. Found in about seventy-five percent of American homes, peanut butter is considered a staple in early childhood programs as well. Peanut butter and jelly serves to comfort and nourish us. It's a food that carries us from childhood through our entire lives. There are many variations on the theme — we each prefer different kinds of jelly and various types of bread. Some like lots of jelly, some prefer an overload of peanut butter, and of course there is always the crunchy versus creamy debate. Though we can easily go to our nearest grocery store and pick up all the necessary ingredients for this quintessential sandwich, none of those items would appear on the shelves without the help of God. The grapes, berries, nuts, and wheat grow in a delicate partnership between people and God, involving both human labor and elements beyond our control, such as the existence of seeds and the proper amount of rain. This partnership is a *brit*, a covenant, between people and God. So with each bite of a delicious peanut butter and jelly sandwich, we are reminded of the *brit*, the partnership between people and God.

Jewish Values

Sometimes, the activities we are involved in with children are Jewish moments, even if it's not readily apparent. Jewish values lead to Jewish behaviors. Eating and exploring peanut butter and jelly sparks lots of Jewish values. These values include:

Ahavah	Love	אַהֲבָה
Brit	Partnership with God	בְּרִית
Chesed	Kindness	חֶסֶד
Hachnasat Orchim	Hospitality/Welcoming Guests	הַכְנָסַת אוֹרְחִים
Hazan et Hakol	Feeding Everyone	הַזָּן אֶת הַכֹּל
Shmirat HaGuf	Caring for the Body	שְׁמִירַת הַגּוּף

When children make a peanut butter and jelly sandwich, they are literally embodying Jewish values. Children's explorations are richest when the children are partners in their own learning. To engage children in these Jewish values and to deepen their learning, take time to investigate what children already know about peanut butter and jelly. Observe children's play and analyze their comments. Seek out the children's questions and interests. Based on the children's questions, you might:

➤ Explore with children the nutritional value and variations of peanut butter and jelly. Peanut butter is high in protein, but it is also high in fat. Jellies come in many different flavors, some with high sugar content and some lower. Breads also offer varying nutritional content. Invite children to bring from home their favorite peanut butters, jellies, and breads and see if your class can make the healthiest sandwich. (Shmirat HaGuf)

➤ Remember that many children have peanut allergies, and be very sensitive to allergies in your class and your school. Explore peanut alternatives and use those when peanut allergies exist. (Shmirat HaGuf)

➤ Invite parents to help make peanut butter and/or jelly from scratch. (You can search web sites such as www.allrecipes.com or www.recipesource.com for jelly and peanut butter recipes) As you crush peanuts or boil grapes or berries, talk about where these ingredients came from, and what kind of work (and by whom) goes into getting a jar of grape jelly to the grocer's shelf. (Brit)

➤ After insuring that there are no allergy risks, invite another class in to have a peanut butter and jelly tasting and making party. Have several different varieties of peanut butter, jelly, and bread available, and let the children make and taste their own sandwiches. Encourage the children to help each other in their sandwich preparations. (Hachnasat Orchim, Hazan et Hakol, Chesed)

➤ Talk about how peanut butter and jelly is a "comfort food." What other foods are comfort foods? Who gives us comfort foods? How else can we find comfort (other than food)? (Ahavah, Shmirat HaGuf)

Israel Connection

Peanuts are not really nuts at all, but legumes. Peanuts are grown is Israel, but in small quantities because cultivation requires a lot of water. Israeli peanuts are used primarily for oil and for animal feed. While in America a peanut butter and jelly sandwich is a standard lunchbox food, in Israel, kids seek pita and hummus for their comfort food. Hummus is made from ground chick peas (also known as garbanzo beans) which originated in the Middle East and are the most widely consumed legume in the world. A bag of warm pita purchased at the *shuk* (open-air market) can disappear quickly as kids rip pieces of pita and dip it generously into a container of hummus. In your class, warm up some pita (without quite toasting it, just warm it in the oven for a few minutes) and let kids enjoy a pita and hummus snack.

Hebrew Vocabulary

Here are some Hebrew words and phrases you can use to talk about peanut butter and jelly:

Peanut	*Bo-ten*	בּוֹטֶן
Peanut butter	*Chem-at bot-nim*	חֶמְאַת בּוֹטְנִים
Jelly	*Ri-bah*	רִבָּה
Grape	*A-nav*	עֵנָב
Strawberry	*Toot sa-deh*	תּוּת שָׂדֶה
Sandwich	*Ka-rich*	כָּרִיךְ
Bread	*Le-chem*	לֶחֶם
More jelly, please!	*Od ri-bah, b'va-ka-sha!*	עוֹד רִבָּה בְּבַקָשָׁה!
My hands are sticky!	*Ya-da-yim she-li d'vi-kot!*	הַיָדַיִם שֶׁלִי דְבִיקוֹת!

Songs and Poems

The PB & J Partnership
By Maxine Handelman. Sung to the tune of "Frère Jacques."

Peanut butter, peanut butter
Jelly too, jelly too.
I lo-ove to eat them
Eat them in a sandwich
Yes I do, yes I do.

We grow peanuts, we grow peanuts,
In the ground, in the ground.
With God's help we grow
The peanuts oh so yummy
Crush them up, crush them up.

Pick the berries, pick the berries
From the bush, from the ground,
God will bring the rain and
God will bring the sun
To help them grow, to help them grow.

To make a sandwich, to make a sandwich
It's not a race, it's not a race
With God as our partner, with God as our partner
The world's a better place, the world's a better place.

Blessings

When we eat a peanut butter and jelly sandwich, we say:

בָּרוּךְ אַתָּה יְיָ אֱלֹהֵינוּ מֶלֶךְ הָעוֹלָם הַמּוֹצִיא לֶחֶם מִן הָאָרֶץ.

*Ba-**ruch** A-**tah** A-do-**nai** E-lo-**hei**-nu **Me**-lech Ha-O-**lam** Ha-**mo**-tzi **Le**-chem Min Ha-**A**-retz.*
We praise You, our God, Creator of the universe, Who brings forth bread from the earth.

For just a spoonful of peanut butter or jelly, we say:

בָּרוּךְ אַתָּה יְיָ אֱלֹהֵינוּ מֶלֶךְ הָעוֹלָם שֶׁהַכֹּל נִהְיֶה בִּדְבָרוֹ.

*Ba-**ruch** A-**tah** A-do-**nai** E-lo-**hei**-nu **Me**-lech Ha-O-**lam** She-ha-**Kol** N'hi-**yeh** Bid-va-**ro**.*
We praise You, our God, Creator of the universe, Who made everything with a word.

Story: Made with Love

By Maxine Handelman, based on a United Way Success Story about senior volunteers at the Heritage Jewish Community Center in Overland Park, KS.

Helen knows it's Tuesday when she walks into her Jewish Community Center, because she can smell the fruity scents of jelly and the peanuty odors of peanut butter. Helen's white stick goes tap tap tap as she makes her way into the room. "Hello, Joe!" Helen says to a man, who is spreading grape jelly onto a slice of whole wheat bread. "Good morning, Sylvia," Helen says to a woman smearing peanut butter onto a slice of white bread. Helen taps her stick until she comes to the end of the table. She sits down, and feels on the table. She finds plastic gloves, sandwich bags, and an already growing pile of peanut butter and jelly sandwiches. Helen can't see with her eyes, but using her nose and her fingers to guide the way, Helen gently takes each sandwich and puts it in a bag.

Every Tuesday, Helen joins her friends at the JCC. Every Tuesday, they make 500 pb&j sandwiches for hungry people in their town. They use eight huge jars of peanut butter, six large cans of jelly, and fifty loaves of bread! Each person has his or her own job. Some people like to spread the jelly, others prefer to shmear the peanut butter. It is hard for Helen to see if she's getting the right amount of jelly on the bread, but she has an important job just the same: putting the sandwiches in the bags.

Helen bags the finished sandwiches and chats with her friends Marian, Stan, and Shirley as they all work together to make the sandwiches. Marian's job is the jelly, Stan's is the peanut butter, and Shirley cuts the sandwiches before giving them to Helen to bag. Suddenly Helen stops — bag in one hand and sandwich in the other. Her nose twitches. "Stan, are you feeling okay? There's barely any peanut butter on this sandwich." "Oh Helen, you have a very powerful nose! My jar is almost empty, but I was feeling too lazy to get up and get another." The friends all laugh, and Helen says, "We'll wait." Stan gets up and saunters over to the supply shelf, where he gets a new four-pound jar of peanut butter.

After a long while, Helen hears the sounds of spreading and chatting fade away, and she can tell that the tables are being cleaned up. As Helen leaves the JCC that day, over the tap tap tap of her white stick, she hears the sounds of vans, carrying 500 peanut butter and jelly sandwiches to hungry people all over the city. Helen smiles to herself, and goes home to make herself some lunch — a peanut butter and jelly sandwich, of course!

Questions and Suggestions:

➤ Why do Helen and her friends come every week to make peanut butter and jelly sandwiches? Talk with your children about *tzedakah*, the importance of helping others, and the ability of each person to help.

➤ Find a homeless shelter or soup kitchen in your town that would appreciate the donation of peanut butter and jelly sandwiches, and set up an assembly line in your classroom. Invite the parents to help with supplying the ingredients, making the sandwiches, and delivering them to hungry people.

Resources

Books

Rosenfeld, Dina. *Peanut Butter & Jelly for Shabbos.* New York: Hachai Publishing, 1995.

> *One Friday afternoon, Yossi and Laibel are confronted with a seemingly impossible task: preparing a make-shift Shabbat meal when they think a snowstorm will delay their parents' arrival home from the hospital with their new baby sister. With the right attitude and a little ingenuity, the two brothers find out that they can try hard and succeed.*

On the Web

www.peanutbutterlovers.com

> *This web site is dedicated to all those who love peanut butter. Includes history, recipes, and details of how peanut butter is made.*

www.allrecipes.com
www.recipesource.com

> *Search these sites for recipes for making peanut butter and jelly from scratch, as well as other recipes using peanut butter or jelly.*

6. What's Jewish about Potatoes?

Potatoes are a commonly known and appreciated food for many people of the world, especially those who live in colder climates. Potatoes are easy to grow, grow in abundance, and have sustained people as a food staple. In America, we enjoy potatoes in the form of French fries, baked potatoes with butter and sour cream, and sweet potatoes for Thanksgiving. But what is Jewish about potatoes?

The Big Idea

For many Jews, the potato is best represented in traditional Ashkenazi Jewish recipes (recipes handed down from Jews from Eastern Europe). Potato *latkes*, made and served during the winter holiday of Chanukah, are fried in oil, connecting them to the holiday where, legend has it, a small amount of oil burned for eight days. Potato *kugel* (pudding) is often served on Shabbat or other special Jewish holidays, especially Rosh HaShanah. During Pesach, potatoes might be eaten after *b'dikot chametz* (cleaning the house for *chametz*), or dipped in salt water during the Seder. Because the potato is linked to so many Jewish celebrations, it helps mark Jewish time, especially for those living in the Diaspora (outside Israel). So, when we think about potatoes, we are made aware of Jewish time.

Jewish Values

Sometimes, the activities we are involved in with children are Jewish moments, even if it's not readily apparent. Jewish values lead to Jewish behaviors. Potatoes are filled with Jewish values, including:

Bal Tashchit	Do not Destroy	בַּל תַּשְׁחִית
Brit	Partnership with God	בְּרִית
Hachnasat Orchim	Hospitality/Welcoming Guests	הַכְנָסַת אוֹרְחִים
Hazan et Hakol	Feeding Everyone	הַזָּן אֶת הַכֹּל
"Jewish Time"	Making the Ordinary Sacred	
Mishpacha	Family	מִשְׁפָּחָה

When children explore potatoes, they are literally embodying Jewish values. Children's explorations are richest when the children are partners in their own learning. To engage children in these Jewish values and to deepen their learning, take time to investigate what children already know about potatoes. Observe children's play and analyze their comments. Seek out the children's questions and interests. Based on the children's questions, you might:

➤ Make potato *latkes*, French fries, baked potatoes or potato kugel. Then invite friends or family members to share them with you. *(Hachnasat Orchim, Hazan et Hakol, Mishpacha)*

➤ Plant potatoes, care for them, and watch them grow outdoors. Two Web sites listed in the "Resources" section below offer two different approaches. *(Brit)*

➤ Harvest your potatoes and share the harvest with a food bank. *(Hazan et Hakol)*

➤ Stick three or four toothpicks into the sides of an old potato (one with eyes), and suspend it over a clear glass container of water. Fill the container with water until it just touches the bottom tip of the potato. Keep the water clean, and watch the roots and plant grow. Using a sweet potato (which is not really a potato at all!) results in a leafy vine with beautiful purple flowers. For details, visit http://www.verybestkids.com and type "sweet potato" in the "search" box. *(Brit)*

➤ Put unused potatoes into a cool place so that not even one potato is wasted. *(Bal Tashchit)*

Israel Connection

The Hebrew word for potato is *tapuach adamah*, literally "apple of the earth." The *tapuach adamah* was first planted in Israel during the 1920s, at which time the growing period was limited to winter. At the onset of the Jewish communal settlements *(Kibbutzim)* in the 1930s, irrigation by sprinklers was introduced, greatly increasing Israel's *tapuach adamah* production. Today, Israel grows a variety of potatoes throughout the entire year from the Golan Heights to the Negev. Most of Israel's potato production is consumed as fresh boiled potatoes. You can find more information about Israel's *tapuach adamah* from the following web site: http://lanra.dac.uga.edu/potato/mideast/israel.htm. In your class, you can boil up some potatoes and eat them Israeli style.

Hebrew Vocabulary

Here are some Hebrew words and phrases you can use as you talk about and eat potatoes:

Potato/es	*Ta-**pu**-ach a-da-**mah**/* *ta-**pu**-chei a-da-**mah***	תַּפּוּחַ אֲדָמָה/ תַּפּוּחֵי אֲדָמָה

Roots	Shor-a-**shim**	שׁוֹרָשִׁים
Plant	Tza-**mach**	צֶמַח
I like to eat *latkes* (m/f)	A-**ni** o-**hev**/o-**hev**-et l'e-**chol** l'vi-**vot**.	אֲנִי אוֹהֵב/אוֹהֶבֶת לֶאֱכֹל לְבִיבוֹת.
Let's plant potatoes.	Bo-**u** lin-**to**-ah ta-**pu**-chei a-da-**mah**.	בֹּאוּ לִנְטֹעַ תַּפּוּחֵי אֲדָמָה.

Songs and Poems

Tapuach Adamah

By Deborah Schein. Because this poem plays on the words "apple from the earth," it would be fun to have in hand both an apple and a potato when you introduce the poem.

Tapuach adamah
An apple from the earth
Isn't red and juicy
And wasn't eaten first
It's common, round and brown
To eat it must be cooked
Tapuach, tapuach,
Tapuach adamah
Here I'm holding both up
Please come take a look.

Take a Potato

Author unknown. Found on the recording, Just In Time For Chanukah *by Ilene Safyan and Margie Rosenthal.*

Take a potato, pat, pat, pat
Roll it and make it flat, flat, flat
Fry it in a pan with fat, fat, fat
Chanukah latkes just like that!

Watch the dreidel spin, spin, spin
It will land on nun, gimel, hey, or shin
Play it with your friends and win, win, win
Chanukah dreidels spin, spin, spin!

Blessings

When we eat potatoes, this is the blessing we say:

בָּרוּךְ אַתָּה יְיָ אֱלֹהֵינוּ מֶלֶךְ הָעוֹלָם בּוֹרֵא פְּרִי הָאֲדָמָה.

Ba-**ruch** A-**tah** A-do-**nai** E-lo-**hei**-nu **Me**-lech Ha-O-**lam** Bo-**rei** P'**ri** Ha-A-da-**mah**.
We praise You, our God, Creator of the universe, Who creates fruit from the earth.

Story: Growing Potatoes

By Deborah Schein

My teacher and my entire class came to my house last Sukkot. My garden was almost all harvested. All that was left were a handful of potatoes buried in the ground. Abe and Zach discovered them while they were digging. *Morah* Devorah was excited and asked my *Ima* if we might take the potatoes back to school so we could plant them in the spring time. Naturally, *Ima* said yes, so we returned to school with eight brown dirt-covered potatoes.

We took one potato and stuck it with a few toothpicks and put it in a glass jar of water. It sat on our science table all year. It is now a lovely green plant. It has a few baby potatoes growing from its side. The rest of the potatoes were carefully placed in our dark storage closet. We all asked *Morah* Devorah, "When will we get to see the potatoes again?" She told us to remind her about the potatoes when the snow melted and then we would find out.

But during winter, right before Chanukah, *Morah* Devorah took out the potatoes. We told her, "It isn't spring yet. There is still lots of snow outside. It is way too early to plant the potatoes!"

Morah Devorah smiled and said, "But it is Chanukah and we need the potatoes to make something special. Can you guess what I am thinking of?"

We knew and we all answered with excitement — *latkes*! We took the bag of potatoes out of the closet and carefully counted them. There were seven left.

Morah Devorah asked us to count out just five potatoes and to tell her how many were left. We had just two potatoes left for growing. Would that be enough for planting? There was no time then to worry. It was Chanukah so we made delicious potato *latkes* and celebrated the holiday with candles, singing, and a retelling of the story of the Maccabees.

Spring finally came and we went looking for those two lonely potatoes. They were full of eyes — potato eyes and sprouts. We cut the potatoes so each piece had an eye and sprouts and we planted them with some help from a local farmer.

Summer came, and when I returned to school in the fall, *Morah* Devorah was no longer my teacher. My classmates and I did not forget about the potatoes, though, and neither did *Morah* Devorah. Right before Sukkot we received an invitation from

Morah Devorah's class to please help them dig for potatoes. There were shovels and kids and parents and teachers and we were all digging in the right place. All we found that day was one teeny tiny potato. *Morah* Devorah said not to worry, my *Ima* had already promised her more potatoes from our garden so that she and her class could try again. Next time they will say a blessing when they plant, "We praise You, our God, Creator of the universe, Who makes all of creation. Please be our partner and help our potatoes grow!" Maybe this time, more potatoes will grow!

Questions and Suggestions:

➤ Why do you think only one potato grew?

➤ What potato planting tips would you offer *Morah* Devorah?

➤ Try growing some potatoes with your class to use for making *latkes*.

Resources

Books and Music

Back, Christine and Barrie Watts. *Potato*. New Jersey: A & C Black Publishers Limited, 1984.
> *Follows the development of a potato plant, using clear and real illustrations, as well as clear and suitable text for young children.*

Hirsch, Marilyn. *Potato Pancakes All Around*. Philadelphia, PA: The Jewish Publication Society of America, 1982.
> *A wandering peddler teaches the villagers how to make potato pancakes from a crust of bread.*

Manushkin, Fran. *Latkes and Applesauce — A Hanukkah Story*. New York: Scholastic, Inc. 1990.
> *A blizzard leaves a peasant family housebound at Hanukkah with the potatoes for latkes buried under the snowdrifts. But when the family takes in first a stray cat and later a stray dog, the two animals return the favor.*

Safyan, Ilene and Margie Rosenthal. *Just in Time for Chanukah*. Portland, OR: Sheera Recordings, 1987.
> *A delightful collection of thirteen Chanukah tunes, including "Take a Potato." Available from Sheera Recordings, http://www.sheeramusic.com.*

On the Web

Information on Potato Production in Israel
http://lanra.dac.uga.edu/potato/mideast/israel.htm
> *All about potato growing in Israel.*

Growing Potatoes
http://www.hdra.org.uk/factsheets/gg9.htm
   Information on how to sprout, plant, and harvest potatoes.

How to grow potatoes without digging
http://www.hdra.org.uk/organicgardening/nd_spuds.htm
   An alternate way of growing potatoes.

Potato Battery
http://www.quantumscientific.com/pclock.html
   A neat science experiment that uses a potato to generate electricity.

Very Best Kids
http://verybestkids.com
   Type "sweet potato" in the "search" box for instructions on how to grow a beautiful leafy vine from a sweet potato.

7. What's Jewish about Pumpkins and Gourds?

Each and every fall season, children in North America see pumpkins and gourds being sold in supermarkets and grocery stores. If they are lucky, someone will take them for a ride in the country where they might see farm fields covered with big orange pumpkins or smaller, harder gourds, the pumpkin's cousin. But what is Jewish about pumpkins and gourds?

The Big Idea

When God told Noah to gather two of each type of animal for his ark, it is also said that God asked Noah's wife, Naamah, to gather all the seeds so that flowers, fruits, and vegetables might once again grow in abundance after the flood. Pumpkins and gourds must have been on the list, because every fall, just in time for Sukkot, it is common to see pumpkins and gourds growing in the fields, being sold in the markets, and hung as decoration in many a *sukkah*. This is the time of year when the Book of Ecclesiastes is read by Jews the world over — a time for every season, a time for every purpose under heaven. Sukkot, harvesting, and pumpkins and gourds go hand in hand in exemplifying Jewish time. So when we think about pumpkins and gourds, we are made aware of how many things in our world help us appreciate and realize Jewish time.

Jewish Values

Sometimes, the activities we are involved in with children are Jewish moments, even it it's not readily apparent. Jewish values lead to Jewish behaviors. Pumpkins and gourds are filled with Jewish values, including:

Bal Tashchit	Do not Destroy	בַּל תַּשְׁחִית
Brit	Partnership with God	בְּרִית
Hazan et Hakol	Feeding Everyone	הַזָּן אֶת הַכֹּל
"Jewish Time"	Making the Ordinary Sacred	
Ma'aseh B'reishit	Miracle of Creation	מַעֲשֵׂה בְּרֵאשִׁית
V'Samachta B'chagecha	Rejoicing in our Festivals	וְשָׂמַחְתָּ בְּחַגֶּיךָ

When children explore pumpkins and gourds, they are literally embodying Jewish values. Children's explorations are richest when the children are partners in their own learning. To engage children in these Jewish values and to deepen their learning, take time to investigate what children already know about pumpkins and gourds. Observe children's play and analyze their comments. Seek out the children's questions and interests. Based on the children's questions, you might:

➤ Place a pumpkin and some gourds on your science table and invite the children to observe them, draw them, and make predictions about what is inside. (You will be surprised!) When the time is right, cut open the pumpkin and gourds and record the children's observations. *(Ma'aseh Bereishit)*

➤ Remove the seeds from the pumpkins and gourds. Cook some for eating, save some for planting, and dry some to feed to the birds and squirrels during the winter months. *(Brit, Bal Tashchit)*

➤ Use pumpkins and gourds for making print designs, or for decorating your *sukkah*. They can also be hollowed out and dried to be used as containers. *(V'Samachta B'chagecha, "Jewish Time")*

➤ Let some gourds dry to become maracas. Be patient, this can take several months. *(Brit, Bal Tashchit)*

➤ Plant some of the seeds and watch what happens. Eventually, plant them in a garden so that the children are able to witness the complete cycle of a plant's life. *(Brit)*

➤ Put the scooped out pumpkin into your garden and let the birds eat from it. *(Bal Tashchit)*

➤ Use the meat from a scooped out pumpkin to make soup and invite friends for lunch — try the recipe below. *(Bal Tashchit, Hachnasat Orchim, Hazan et Hakol)*

Jacob's Creamy Pumpkin Soup
By Jacob Handelman, used with permission. This is a dairy recipe. To make it parve, substitute margarine for the butter, and rice or soy milk for the milk.

Ingredients
    1 small butternut squash or baking pumpkin (approx. 1 lb.)
    2 tbsp honey
    1 tbsp butter
    2 small onions, minced
    2 fresh rosemary leaves, minced
    4 C milk
    salt, pepper, and honey to taste

Directions

1. Cut squash/pumpkin in half. Remove seeds.

2. Squeeze honey on squash/pumpkin meat. Roast in preheated oven at 350 degrees until tender (approx. 1-1/2 hours). Cool and cut flesh from skin.

3. Melt butter in a large saucepan. Add minced onions. Cook over low heat until translucent.

4. Add squash/pumpkin and milk. Raise heat to medium until the soup lightly boils.

5. Reduce heat to low and add rosemary. Simmer for 10 minutes.

6. Puree soup in a blender. Soup will be thick and rich.

Israel Connection

Pumpkins and gourds have been growing in Israel and surrounding lands since ancient times. Pumpkins and gourds are thought to be one of the first fruits to be harvested by farmers. They provide nourishment and can be cooked in a myriad of ways (breads, pies, stews). Also, the outer shell of a gourd can be used to scoop and hold water. With a piece of cleaned animal skin stretched tightly over an opening, hollowed gourds make fine drums. The book *Making Gourd Musical Instruments* by Ginger Summit and Jim Widess is a great resource. See http://shop.welburngourds.com for more gourd ideas.

Neomy Selman, of Moshav Ramot Hashavim, near near Kfar Saba, Israel, grows gourds and then makes wonderful creations by painting them. The process is long — three months for growing the gourds and another three months to let them dry. Finally they are hollowed and then painted. These gourds can be bought on any Tuesday or Friday at the art fair held on Nachalat Benjamin Street in Tel Aviv, Israel.

In your classroom, invite the children to create their own painted gourds or instruments.

Hebrew Vocabulary

Here are some Hebrew words and phrases you can use as you explore pumpkins and gourds:

Pumpkin	*D'la-at*	דְּלַעַת
Gourd	*D'la-at*	דְּלַעַת
Fruit (sing/pl)	*P'ri/Pei-rot*	פְּרִי/פֵּרוֹת
Garden	*Gan*	גַּן
Seed	*Ze-ra*	זֶרַע
We planted pumpkins.	*Sha-tal-nu d'lu-im.*	שָׁתַלְנוּ דְּלוּעִים.
What's inside the pumpkin?	*Ma bif-nim ha-d'la-at?*	מַה בִּפְנִים הַדְּלַעַת?

A note about Halloween: While there are many ways to enjoy pumpkins without relating them to the holiday of Halloween, it is important to mention here why

Halloween is not an appropriate holiday to celebrate in a Jewish early childhood classroom. The origins of Halloween can be traced back to the fifth century B.C.E. to a holiday called Samhain, the Celtic New Year, which fell on October 31, the last day of the Celtic year. On Samhain, the curtain dividing the realms of the living and the dead was believed to be at its thinnest. This allowed spirits to spend this night visiting the world of the living and possibly finding bodies to possess. Celtic tradition involved dressing up in costume, mostly by adults, to avoid being recognized by the spirits. Centuries later, medieval Christian authorities adapted the holiday to be the church-sanctioned holiday of All Hallows Day. Now, you might argue that nobody's trick-or-treating nowadays to honor the dead, and we aren't dressing up to hide from Celtic spirits anymore. What's the harm in dressing up and eating a little candy? There probably is no harm, but there's no benefit either. Why spend precious classroom time on Halloween when there are so many beneficial, more interesting things you could be exploring with your children? Plus, we have the holiday of Purim coming later in the year, a wonderful opportunity to dress in costume and eat treats within a Jewish context. To explore this issue more, see www.zipple.com/holidays/20001027_halloween.shtml.

Songs and Poems

The Pumpkin
By Deborah Schein

From deep within the pumpkin shell
We can not see the seed, oh well,
Then out it comes that little seed
And quietly, slowly food to feed
That pumpkin can be lots of things
In the sukkah it hears us sing
From seed to fruit
From fruit to wall
God made the pumpkin
God made it all

Jonah, Jonah Pumpkin Eater
Adapted by Deborah Schein

Jonah, Jonah pumpkin eater
Had a pumpkin, couldn't keep her
Put her in a sukkah tall
And there she hung a week in fall.

Blessings

When we eat pumpkins and gourds, this is the blessing we say:

בָּרוּךְ אַתָּה יְיָ אֱלֹהֵינוּ מֶלֶךְ הָעוֹלָם בּוֹרֵא פְּרִי הָאֲדָמָה.

Ba-ruch A-tah A-do-nai E-lo-hei-nu Me-lech Ha-O-lam Bo-rei P'ri Ha-A-da-mah.
We praise You, our God, Creator of the universe, Who creates fruit from the earth.

Story: A Study of a Small Pumpkin

A true story, by Deborah Schein, about a pre-K Class from Cleveland, Ohio.

It was almost time for Sukkot, and the pumpkin and gourds sat on the science table. We all looked at them and wondered about them. One day Zoe came in, picked up the small pumpkin-looking gourd and asked *Morah* Devorah, "Is this a little pumpkin or a gourd?" *Morah* Devorah answered as she usually did, with another question, "What do you think it is, Zoe?" When Zoe shrugged, *Morah* Devorah asked, "Well, what can we do to find out?" At this Zoe's face lit up as she responded with, "I know, let's cut it open!"

Before the class cut open the pumpkin, *Morah* Devorah invited any interested students to first draw and then dictate their predictions. Zoe drew a picture of a little pumpkin inside a big pumpkin. This is what she thought would be found within the small pumpkin she held that morning. Eli thought there would be a big pumpkin inside the little pumpkin. Many of the children agreed with Zoe, some with Eli. Only Eliza suggested that there might be seeds inside the pumpkin.

When it was time to make the cut, all the children were curious and came to watch. The outside was hard to cut, but once the knife was through the shell, it slid around the circumference smoothly and easily. Finally it was time to look inside the pumpkin. Everyone held their breath. Whose predictions would be correct? Would Zoe's question be answered? *Morah* Devorah lifted the top and . . . what do you think she and the children found? Was it pumpkins or seeds? Was this a pumpkin or a gourd? The answer is not written here. You should go and make your own predictions. Keep in mind that no answer is silly, no question should be left unasked. God created the pumpkin and our minds. So have fun with your exploration of pumpkins and gourds!

Questions and Suggestions:

➤ Discuss why all the children's predictions make good sense. (Zoe's answer makes sense because the pumpkin inside would have to be smaller. Eli's answer makes sense, because most pumpkins the children see are large. Eliza's answer makes sense because we know it to be true, but Eliza only knows this because she has experience working in a garden with her grandmother.)

➤ It is important to let children make their own discoveries. Real understanding for children of this age comes from hands-on experience, not by being given the answer.

➤ Have children compare fruits and vegetables. Sorting them may be confusing. Here is why: the word "fruit" is a scientific term given to all plants that bear seeds. The word "vegetable" is not a scientific term. Some fruits are called vegetables such as pumpkins and gourds, but they are also fruit.

➤ Point of information: a pumpkin is a type of gourd, but not all gourds are pumpkins. The small pumpkin that Zoe picked up was indeed a small pumpkin, but it also was a gourd. Pumpkins are gourds with softer shells. Harder shelled gourds are not pumpkins. In fact the Hebrew word for both pumpkin and gourd are the same: *d'la-at*.

Resources

Books and Music

King, Elizabeth. *The Pumpkin Patch*. New York: Puffin, 1996.
  Text and photos describe the activities in a pumpkin patch, as pink colored seeds become a fat pumpkin. The last pages display Halloween, but the pictures are worthy of showing to a class of Jewish children.

Levenson, George. *Pumpkin Circle*. Berkley, California: Tricycle Press, 1999.
  This book has wonderful pictures of seeds, leaves, blossoms, and pumpkins, plus instructions on how to grow pumpkin seeds.

Sasso, Sandy. *Noah's Wife: The Story of Naamah*. Woodstock, VT: Jewish Lights Publishing, 2002.
  Naamah is asked by God to gather all the seeds before the flood so that all flower and fauna can once again grow upon the earth. Also available in an abbreviated board book form titled Naamah, Noah's Wife *(2002).*

Summit, Ginger and Jim Widess. *Making Gourd Musical Instruments: Over 60 String, Wind & Percussion Instruments & How to Play Them*. New York: Sterling, 2002.
  Legitimate musical instruments made from traditional materials, fully playable as well as being beautifully crafted.

On the Web

California Gourds
http://shop.welburngourds.com
  An online store featuring gourds, gourd books, craft projects, and supplies.

Growing Pumpkins

http://www.sadako.com/pumpkin/growing.html

This web site offer pictures, directions for growing pumpkins, the history of pumpkins, and anything else you need to know about pumpkins.

Is Halloween Kosher?

http://www.zipple.com/holidays/20001027_halloween.shtml

An interesting history of Halloween, and a discussion of whether or not Jews should celebrate Halloween.

8. What's Jewish about Soup?

Soup is fun and easy to make with young children. It is magical to watch a pot of water and added ingredients boil and steam and then transform into something good to eat. It has become a traditional part of many early childhood curricula to read several versions of the folk tale "Stone Soup," and then to make soup with the children on a cold fall morning. But what is Jewish about soup?

The Big Idea

Making soup with a young child is usually seen as an exercise in math (measuring) and science (combining ingredients and observing change). When you wear a Jewish lens, however, cooking soup becomes much more than this. The ingredients used will determine what blessing to recite before eating. Deciding with whom it is shared and how it is shared can transform the eating of soup into an exercise in Jewish values. We depend on our partnership with God to make the soup. God provides us with the water and the seeds for many of the ingredients. We grow the vegetables and raise the chickens. We cook and share the soup. So when we think about soup, we are made aware of our partnership with God.

Jewish Values

Sometimes, the activities we are involved in with children are Jewish moments, even if it's not readily apparent. Jewish values lead to Jewish behaviors. Soup is filled with Jewish values, including:

Bal Tashchit	Do not Destroy	בַּל תַּשְׁחִית
Bikur Cholim	Visiting the Sick	בִּקוּר חוֹלִים
Brit	Partnership with God	בְּרִית
G'milut Chasadim	Acts of Loving-kindness	גְּמִילוּת חֲסָדִים
Hachnasat Orchim	Hospitality/Welcoming Guests	הַכְנָסַת אוֹרְחִים
Hazan et Hakol	Feeding Everyone	הַזָּן אֶת הַכֹּל
Hoda'ah	Appreciation	הוֹדָאָה
"Jewish Time"	Making the Ordinary Sacred	
Lichvod Shabbat	To Honor Shabbat	לִכְבוֹד שַׁבָּת
Ma'aseh B'reishit	Miracle of Creation	מַעֲשֵׂה בְּרֵאשִׁית
Shmirat HaGuf	Caring for the Body	שְׁמִירַת הַגוּף
V'achalta V'savata	To Eat and be Satisfied	וְאָכַלְתָּ וְשָׂבָעְתָּ

When children explore soup, they are literally embodying Jewish values. Children's explorations are richest when the children are partners in their own learning. To engage children in these Jewish values and to deepen their learning, take time to investigate what children already know about soup. Observe children's play and analyze their comments. Seek out the children's questions and interests. Based on the children's questions, you might:

➤ Create classroom provocations where the children will suggest that the class make soup. Do this by reading several versions of "Stone Soup," including *Bone Button Borscht* by Aubrey Davis (a Jewish variation), by helping to harvest a garden or by having carrots, celery, or onions sitting on the science table, or by placing a large pot in the Dramatic Play Area. Invite parents to come help when you do make the soup. (*Brit, Bal Tashchit, Ma'aseh B'reishit*)

➤ Take time to sit and enjoy the soup. Revisit the process and the benefits soup brings. (*V'achalta V'savata, Shmirat HaGuf, Hoda'ah*)

➤ Say a blessing before eating. This blessing will be determined by the ingredients used in the soup. For ingredients such as carrots, celery, and onions, which all grow inside the earth, you say "*Borei P'ri HaAdamah.*" If the soup has noodles, you can say the blessing, "*Borei Minei M'zonot.*" (*Brit, Ma'aseh B'reishit, Hoda'ah*)

➤ Say a blessing when the soup is finished. This blessing (*Birkat HaMazon*) thanks God for the entire process of making the soup, including the growing of the seed, for the farmer, the sun and the rain, the harvesting of the food, the grocer, the preparation, and the satisfaction of eating. *Birkat HaMazon* appreciates and thanks God who makes it all possible. (*Brit, Ma'aseh B'reishit, Hoda'ah*)

➤ Learn about foods that are healthy for the body. Fresh vegetables are definitely on this list! Use these foods in your soup. (*Shimrat HaGuf*)

➤ Share the soup with others. Invite guests or another class to join your class, or bring some soup to those that are less fortunate or those that are sick. (*Hachnasat Orchim, Hazan et Hakol, G'milut Chasadim, Bikur Cholim*)

Israel Connection

People often think of chicken soup when they think about Jewish soup. Israelis, though, make many types of soup. Included here are two recipes, one for chicken soup and one for fruit soup. The chicken soup recipe comes from the Israeli Embassy. It might be cooked and served on Shabbat or Rosh HaShanah, or brought to those sick with a cold. The fruit soup would be cool and delicious on a warm Israeli day. It might be prepared and served for any of the harvest holidays such as Sukkot, Shavuot, and Pesach. Enjoy!

Israeli Embassy Chicken Soup

Source: San Francisco Examiner

Yield: 2-1/2 Quarts

Ingredients

1 soup chicken	3 carrots, cut in pieces
Chicken feet	3 stalks celery, cut in pieces
3-1/2 qt water	2 sprigs dill
2 onions, cut in pieces	3 sprigs parsley
1 tbsp salt	

Directions:

Clean the chicken and the feet thoroughly. (The feet add strength to the soup, so use as many as you can get.) Combine in a deep saucepan with water and onions. Bring to a boil and cook over medium heat for 1-1/2 hours.

Add remaining ingredients. Cover and cook over low heat for 1 hour longer or until chicken is tender. Remove chicken and strain soup. Use the chicken in other dishes or serve with the soup.

Israeli Fruit Soup

Source: www.gourmed.gr/recipes/israeli/

Ingredients

2 oranges, peeled	1 cup brown sugar or honey
2 stalks rhubarb, cut in pieces	1/2 tsp salt
4 slices fresh pineapple	1/2 tsp cinnamon
1 cup strawberries	2 tbsp lemon juice
1 cup pitted cherries	1 cup sour cream
6 cups water	

Directions:

Combine all the ingredients except the sour cream. Adjust to taste. Simmer covered for about 20 minutes, or until the fruit is tender. Puree or force through a sieve. Chill and add sour cream before serving.

Note: Other fruits may be substituted, but make sure there is a combination of tart and sweet.

Hebrew Vocabulary

Here are some Hebrew words and phrases you can use as you explore soup:

Soup	Ma-rak	מָרָק
Carrots	Ge-za-rim	גְּזָרִים
Water	Ma-yim	מַיִם
Pot	Sir	סִיר
Stone	E-ven	אֶבֶן
We are stirring.	A-nach-nu m'ar-bei-vim.	אֲנַחְנוּ מְעַרְבְּבִים.
We are eating.	A-nach-nu och-lim.	אֲנַחְנ אוֹכְלִים.
I (m/f) am making soup.	A-ni m'va-shel/ m'va-she-let ma-rak.	אֲנִי מְבַשֵּׁל/ מְבַשֶּׁלֶת מָרָק.
Would you like (m/f) some soup?	A-tah ro-tzeh/ at ro-tzah ma-rak?	אַתָּה רוֹצֶה/ אַתְ רוֹצָה מָרָק?

Songs and Poems

This Is the Way We Make Our Soup
*By Deborah Schein. Sung to the tune of "Here We Go 'Round the Mulberry Bush,"
the music and words to which can be found in* A Treasury of Children's Songs *by Dan
Fox. A sound clip of the melody can be found at*
http://www.niehs.nih.gov/kids/lyrics/mulberry.htm.

This is the way we make our soup
Make our soup, make our soup
This is the way we make our soup,
So early in the morning

This is the way we gather vegetables
Gather vegetables, gather vegetables
This is the way we gather vegetables
So early in the morning

This is the way we cut our vegetables
Cut our vegetables, cut our vegetables
This is the way we cut our vegetables
So early in the morning

This is the way we stir in the water
Stir in the water, stir in the water

This is the way we stir in the water
So early in the morning

Add other steps (cover the pot, serve the soup, etc.) and change the time of day, if desired, until:

This is the way we say our *bracha*
Say our *bracha*
Say our *bracha*
This is the way we say our *bracha*
Just before we eat

Soup
By Deborah Schein

I think soup is rather nice.
It's good to eat when there's snow and ice.
It fills me up and makes me sing,
"Thank you God for everything."
The veggies, the pot, the taste, the hot
The friends to share, and all the care
That goes into the soup I eat
Now everyone come have a seat.
The soup is ready, it's time to eat!

Blessings

When we eat soup made from vegetables that grow in the ground, this is the blessing we say:

בָּרוּךְ אַתָּה יְיָ אֱלֹהֵינוּ מֶלֶךְ הָעוֹלָם בּוֹרֵא פְּרִי הָאֲדָמָה.

*Ba-**ruch** A-**tah** A-do-**nai** E-lo-**hei**-nu **Me**-lech Ha-O-**lam** Bo-**rei** P'ri Ha-A-da-**mah**.*
We praise You, our God, Creator of the universe, Who creates food from the ground.

When we include rice or noodles in our soup, this is the blessing we say:

בָּרוּךְ אַתָּה יְיָ אֱלֹהֵינוּ מֶלֶךְ הָעוֹלָם בּוֹרֵא מִינֵי מְזוֹנוֹת.

*Ba-**ruch** A-**tah** A-do-**nai** E-lo-**hei**-nu **Me**-lech Ha-O-**lam** Bo-**rei** Mi-**nei** M'zo-**not**.*
We praise You, our God, Creator of the universe, Who creates all kinds of food.

When we finish eating, we say *Birkat Hamazon* (the Blessing after the Meal) which gives thanks to God who created the farmer and garden, the sun and the rain, and gave us the ability to make and share the soup. Here is an abbreviated version of *Birkat Hamazon*:

בָּרוּךְ אַתָּה יְיָ הַזָּן אֶת הַכֹּל.

Ba-ruch A-tah A-do-nai Ha-zan et Ha-kol.
We praise You, our God, Who provides our food.

Story: Shabbat Soup

Adapted by Maxine Handelman from a traditional Jewish folktale.

Chaya Leah made the most wonderful Shabbat soup. Every Shabbat, she would make a huge pot of her famous soup. Her friends' mouths watered every week, hoping for an invitation to Chaya Leah's house for Shabbat soup.

Mara lived next door to Chaya Leah. Mara didn't have many friends. She found it hard to smile. One day, Mara marched over to Chaya Leah's house and knocked on the door. BANG! BANG! Chaya Leah opened the door and smiled when she saw Mara. "Mara, how nice to see you," Chaya Leah said.

"Give me your recipe for your soup," demanded Mara.

"Why, certainly," said Chaya Leah. She invited Mara in and gave her the recipe for her soup.

Mara marched directly to the store, recipe in hand. "Let's see," she muttered as she shopped. "I need onions . . . potatoes . . . carrots . . ." She bought all the ingredients, went home, and made the soup. It took hours to prepare and when it was finally steaming and ready she sat down to try it. She tasted it and UGH! It tasted horrible.

Mara stomped over to Chaya Leah's house and banged on the door. Chaya Leah opened the door with a smile, but Mara shook her finger and said, "You gave me the wrong recipe. That soup tasted terrible!"

Chaya Leah said, "Oh, did you make the soup just now? That soup is only for Shabbat." And then she asked Mara, "And did you eat it by yourself? That soup needs to be shared with friends."

"Oh" said Mara, "I don't have any friends."

"Tell you what," said Chaya Leah, "I'll bring my friends to your house on Shabbat and you can remake the soup."

"Okay," said Mara, and she stomped away without even saying thank you.

Mara went back to the grocery store and bought all the ingredients for more soup. She waited until just before Shabbat to make the soup.

On Shabbat, Mara heard a knock at her door. She opened the door and there stood Chaya Leah and her friends.

"Shabbat Shalom," said Chaya Leah.

"Shabbat Shalom," said Mara. She tried to smile.

Everyone came in and sat around the table. Each person was afraid to be the first one to taste the soup.

Finally, Chaya Leah took a big sip and a smile broke out on her face. "This soup is wonderful!"

Everyone smiled and began to eat their soup.

"Wonderful!"

"So delicious!"

From then on, Mara knew to make Shabbat soup on Shabbat, and to always share it with friends.

Questions and Suggestions:

➤ Why did the soup taste better on Shabbat and with friends?

➤ What did Mara learn from Chaya Leah?

➤ What other things could be done with soup to make it taste better?

➤ What makes soup taste good to you?

➤ Make some soup and eat it at different times to see if the story is true.

Resources

Books and Music

Brown, Marcia. *Stone Soup.* Upper Saddle River, NJ: Scott Foresman, 1947.
This French tale about soldiers who trick miserly villages into making them a feast won a Caldecott Medal.

Davis, Aubrey. *Bone Button Borscht.* Buffalo, NY: Kids Can Press Ltd., 1995.
A Jewish version of the folktale "Stone Soup."

Fox, Dan. *A Treasury of Children's Songs.* New York: Henry Holt & Company, Inc., 2003.
In this popular songbook, forty classic childhood songs are imaginatively illustrated with treasures from the Metropolitan Museum of Art. All of the selections include simple arrangements for musical accompaniment. Includes "Here We Go 'Round the Mulberry Bush."

Heymsfeld, Carla. *The Matzah Ball Fairy.* New York: Union of American Hebrew Congregations, 1996.
When Frieda Pinsky uses some magic powder to help make the matzah balls for her Passover seder light and fluffy, it works too well.

Hershenhom, Esther. *Chicken Soup by Heart*. New York: Simon & Schuster Children's Publishing, 2002.

This look at an intergenerational friendship is as satisfying as a bowl of chicken soup. When Rudie Dinkins discovers that his elderly sitter, Mrs. Gittel, has the flu, he decides that it's time for him to take care of her for a change and gets ready to cook her a batch of her own medicine. A recipient of a Sidney Taylor Award.

McGovern, Ann. *Stone Soup*. New York: Scholastic. 1986.

A clever young man tricks an old woman into believing that soup can be made from a stone. As the pot of water boils with the stone in it, he urges her to add more and more ingredients until the soup is a feast "fit for a king."

Muth, Jon J. *Stone Soup*. New York: Scholastic, 2003

Three wise monks trick a poor, frightened community into finding happiness by teaching them the magic of generosity.

On the Web

Soup of the Evening . . . Beautiful Soup
http://www.soupsong.com

A witty and substantive research effort on the history of soup and food in all cultures, with over 400 pages of recipes, quotations, stories, songs, traditions, and more.

Part II: Animals

9. What's Jewish about Birds?

Outside the window a small bird perches on a tree branch. It cleans its wing with its beak, hops a few steps, and then flies away. Birds are captivating and fascinating creatures, but what is Jewish about birds?

The Big Idea

On the fifth day of creation, God created birds that could fly across the sky. Some birds add color to the world such as multicolored peacocks, blue jays, and red cardinals. Other birds are unique — swimming penguins, fast running ostriches, and talking parrots. Some birds, most birds in fact, were given the gift of song — the hooting of the owl, the haunting cry of the whippoorwill, and the sweet songs of the robin, sparrow, and chickadee. The rabbis tell us that the song of birds is meant as praise to God.

Birds are mentioned many times in the Torah. The raven and the dove are both featured in the story of Noah. In Deuteronomy it states that an egg or a young bird may not be taken from its mother. And in the Torah portion *Vayikra*, it clearly states that birds of prey and scavengers, such as herons, hawks, pelicans, and swans, should not be eaten. Birds definitely bring variety and beauty to the world. So when we learn about birds, we appreciate and are reminded of God's creations.

Jewish Values

Sometimes, the activities we are involved in with children are Jewish moments, even if it's not readily apparent. Jewish values lead to Jewish behaviors. Birds are filled with Jewish values, including:

Brit	Partnership with God	בְּרִית
Hoda'ah	Appreciation	הוֹדָאָה
Ma'aseh B'reishit	Miracle of Creation	מַעֲשֵׂה בְּרֵאשִׁית
Ohev et HaBriyot	Loving all Creatures	אוֹהֵב אֶת הַבְּרִיּוֹת
Tza'ar Ba'alei Chayim	Kindness to Animals	צַעַר בַּעֲלֵי חַיִּים

When children interact with birds, they are literally embodying Jewish values. Children's explorations are richest when the children are partners in their own learning. To engage children in these Jewish values and to deepen their learning, take time to investigate what children already know about birds. Observe children's play and analyze their comments. Seek out the children's questions and interests. Based on the children's questions, you might:

➤ Go on a bird walk to see what types of birds live near you. Record what you see using drawings, photographs, and dictation. Alternatively, put up a bird feeder or bird house to attract birds to come to you. *(Ma'aseh B'reishit, Hoda'ah)*

➤ Adopt a bird who frequents a nearby tree and continue to observe and study this bird so you might discover its uniqueness and it similarities to other creatures. *(Ma'aseh B'reishit, Hoda'ah)*

➤ Based on your study of birds, carefully select ways in which you may develop a relationship with this bird. It might be by laying out straw for a nest or by not getting too close when it comes near. *(Brit, Tza'ar Ba'alay Chayim, Ohev et HaBriyot)*

➤ Make bird feeders during winter, or bird baths in the summer. See the "Resources" section below for more information. *(Brit, Tza'ar Ba'alei Chayim)*

➤ Place binoculars near a classroom window so that children may look for birds throughout the day. *(Ma'aseh B'reishit)*

➤ Invite a bird watcher to your school to help you identify birds and/or to create a bird sanctuary in an outdoor space of your school environment. *(Brit, Tza'ar Ba'alei Chayim)*

➤ Discuss with children why God might have created all sorts of different birds. *(Ma'aseh B'reishit, Hoda'ah)*

Israel Connection

Because of its location and climate, Israel is a bird watchers paradise. Located between Africa, Europe, and Asia, Israel is a super-highway for migratory birds on their way to and from their seasonal habitats. Eilat, at the southern tip of Israel, is a particularly good place to see migrant birds because of its oasis-like qualities. The Hula valley, in northeast Israel between the Galilee mountains and the Golan Heights, is one of the prime wintering sites in the Middle East for a wide variety of birds. The southern part of the valley was established as a nature preserve in 1961.

The Web site www.birdingisrael.com offers beautiful pictures of birds in their Israeli habitat. One entry at this web site stated that 264 species of birds were spotted in a three month span! You will also learn that Kibbutz Lotan, located forty-five miles north of Eilat, is a center for bird watching in Israel. In the classroom, provide children with pictures of birds from Israel, binoculars, and clipboards and so they can pretend to be birdwatchers at Kibbutz Lotan. Learn more about bird watching at Kibbutz Lotan at http://www.birdingisrael.com/birdsOfIsrael/birdingLotan/index.htm.

Hebrew Vocabulary

Here are some Hebrew words and phrases you can use as you explore birds:

Bird	*Tzi-por*	צִפּוֹר
Song	*Shir*	שִׁיר
Wing/s	*Ka-naf/k'na-fa-yim*	כָּנָף/כְּנָפַיִם
Feather	*No-tzah*	נוֹצָה
I see (m/f) a bird	*A-ni ro-eh/ro-ah tzi-por.*	אֲנִי רוֹאֶה/רוֹאָה צִפּוֹר.
The bird is flying in the sky.	*Ha-tzi-por ahf ba-sha-ma-yim.*	הַצִפּוֹר עָף בַּשָׁמַיִם.

Songs and Poems

Al Ha-Etz (On The Tree)

From Songs of Childhood *by Judith Eisenstein and Frieda Prensky. Used with permission.*

Al ha-etz, al ha-etz,	*On the tree, on the tree,*
Al ha-etz tzipor.	*On the tree, sits a bird.*
Tzi, tzif, tzif	*Chirp, chirp, chirp*
Tzif, tzif, tzif,	*Chirp, chirp, chirp*
Sharah ha-tzi-por.	*Sings the bird.*
Al ha-etz, al ha-etz,	*On the tree, on the tree,*
Al ha-etz tzipor.	*On the tree, sits a bird.*
Uf, uf, uf,	*Fly, fly, fly,*
Uf, uf, uf,	*Fly, fly, fly,*
Afah ha-tzipor.	*The bird flies.*

The authors suggest that the children sing while pretending to be birds. Each child finds a spot to be his/her tree. First, the children sit on the tree and sing, "Tzi, tzif, tzif" when the song tells about chirping. When the song says "fly", off they go with outstretched wings. When the music stops, they fly back to their trees.

How Do Birds Know?

By Deborah Schein

How do birds know
When to build their nests?
Does God whisper to them,

"This time is best"?

And how do they know
When to lay their eggs?
Does God tell them
"These are the days"?

What tells the birds
Which way to fly?
Does God direct them
Across the sky?
It's more than God's voice
It is something quite grand
That changes the weather
Animals and land
The birds feel the changes
And know what to do
Because God creates order
For birds, and for us too.

Blessings

When we study and appreciate birds, this is the blessing we can say:

בָּרוּךְ אַתָּה יְיָ אֱלֹהֵינוּ מֶלֶךְ הָעוֹלָם שֶׁכָּכָה לוֹ בְּעוֹלָמוֹ.

*Ba-**ruch** A-**tah** A-do-**nai** E-lo-**hei**-nu **Me**-lech Ha-O-**lam** She-**ka**-cha Lo B'O-la-**mo**.*
We praise You, our God, Creator of the universe, Who has made such things as
these in the world.

Story: Shabbat Shira

By Deborah Schein

Tzippi loved birds. One reason she loved birds so much was because
of their beauty. She would often see a blue jay sitting up in a tree singing.
Even in winter that jay could be seen scratching the ground clothed in blue
feathers. Tzippi loved the red of the robin, the yellow of the finch, and the
green-blue heads of the Canadian Geese. She was also aware that her name
itself came from *tzipur*, meaning bird.

One day, when Tzippi was four years old, her parents and her grandparents took her to synagogue. They often went together, but today they
said there will be something special. Tzippi tried to guess . . . would there be
singing? Her mother answered, "Yes, but there is always singing in the synagogue

on Shabbat." Tzippi guessed, "Will there be a special treat?" Her father answered, "Yes, but there is always a special treat on Shabbat." Tzippi asked, "Will I see my friends?" Her grandparents answered, "Yes, but you almost always see your friends at synagogue on Shabbat." Tzippi could not guess, so she had to wait.

When they arrived, everything seemed as it always did. People greeted each other, "Shabbat Shalom. How was your week?" Children were already sitting down looking at books or playing tag. It felt good, as it always did coming to the synagogue on Shabbat. But today, Tzippi kept looking and waiting for something special to happen. During the beginning part of the service she sang and stood and sat at the appropriate times. She sat quietly and listened to the rabbi speak and the grown-ups read. She watched as the Torah was taken from the ark and paraded around. She heard the rabbi say something about Moses and the Israelites singing songs of praise to God for leading them to freedom. And then Tzippi heard the rabbi say, "And today is *Shabbat Shira* — a special day for us to feed the birds. On *Shabbat Shira*, we read the Torah portion *Beshalach*. The custom of feeding the birds comes from a *midrash* about this portion. Moses told the people to gather a double portion of manna on Fridays, because no manna would fall on Shabbat. A few people with a grudge against Moses spread out some manna on Shabbat, to make the people think Moses had lied to them. But the birds came and ate the manna, foiling the plot. Today, we feed the birds on *Shabbat Shira* to reward them for their good deed." Now Tzippi knew why her parents and grand-parents thought the day would be special for her.

After the Torah reading, everyone went outside. It was a bit chilly and gray, but no one seemed to care, certainly not Tzippi. Everyone was given some breadcrumbs to scatter around the yard and a new bird feeder was placed in the tree sitting behind the synagogue. Tzippi felt so happy that she was big enough to participate in this special day. When everyone began singing, she joined in singing the words when she knew them and humming when she didn't. Tzippi sang with a voice as sweet as any bird, and on her face was a smile for all to see.

Questions and Suggestions:

➤ What else do birds give us? What other reasons do we have to appreciate birds?

➤ Brainstorm ways to celebrate *Shabbat Shira* — ways to show appreciation to birds — such as drawing pictures for the birds to look at through your classroom window.

➤ Make a present for the birds — see the "Resources" section on the next page.

Resources

Books and Music

Aroner, Miriam and Shelly O. Haas. *The Kingdom of Singing Birds.* Rockville, MD: Kar Ben Publishing, 1993.
> *A new king inherits a magnificent royal aviary in which dwell birds from all over the world, beautiful but utterly silent.*

Eisenstein, Judith Kaplan, Frieda Prensky, and Ayala Gordon. *Songs of Childhood.* New York: United Synagogue Commission on Jewish Education, 1955.
> *A wonderful book filled with Hebrew songs of childhood for all occasions including everyday activities, community workers, holidays, trips, and seasons. The Hebrew words are all written in transliteration, include simple translation, and are easy to read. Out of print, may be found in libraries or resource centers.*

Oberman, Sheldon. *The Wisdom Bird: A Tale of Solomon and Sheba.* Honesdale, PA: Boyds Mill Press, 2000.
> *King Solomon learns a lesson from a little bird in this story based on Jewish and African tales.*

Spier, Peter. *Noah's Ark.* New York: Yearling Books, 1992.
> *This is a Caldecott award winning book where the illustrations alone were used to depict the story of Noah.*

Westervelt, Linda. *Roger Tory Peterson's ABC of Birds.* New York: University Publishing, 1995.
> *A book for young birdwatchers.*

On the Web

Backyard Bird Feeding
http://baltimorebirdclub.org/by/feed.html

Backyard Birding
http://www.bcpl.net/~tross/by/backyard.html

> *These two Web sites have everything you need to know about watching, feeding, and building homes for birds in your backyard.*

10. What's Jewish about Butterflies?

In the springtime, many classes take the opportunity to raise caterpillars to butterflies. If we are lucky, we live in a place where we see many different kinds of butterflies flying around in the fresh spring weather. So, what's Jewish about butterflies?

The Big Idea

There are more than 160,000 species of butterflies, found all over the world. Each species varies in color, size, and survival techniques. According to the Creation story in the Torah, butterflies were created by God on the sixth day, the same day that humans were created. Observing butterflies in nature is a lesson in the awe of creation. As one watches butterflies soar, flutter, dip, land, and take off once more, one cannot help but be amazed by the beauty and delicateness of butterflies, as well as be awed by the skill of the butterfly's creator.

Ideally, a unit about butterflies will include actually growing caterpillars into butterflies (some resources for butterfly kits are listed at the end of this unit). As children engage in the transformation of caterpillars into butterflies, the partnership between the children and God becomes concrete and apparent. Becoming a butterfly (in a classroom) requires help from God and help from the children in the class — a partnership that children can engage in on a daily basis. Studying and caring for butterflies, be it in nature or in the classroom, leads us to think about Creation and the *brit*, the partnership between God and people.

Jewish Values

Sometimes, the activities we are involved in with children are Jewish moments, even if it's not readily apparent. Jewish values lead to Jewish behaviors. Observing butterflies, and caring for caterpillars as they grow into butterflies, sparks several Jewish values, including:

Bal Tashchit	Do not Destroy	בַּל תַּשְׁחִית
Brit	Partnership with God	בְּרִית
G'milut Chasadim	Acts of Loving-kindness	גְּמִילוּת חֲסָדִים
Ma'aseh B'reishit	Miracle of Creation	מַעֲשֵׂה בְּרֵאשִׁית
Tza'ar Ba'alei Chayim	Kindness to Animals	צַעַר בַּעֲלֵי חַיִּים

When children learn about butterflies, they are literally embodying Jewish values. Children's explorations are richest when the children are partners in their own learning. To engage children in these Jewish values and to deepen their learning, take time to investigate what children already know about butterflies. Observe children's play and analyze their comments. Seek out the children's questions and interests. Based on the children's questions, you might:

➤ Keep track of the varieties of butterflies you spot around your school. Take pictures when you can. *(Ma'aseh B'reishit)*

➤ If possible, take a field trip to a nature conservatory or local institution with live butterflies, or invite a butterfly expert to visit your class. Allow the children to get as close to live butterflies as possible. *(Ma'aseh B'reishit)*

➤ Name the job of feeding the caterpillars (and other animals in your room) "*Tza'ar Ba'alei Chayim.*"

➤ Discuss what we can do for butterflies and what butterflies do for people. *(G'milut Chasadim, Tza'ar Ba'alei Chayim)*

➤ Discuss what role God plays in helping caterpillars become butterflies (i.e. giving the caterpillars the wisdom and ability to build a chrysalis) and what role the children play (providing appropriate nourishment, being careful not to knock over the container, eventually setting the butterflies free). *(Brit)*

➤ If we keep the butterflies in the classroom too long, they will die. When you set your butterflies free, tell the children they are participating in the *mitzvot* of *Bal Tashchit* and *Tza'ar Ba'alei Chayim.*

Israel Connection

Butterflies and moths belong to the order *Lepidoptera*, which is part of the class *Insecta*. To date, more than 160,000 species have been identified by science, of which around 2300 are found in Israel. The reason for so many species of butterflies and moths in such a small area is the geographical location of Israel at the "junction" of three continents: Asia, Africa and Europe. To see lists and pictures of Israeli butterfly species, go to the home page of The Israeli Lepidopterists Society at http://www.geocities.com/RainForest/1153/. Another web site with lots of pictures of butterflies, moths, and other insects from Israel and worldwide can be found at http://www.nature-of-oz.com/butterflies.htm. As you spot local butterflies or grow some in your classroom, be on the lookout for butterflies that look like any of the butterfly species found in Israel.

Hebrew Vocabulary

Here are some Hebrew words and phrases you can use as you talk about your caterpillars and butterflies:

Butterfly	*Par-**par***	פַּרְפָּר
Caterpillar	*Za-**chal***	זַחַל
Cocoon	*P'ka-**at***	פְּקַעַת
Chrysalis	***Go**-lem*	גֹּלֶם
Sugar	***Su**-kar*	סֻכָּר
Sugar-water	*Mei-**su**-kar*	מֵי-סֻכָּר
Flower	*Pe-**rach***	פֶּרַח
Fly!	*Oof!*	עוּף
Butterflies are flying.	*Par-par-**im** A-**fim**.*	פַּרְפָּרִים עָפִים

Songs and Poems

This very popular Israeli children's song in Hebrew about a butterfly is written below in transliteration with suggested hand movements. If there is an Israeli teacher in your school, ask him or her to sing it for you. You can also find the music on the CD 100 Shirim Rishonim (100 First Songs) *by Daniela Gardosh and Talma Alyagon, and the poem in the book* Bo Alay Parpar Nechmad (Sweet Butterfly) *by Fania Bergstein.*

Bo Alay Parpar Nechmad
Israeli folksong

Bo a-lay parpar nech-mad   (butterfly movements with both hands)
Shev etz-lee al kaf ha-yad   (butterfly landing on the palm of the hand)
Shev, tanu-ach, al tee-rah,   (butterfly sitting on the palm of the hand)
V'ta-oof ba-cha-za-rah.   (butterfly flying away)

Come to me, nice butterfly.
Sit with me in the palm of my hand.
Sit, rest, don't fear,
And fly away again.

Blessings

When you free your butterflies, you can wish them well and acknowledge the beauty of God's creations with this blessing:

בָּרוּךְ אַתָּה יְיָ אֱלֹהֵינוּ מֶלֶךְ הָעוֹלָם עֹשֶׂה מַעֲשֵׂה בְרֵאשִׁית.

Ba-ruch A-tah A-do-nai E-lo-hei-nu Me-lech Ha-O-lam O-seh Ma-a-seh V'rei-shit.
We praise You, our God, Creator of the universe, Who makes all of creation.

You can also recite the *Shehecheyanu*, the blessing we say upon experiencing something wonderful for the first time (or the first time in a long time):

בָּרוּךְ אַתָּה יְיָ אֱלֹהֵינוּ מֶלֶךְ הָעוֹלָם שֶׁהֶחֱיָנוּ וְקִיְּמָנוּ וְהִגִּיעָנוּ לַזְּמַן הַזֶּה.

Ba-ruch A-tah A-do-nai E-lo-hei-nu Me-lech Ha-O-lam She-he-che-ya-nu,
V'ki-y'ma-nu, V'hi-gi-ya-nu Laz'man HaZeh.
We praise You, our God, Creator of the universe, for giving us life, sustaining us, and helping us to reach this moment.

Story: Caring for the World

By Maxine Handelman. This story illustrates the Jewish values of Tza'ar Ba'alei Chayim and our partnership with God.

When God created the world, God created the first man and woman, Adam and Eve. God created a beautiful garden, *Gan Eden*, for Adam and Eve to live in. After some time, it was time for Adam and Eve to leave *Gan Eden* and go out into the world. God said to Adam and Eve, "It is your job to take care of all the trees and flowers and plants in the world." God also said to Adam and Eve, "It is your job to take care of all the animals, and the fish, and even the bugs and butterflies."

Adam and Eve were not quite sure how to take care of God's world, of all the trees, flowers, animals, and even the butterflies. First they tried singing to the trees to make them feel happy and well cared for. The trees seemed to like their singing, but after a while their leaves started to droop and turn brown. "What are we doing wrong?" Eve asked Adam. "I don't know," said Adam. "Maybe we should try a different song." But while Adam and Eve were deciding on a new song, a butterfly fluttered into Eve's face and flew back and forth until Eve followed her. The butterfly led Eve to a stream. "Adam!" cried Eve. "The trees need water, not a different song!" Adam and Eve watered all the trees and plants, and soon they were not drooping or brown anymore.

With the help of the butterfly, Adam and Eve figured out the best ways to take care of all God's creations. After a day of watering, feeding, pruning, and grooming,

Adam and Eve still liked to sing to the trees, plants, animals, and fish. The butterfly liked their songs best of all.

Questions and Suggestions:

➤ How can we take care of the trees?

➤ How can we take care of the animals? How do we take care of our caterpillars?

➤ How will we take care of the butterflies when they come out of their chrysalises? (Note that the larval stage of a butterfly is called a chrysalis. Moths and other insects build cocoons, butterflies do not.)

➤ Using lots of different recycled materials (especially scraps of construction paper left over from other projects), invite the children to create the butterfly that helped Adam and Eve. Why did the butterfly help them?

Resources

Books and Music

Bergstein, Fania. *Bo Alay Parpar Nechmad.* Tel Aviv: HaKibbutz Hameuchad Publishing House, 2001.
    Originally published in 1945, this classic Israeli song is also a book (in Hebrew).

Gardosh, Daniela and Talma Alyagon. *100 Shirom Rishonim (100 First Songs).* Tel Aviv, Israel: Kineret Publishing House, 1970.
    Includes the song, "Bo Alay Parpar Nechmad." Compact disc and songbook, available at http://www.israeliscent.com.

Watson, Mary. *The Butterfly Seeds.* New York: Tambourine Books, 1995.
    A little boy comes to New York's Lower East Side with a package of seeds given him by his grandfather, who has stayed behind. Grandpa has told Jake to plant the seeds in his new garden and "like magic, you'll have hundreds of butterflies."

Materials and Supplies

The Nature Store — Butterfly Kits and Larvae
http://www.thenaturestore.com/raisingkitslarva.htm or (800) 345-1638
    Offers Painted Lady and Monarch butterfly kits.

abc School Supply
http://www.abcschoolsupply.com or (800) 669-4222
    Butterfly Garden Kit grows Painted Lady Butterflies. Type "Butterfly Garden Kit" in the "Search" box.

On the Web

Butterflies and Moths of Israel
http://www.geocities.com/RainForest/1153/
   The home page of the Israel Lepidopterists Society

Oz's Insect World: Butterflies, Moths and other Insects from Israel and Worldwide
http://www.nature-of-oz.com/butterflies.htm
   Stunning pictures of butterflies found in Israel.

11. What's Jewish about Cats and Dogs?

Dogs and cats are adorable, furry pets. They come in a variety of colors and sizes, have an assortment of names, and need to be loved and cared for. It is quite common for a cat or dog to become an adored, loving member of a family. But what is Jewish about cats and dogs?

The Big Idea

There is a selection from the Talmud (*Eruvim* 100b) that states, "One can learn modesty from a cat." Children can and do learn much more than modesty if they are fortunate to care for a cat or a dog. Such care requires devotion and a compassionate attitude. If a small animal is thirsty, Judaism tells us it is a *mitzvah* (commandment) to give it water before attending to our own needs. If a puppy threatens to run into the street, you must protect it. Cats and dogs need to be fed regularly and taught how to behave. They need walks, sleeping space, and a time to play. When we think about cats and dogs, we are appreciative to God for creating them. Even young children can become aware of the *mitzvot* required to care for something smaller than themselves such as cats and dogs, and partake in a partnership with God.

Jewish Values

Sometimes, the activities we are involved in with children are Jewish moments, even if it's not readily apparent. Jewish values lead to Jewish behaviors. Cats and dogs are filled with Jewish values, including:

Brit	Partnership with God	בְּרִית
G'milut Chasadim	Acts of Loving-kindness	גְּמִילוּת חֲסָדִים
Ma'aseh B'reishit	Miracle of Creation	מַעֲשֵׂה בְּרֵאשִׁית
Mishpacha	Family	מִשְׁפָּחָה
Ohev et HaBriyot	Loving All Creatures	אוֹהֵב אֶת הַבְּרִיּוֹת
Tza'ar Ba'alei Chayim	Kindness to Animals	צַעַר בַּעֲלֵי חַיִּים

When children explore cats and dogs, they are literally embodying Jewish values. Children's explorations are richest when the children are partners in their own learning. To engage children in these Jewish values and to deepen their learning, take time to observe children's play and analyze their comments. Seek out the children's questions and interests. Based on the children's questions you might:

➤ Invite those children who have pet dogs and cats at home to bring in a picture of their pet and to share how they care for their pet at home. *(Brit, Mishpacha, Ma'aseh B'reishit, G'milut Chasadim, Tza'ar Ba'alei Chayim)*

➤ If possible, invite one or two pets to visit the classroom. *(Brit, Mishpacha, Ma'aseh B'reishit, G'milut Chasadim, Tza'ar Ba'alei Chayim)*

➤ Collect food or toys for an animal shelter. *(Tza'ar Ba'alei Chayim)*

➤ Discuss the *mitzvah* of caring for animals before yourself, and then be sure to feed classroom animals before having snack or lunch. *(Brit, Ohev et HaBriyot)*

➤ Make a toy for a pet that will help the pet grow and develop strength and skill e.g., a stuffed sock for a dog to play catch with, or a flexible stick with shiny streamers for a cat. *(Brit)*

➤ Place stuffed dogs and cats in the Dramatic Play Area so children can practice and pretend caring for pets. *(Brit, G'milut Chasadim, Tza'ar Ba'alei Chayim)*

Israel Connection

If you ever travel to Israel you will be sure to see many cats roaming the streets. The cats were brought in by the British in the 1920s to rid the streets of mice. Now, instead of mice there are cats everywhere — in the streets, alleys and courtyards. It is estimated that there are over one million cats living on the streets of Israel, cats that belong to nobody and to everyone. You may delight in seeing them, but the reality is that a cat's life in Israel is very difficult. Many get sick, are poisoned, or worse. While some cities use drastic "animal-unfriendly" measures to reduce their cat populations, there are some "animal-friendly cities" as well, as designated by The Cat Welfare Society of Israel. In the animal-friendly cities you will find sanctuaries for stray animals and free spay/neutering and vaccines for homeless cats. The cities of Hadera and Nes-Ziona are known to be animal-friendly Israeli cities. You can find more information about cats in Israel at http://www.cats.org.il/eng/index.html.

Did you know that dogs in Israel say "How! How!" instead of "Ruff Ruff"? Cats in Israel say "Meow" just like their American counterparts.

Invite the children to pretend to be cats or dogs in animal-friendly Israeli cities. Record the children's stories and make into books to be re-read and acted out. Also consider collecting *tzedakah* from the children to support cat friendly Israeli cities.

Hebrew Vocabulary

Here are some Hebrew words and phrases you can use when you talk about cats and dogs:

Dog	*Ke-lev*	כֶּלֶב
Puppy	*K'lav-lav*	כְּלַבְלָב
Cat	*Cha-tul*	חָתוּל
Kitten	*Cha-tal-tul*	חֲתַלְתּוּל
The dog barks.	*Ha-ke-lev no-vei-ach.*	הַכֶּלֶב נוֹבֵחַ.
The cat meows.	*Heh-cha-tul m'ya-lel.*	הֶחָתוּל מְיַלֵּל.
I have a dog.	*Yesh li ke-lev.*	יֵשׁ לִי כֶּלֶב.
I have a cat.	*Yesh li cha-tul.*	יֵשׁ לִי חָתוּל.

Songs and poems

Ha-ke-lev (The Dog)
From Songs of Childhood *by Judith Kaplan Einstein, Frieda Prensky, and Ayala Gordon. Used with permission.*

Yesh li, yesh li ke-lev, m'od, m'od pi-ke-ah
Ani o-mer, "Rutz, rutz, rutz!" v'hu mi-yad bo-re-ah.
Yesh li, yesh li ke-lev, m'od, m'od pi-ke-ah.
A-ni o-mer, "Da-ber, da-ber!" V'hu mi-yad no-vea-ch.

I have a dog, a very smart dog.
I tell him to run, off he dashes.
I have a dog, a very smart dog.
I tell him to talk, and he barks!

Chatul M'yalel (The Cat Meows)
From Songs of Childhood *by Judith Kaplan Einstein, Frieda Prensky, and Ayala Gordon. Used with permission.*

Meow - meow, cha-tul m'ya-lel, kol ha-lai-lah, kol ha-leil.

Meow - meow, cha-tul m'ya-lel, kol ha-lai-lah, kol ha-leil.

Meow - meow, m'ya-lel cha-tul, meow - meow, m'ya-lel cha-tul.

Meow, meow, cries the cat, all night long.

Blessings

When we think about dogs and cats, we can acknowledge the beauty of God's creations with this blessing:

בָּרוּךְ אַתָּה יְיָ אֱלֹהֵינוּ מֶלֶךְ הָעוֹלָם עֹשֶׂה מַעֲשֵׂה בְרֵאשִׁית.

Ba-ruch A-tah A-do-nai E-lo-hei-nu Me-lech Ha-O-lam O-seh Ma-a-seh V'rei-shit.
We praise you, our God, Creator of the universe, Who makes all of creation.

Story: Shofar, the Jewish Beagle

By Deborah Schein

Our dog Shofar is not your ordinary dog. Like most beagles she is tri-colored tan, black, and white. She has lovely silky ears and a long pointed tail. Her legs are short, her body long, and as beagles go, she is quite a beauty. It is not her looks, though, that make her special, but the fact that she is a Jewish dog. So, we ask her, "Shofar, are you a Jewish dog?" Shofar looks at us with big questioning eyes.

For treats we feed Shofar bits and pieces of kosher meat and she adores *challah*. She puts her nose to the floor during Shabbat and cleans up every *challah* crumb to be found. On Saturday mornings, in honor of Shabbat, Shofar receives not one, but two dog bones. Then we ask her, "Shofar, are you a Jewish dog? She still looks up not understanding what our words mean.

She also has a Jewish name, which fits her well. During the month of *Elul*, my *Abba* blows the family's shofar, no not Shofar the dog, but the shofar made from a ram's horn. *Abba* blows this shofar for two reasons. First, because its helps to get us all ready for the coming High Holidays of Rosh Hashanah and Yom Kippur. Secondly, we have just returned to school after a long summer vacation and hearing the shofar helps to wake us up. The blast from the shofar sounds just like Shofar the beagle's bark. Obviously, this is why she was given this name. But a name doesn't necessarily make someone Jewish. We ask Shofar, "Hey girl, do you have a Jewish name?" Shofar does not respond.

By now it is clear that Shofar lives in a Jewish house. This, too, makes her Jewish. She knows to sit quietly while we sing our special Shabbat *brachot*. She sleeps with us in the *sukkah* if it is not too cold or rainy. In the winter months she is there when we light the Chanukah candles and later when we dress up in costumes to go to synagogue to hear the Megillah read for Purim. In the springtime, when we rely on sunlight to wake us up rather than *Abba's* shofar blowing, Shofar the beagle looks forward to Grandma Rae's visit. Grandma comes every year when the tulips bloom and just in time for Pesach where Shofar howls and barks very nicely, as we sing *"L'Shanah*

Habaah Birushalayim," next year in Jerusalem. Again we ask, "Shofar, are you a Jewish dog?" and again she looks at us with a confused expression across her doggy face.

Shofar's Jewishness continues to grow. She is kind, thoughtful, and a true friend. She honors us, her family. She is nice to other people and she comforts me whenever I am sad by giving me big wet kisses and furry hugs. Again we ask, "Shofar are you a Jewish dog?" This time, there is no confusion on her face, her eyes are clear. She confidently runs to the basket where *Abba* keeps all of his colorful *kippot*. Shofar takes a *kippa* out of the basket using her paws and her mouth. Pushing her head to the floor, she somehow manages to get that *kippa* upon her head. She sits there with a big beagle smile across her face. Everyone agrees that Shofar is special because she is indeed a Jewish dog. And now, even Shofar agrees.

Questions and Suggestions:

➤ Discuss what makes a person Jewish.

➤ Can an animal be Jewish? How?

➤ Invite the children to share stories of pets they have known.

Resources

Books and Music

Abrams, Leah. *Apples on Holidays and Other Days: Songs and Activities for Young Children… and Their Families.* Cedarhurst, NY: Tara Publications, 1989.
   This recording and songbook includes a cute song called "My Dog - Hakelev Sheli"

Burstein, Chaya. *Hanukkah Cat.* Minneapolis, MN: Kar-Ben Publishing, 2001.
   On the first night of Chanukah, a stray orange kitten appears and despite its mischievous antics endears itself to the family.

Eisenstein, Judith Kaplan, Frieda Prensky, and Ayala Gordon. *Songs of Childhood.* New York: United Synagogue Commission on Jewish Education, 1955.
   A wonderful book filled with Hebrew songs of childhood for all occasions including everyday activities, community workers, holidays, trips, and seasons. The Hebrew words are all written in transliteration, include simple translation, and are easy to read. Out of print, may be found in libraries or resource centers.

Gibbons, Gail. *Dogs.* New York: Holiday House, 1996.
   An introduction to dogs, including their history, types of breads, senses, and ways of communication.

———. *Cats.* New York: Holiday House, 1998.
   Information about the physical characteristics, senses, and behavior of cats, as well as how to care for these animals and some general facts about them.

On The Web

The Cat Welfare Society of Israel
http://www.cats.org.il/eng/index.html.
   The web site of the leading organization in the treatment and care of cats in Israel.

12. What's Jewish about Dinosaurs?

Dinosaurs roamed the earth long before Adam and Eve. Dinosaurs have fascinated young children for years with their strength, diversity, mystery, and names so challenging only children can pronounce them all. So what's Jewish about dinosaurs?

The Big Idea

Dinosaurs take us back to the beginnings of time. They are shrouded in mystery: what did they look like? How and why did they disappear? We are awed by their size and strength. When we think about dinosaurs, we cannot help but think about what the earth might have been like then and how so many different kinds of dinosaurs came to live on the earth. How were dinosaurs created? Although dinosaurs are not listed among the things created in the Torah during the six days of creation, we can still look to God as the creator of these incredible beings. As we study dinosaurs with our children, we can't help but engage in explorations of creation and the role God played in the creation of the dinosaurs.

Jewish Values

Sometimes, the activities we are involved in with children are Jewish moments, even if it's not readily apparent. Jewish values lead to Jewish behaviors. Explorations of the lives and times of dinosaurs can embody Jewish values, including:

Kavod	Respect, Honor	כָּבוֹד
Ma'aseh B'reishit	Miracle of Creation	מַעֲשֵׂה בְּרֵאשִׁית
Talmud Torah	Study/Love of Learning	תַּלְמוּד תּוֹרָה

When children get to know dinosaurs, they are literally embodying Jewish values. Children's explorations are richest when the children are partners in their own learning. To engage children in these Jewish values and to deepen their learning, take time to investigate what children already know about dinosaurs. Observe children's play and analyze their comments. Seek out the children's questions and interests. Based on the children's questions, you might:

➤ How might we treat a dinosaur if one were to show up in the classroom? Discuss with the children what they might do. *(Kavod)*

➤ Learning about dinosaurs requires a lot of investigating and learning of new facts, hard-to-pronounce names, and so on. It is a very important Jewish value to study and to learn. One who is wise is called a *hacham* (m) or a *hachamah* (f). Create a classroom book of all the dino-facts that the *hachamim* (wise ones) bring in. *(Talmud Torah)*

➤ Gather the children's questions about dinosaurs and the world they lived in. Which questions can be addressed through research and study? Which questions are better tackled with creativity and imagination? Make sure you use all sorts of strategies for answering questions. *(Talmud Torah, Kavod)*

➤ One of the ways we learn about dinosaurs is through fossils. After studying about fossils (from almost any children's book about dinosaurs), make your own fossils with shells or bones and plaster of paris. *(Ma'aseh B'reishit, Talmud Torah)*

➤ Dinosaurs came in so many varieties, ranging in size, strength, speed, diet, and features such as neck length, number of horns or armored plates, and so on. As you study different dinosaurs, discuss with the children why God would have made so many different kinds of dinosaurs. *(Ma'aseh B'reishit)*

➤ Plan a field trip to your local Museum of Natural History to view the dinosaur exhibit. Spend time before you go discussing with children what they might see. After returning, have children talk about what they saw and learned. For more ideas of follow-up activities, visit http://www.scholastic.com/magicschoolbus/games/teacher/dinosaurs/index.htm. *(Talmud Torah)*

Israel Connection

There are some findings that dinosaurs existed in Israel millions of years ago. Dinosaur footprints from the Judean Hills near Bet Zayit, Israel, were reported by M. Avnimelech in the 1960's. In recent years, dinosaurs have appeared on Israeli stamps and phone cards (see the "Resources" section below for the address of a Web site where you can see pictures of the phone cards). In any case, archeology — digging to discover the past — is happening constantly all over Israel. As you explore the work of paleontologists as they search for dinosaur fossils, you can also tie in the work that archeologists are doing in Israel.

Hebrew Vocabulary

Here are some Hebrew words and phrases you can use as you investigate dinosaurs:

Dinosaur	*Di-no-za-or*	דִּינוֹזָאוּר
Skeleton	*She-led*	שֶׁלֶד
Bone	*Et-zem*	עֶצֶם
Herbivore	*O-chel ei'sev*	אוֹכֵל עֵשֶׂב
Carnivore	*o-chel ba-sar*	אוֹכֵל בָּשָׂר

Teeth	*Shi-**na**-yim*	שְׁנַיִם
Horn/s	***Ke**-ren/Kar-**na**-yim*	קֶרֶן/קַרְנַיִם
Fossil	*M'u-**ban***	מְאֻבָּן
Egg	***Bei**-tza*	בֵּיצָה
This is a very big dinosaur!	*Zeh di-no-**za**-or*	זֶה דִינוֹזָאוּר
	*ma-**mash** ga-**dol**!*	מַמָּשׁ גָּדוֹל!
Dinosaurs lived long ago.	*Di-no-**za**-rim*	דִינוֹזָאוּרִים
	*ka-ya-**mim** miz-**man**.*	קַיָּמִים מִזְּמַן.

Songs and Poems

There's a popular song by Linda Arnold called "There's a Dinosaur Knocking at my Door." In the Jewish version of this song, written by Andi Joseph and Mimi Greisman, the dinosaur comes to spend Shabbat. You can find the music on the recording I've Got a Shabbat Feeling! by Andi Joseph — lyrics reprinted with permission.

There's a Dinosaur

There's a dinosaur knocking at my door
Knocking one, two three.
There's a dinosaur knocking at my door
And he's come to have Shabbat with me.

First we'll light the candles
Then we'll bless the wine
Then we'll bless the challah
And we'll all have dinner together.

There's a dinosaur knocking at my door
Knocking one, two three.
There's a dinosaur knocking at my door
And he's come to have Shabbat with me.

Blessings

God created so many wonderful, incredible things. As your children become investigators of dinosaurs, and perhaps even creators of their own dinosaurs, you can acknowledge this awesome power of creation with a blessing:

בָּרוּךְ אַתָּה יְיָ אֱלֹהֵינוּ מֶלֶךְ הָעוֹלָם עֹשֶׂה מַעֲשֵׂה בְרֵאשִׁית.

*Ba-**ruch** A-**tah** A-do-**nai** E-lo-**hei**-nu Me-lech Ha-O-**lam** O-**seh** Ma'a-**seh** V'rei-**shit**.*
We praise You, our God, Creator of the universe, Who makes all of creation.

Story: How Do Dinosaurs Celebrate Shabbat?

By Maxine Handelman, inspired by the stories of Jane Yolen.

How does a dinosaur celebrate Shabbat when he comes to your house on Friday night?

Does a dinosaur blow out the candles on his way in the door?

Does he spill the wine all over the floor?

Does a dinosaur toss the challah cover with glee, and eat all the challah before saying *"motzi?"*

Does a dinosaur grimace and fight?

How does a dinosaur celebrate Shabbat when she sees you in synagogue on Saturday morn?

Does a dinosaur run up the aisles and stand on the chairs?

Does she leap from the *bimah* and dance on the stairs?

Does a dinosaur drop the *siddur* on the ground, and giggle with friends as the Torah goes round?

Does a dinosaur cry and complain?

No, dinosaurs don't. They make Shabbat a delight.

They munch on their challah and sip at their wine.

They say, "Shabbat Shalom." They sing Shabbat songs.

They shake hands with the rabbi. They eat special Shabbat treats.

Shabbat Shalom.

Shabbat Shalom, little dinosaur.

Questions and Suggestions:

➤ Invite children to draw pictures for this story, and create a class book.

➤ How else might dinosaurs celebrate Shabbat?

➤ Make up your own story, such as "How Do Dinosaurs Celebrate Sukkot?" or any other holiday. You could even write a story about how dinosaurs do *mitzvot*, such as "How Do Dinosaurs Give *Tzedakah*?"

Resources

Books and Music

Joseph, Andi. *I've Got A Shabbat Feeling! Songs for Shabbat and Everyday Jewish Life.* Broomall, PA: Musical Mommy Productions, 1996.
   Includes the song, "There's a Dinosaur." Compact disc or cassette, available from http://www.musicalmommy.com.

Steinberg, Sari. *And Then There Were Dinosaurs.* New York: Pitspopany Press, 2003.
   Creation fable about how God created the dinosaurs.

VanCleave, Janice. *Janice VanCleave's Dinosaurs for Every Kid: Easy Activities that Make Learning Science Fun.* New York: John Wiley & Sons, Inc., 1994.
   Science activities for learning about dinosaurs. Includes directions for making fossils.

Yolen, Jane. *How Do Dinosaurs Say Goodnight?* New York: Blue Sky Press, 2000.
   Very cute story about the polite way dinosaurs go to bed. When you read this book, you can have the dinosaurs say "Laila tov" rather than "Good night."

———. *How Do Dinosaurs Get Well Soon?* New York: Blue Sky Press, 2003.
   Another cute story about how dinosaurs behave when they go to the doctor.

On the Web

Dinosaurs on Phonecards
http://www.ai.sanu.ac.yu/~jsaric/phonecards/world/dinosaurs_5.html
   Pictures of dinosaurs on phone cards from around the world, including Israel.

Scholastic's The Magic Schoolbus: The Busasaurus
http://www.scholastic.com/magicschoolbus/games/teacher/dinosaurs/index.htm
   Ms. Frizzle and the kids travel back to the Late Cretaceous Period — 67 million years ago. There, they see dinosaurs eat, hunt, rest, and fight. Some even take care of baby dinosaurs! This site includes two fun hands-on suggestions for making "fossils".

13. What's Jewish about Farm Animals?

Some material adapted from the Machon L'Morim: Bereshit curriculum

From the youngest age, children are fascinated with farm animals. Cows, sheep, and pigs are some of the first animals toddlers can identify and make the sounds of. So what is Jewish about farm animals?

The Big Idea

On the sixth day of creation, God created all the animals: cattle, creeping things, and wild beasts of every kind. God knew that people would both depend on animals and also need to care for the animals. Perhaps that is why God created animals and people on the same day. Farm animals give us eggs, milk, wool, and meat. Horses help us plow fields (at least they did before machines largely took over this job) and roosters help us wake up in the morning. Farm animals, as opposed to most animals in a zoo, are tame enough to pet and feed. There is, just as God planned, a wonderful partnership between farm animals and people. When we learn about farm animals, we are learning about the wonder of God's creations, of the animals, and of the world.

Jewish Values

Sometimes, the activities we are involved in with children are Jewish moments, even if it's not readily apparent. Jewish values lead to Jewish behaviors. Interacting with the animals on the farm puts Jewish values into action every day. These values include:

Brit	Partnership with God	בְּרִית
G'milut Chasadim	Acts of Loving-kindness	גְּמִילוּת חֲסָדִים
Ma'aseh B'reishit	Miracle of Creation	מַעֲשֵׂה בְּרֵאשִׁית
Tikkun Olam	Repair of the World	תִּקּוּן עוֹלָם
Tza'ar Ba'alei Chayim	Kindness to Animals	צַעַר בַּעֲלֵי חַיִּים

When children learn about and care for farm animals, they are literally embodying Jewish values. Children's explorations are richest when the children are partners in their own learning. To engage children in these Jewish values and to deepen their learning, take time to investigate what children already know about farm animals. Observe children's play and analyze their comments. Seek out the children's questions and interests. Based on the children's questions, you might:

- Have a pet in the classroom which children help care for. *(Tza'ar Ba'alei Chayim)*
- Match animals to their homes, to the foods they eat, and the things they need for survival. *(G'milut Chasadim)*
- Help children identify with farm animals by walking like the animals to Hebrew music. *(Tza'ar Ba'alei Chayim)*
- Build a barnyard and create animals to live in it using recycled materials. *(Tza'ar Ba'alei Chayim, Tikkun Olam)*
- Incubate chicken eggs. *(Tza'ar Ba'alei Chayim, Ma'aseh Bereshit)*
- Discuss with children what we do for farm animals and what they do for us. How does God fit into this equation? *(Brit)*

Israel Connection

World Farm Animals Day was launched in 1983 to urge the world to more humane treatment of farm animals. The date of October 2 honors the birthday of Mahatma Gandhi, foremost champion of humane farming. World Farm Animals Day is celebrated even in Israel, with street theater and a march in Tel Aviv. Organize some research, celebration, or observation of World Farm Animals Day with the children in your class to make others aware that people are responsible for kind treatment of farm animals.

There are numerous organizations in Israel that are concerned with the welfare of animals. See a comprehensive list at http://worldanimalnet.org/new.asp?co=ISRAEL&geo=as&prov=&cat=. Discuss with your class ways that they can help these causes, and perhaps choose one organization to support with a *tzedakah* contribution.

Hebrew Vocabulary

Here are some Hebrew words and phrases you can use to talk about the animals on the farm:

Goat	*Ta-yish*	תַּיִשׁ
Sheep	*Kiv-sah*	כִּבְשָׂה
Cow	*Pa-rah*	פָּרָה
Horse	*Soos*	סוּס
Pig	*Cha-zir*	חֲזִיר
Duck	*Bar-vaz*	בַּרְוָז
Chicken	*Tar-n'go-let*	תַּרְנְגֹלֶת

Rooster	*Tar-n'gol*	תַּרְנְגֹל
Farmer	*I-kar*	אִכָּר
Egg/eggs	*Bei-tzah/bei-tzim*	בֵּיצָה/בֵּיצִים
Cowshed	*Re-fet*	רֶפֶת
It's time to feed the cows.	*Z'man l'ha-a-chil et ha-pa-rot.*	זְמַן לְהַאֲכִיל אֶת הַפָּרוֹת.

Songs and Poems

Kum Bachur Atzeil

This classic Israeli children's song is found on Judy Caplan Ginsburgh's recording, Boker Tov/Laila Tov and in The Complete Jewish Songbook for Children, edited by Stephen Richards.

Kum bachur atzeil, v'tzei la'a-vo-dah! (2x)
Kum, kum, v'tzei la'a-vo-dah! (2x)
Ku-ku-ri-ku, ku-ku-ri-ku, Tar-n'gol kara. (2x)

Get up lazy youth, and go out to work!
Get up, get up, and go out to work!
Ku-ku-ri-ku, ku-ku-ri-ku, the rooster calls.

Soos Sha-chor, Soos Sha-chor, Et Mi Atah Ro-eh?

By Rachel Talmor, adapted from Brown Bear Brown Bear, What Do You See? *by Bill Martin, Jr. and Eric Carle. Used with permission. Children can make a big book illustrating these Israeli animals.*

Soos sha-chor, soos sha-chor, et mi a-tah ro-eh?
A-ni ro-eh bar-vaz tza-hov o-meid mi-mu-li.
Bar-vaz tza-hov, bar-vaz tza-hov, et mi a-tah ro-eh?
A-ni ro-eh cha-zir va-rod o-meid mi-mu-li.

Black Horse, black horse, who do you see?
I see a yellow duck standing by me.
Yellow duck, yellow duck, who do you see?
I see a pink pig standing by me.

Continue with the following animals:
tar-n'gol ka-tom (orange rooster)
ta-yish la-van (white goat)

(last animal)
Ke-lev chum, kelev chum, et mi a-tah ro-eh?
A-ni ro-eh i-kar o-meid mi-mu-li.

Brown Dog, Brown Dog, who do you see?
I see the farmer standing by me.

Blessings

When we see some of God's wonderful creations, such as farm animals, we can say:

בָּרוּךְ אַתָּה יְיָ אֱלֹהֵינוּ מֶלֶךְ הָעוֹלָם עֹשֶׂה מַעֲשֵׂה בְרֵאשִׁית.

Ba-ruch A-tah A-do-nai E-lo-hei-nu Me-lech Ha-O-lam O-seh Ma'a-seh V'rei-shit.
We praise You, our God, Creator of the universe, Who makes all of creation.

Story: The Goats that Once were Chickens

This story from the Talmud (Ta'anit 25a; adapted by Maxine Handelman from the version in The Family Book of Midrash *by Barbara Diamond Goldin) illustrates the mitzvah of Hashavat Aveydah (returning lost property) as well as the value of Tza'ar Ba'alei Chayim (kindness to animals).*

Once a man named Jacob bought some chickens and was carrying them home in a sack. Jacob was very tired, and even though the chickens were clucking in the bag, he stopped to rest under a tree near a house. Jacob fell into a deep sleep. When he woke up, he saw that it was getting quite late, and he rushed off towards home, completely forgetting the sack of chickens.

Cackle! Cackle! Cackle! The chickens began to squirm and cackle in their bag.

Rabbi Hanina ben Dosa, who lived in the house, heard the noise. "Those chickens sound like they are in our yard," he said. "I'll go see," said Rachel, his wife. Rachel fetched the sack of chickens and brought them to Rabbi Hanina. "What shall we do with this?" she asked. "Probably the owner forgot them," Rabbi Hanina said. "We'll care for his chickens until he comes back."

Rabbi Hanina and Rachel fed the chickens and gave them water. The chickens ran around the yard and in and out of the house.

One day went by. Two. Three. More. Still the owner did not come for his chickens.

The hens began to lay eggs. Rachel showed Rabbi Hanina the eggs. He said, "We mustn't eat any of the eggs. They belong to the owner of the chickens. He'll come back for them." Even though

Rabbi Hanina and Rachel were very poor and were sometimes hungry, they didn't eat any of the eggs. The hens sat on the eggs, and before long, the eggs hatched into active little chicks.

Hens, roosters and chicks filled the yard and the house. Cheep cheep! Cackle cackle!! Cock-a-doodle-doo!

A month went by. Two. Three. More. Still the owner did not come for his chickens.

"We must do something," said Rachel, as she scattered the last of the chicken grain around the yard. "I know." Said Rabbi Hanina. "I know! I'll sell the chickens and buy goats. We won't have to feed the goats. They can graze in the field."

A year went by. Two. Three. More.

Then one day, Jacob was walking near Rabbi Hanina's house with a friend when he stopped. "Say, this place reminds me of the place I lost my chickens, so long ago," said Jacob to his friend. "I went looking for them, but I couldn't find the right house or the sack."

Rabbi Hanina heard Jacob and ran out of his yard. "Friend! Wait a minute! What did you say you lost?" Jacob looked startled, but he answered, "A large sack with five chickens in it." "Then I have something to show you," said Rabbi Hanina, leading Jacob to the goat shed. "Here are your chickens. Please take them with you." "But these are goats!" Jacob looked very confused. Rabbi Hanina laughed. "Your chicken family grew so large that I sold them and bought goats."

"Rabbi Hanina, thank you! You are so kind. I've never met anyone so careful to return lost things," said Jacob. He tied up the goats and led them out of the yard.

And that is how Rachel and Rabbi Hanina returned the lost chickens.

Questions and Suggestions:

➤ Why did Rabbi Hanina and Rachel take such good care of the chickens if the chickens didn't belong to them?

➤ Did the chickens really turn into goats?

➤ This is a wonderful story to make a felt board of, or to tell with puppets, or to have the children act out.

Resources

Books and Music

Edwards, Michelle. *Chicken Man.* New York: Lothrop, Lee and Shepard Books, 1991.
  A delightful story of life with the animals on a kibbutz.

Ginsburgh, Judy Caplan. *Boker Tov/Lailah Tov.* Alexandria, LA: Judy Caplan
Ginsburgh, 1989.
> *Includes the song "Kum Bachur Atzeyl." Compact disc, available from A.R.E.
> Publishing, Inc., (800) 346-7779 or www.arepublish.com.*

Goldin, Barbara Diamond. *The Family Book of Midrash: 52 Jewish Stories from the
Sages.* Northvale, NJ: Jason Aronson, 1998.
> *A* midrash *for every week written in very tellable language.*

Goodman, David R. *Kippa The Dancing Duck.* New York: Geffen Publishing House,
1997.
> *Ari is on his way to Shofarville's animal talent fair when he meets a sad duck
> named Kippa who feels "just so ordinary." But Kippa soon makes a charming
> discovery that he and all of Hashem's creatures are "special."*

Machon L'Morim: Bereshit Curriculum Guides. Baltimore, MD: Center for Jewish
Education, 1998.
> *A professional development program designed to facilitate the integration of
> Jewish concepts and values into everyday secular themes. Available from the
> Center for Jewish Education, 5708 Park Heights Avenue, Baltimore, MD 21215,
> (410) 578-6943 or http://www.machonlmorim.org.*

Martin, Bill and Eric Carle. Brown Bear, Brown Bear, What Do You See? New York:
Holt, Rinehart, and Winston, 1983.
> *This classic children's book introduces animals and colors through a simple
> repetitive rhyme.*

Richards, Stephen, ed. *The Complete Jewish Songbook for Children: Manginot.* New
York: Transcontinental Music Publications, 2002.
> *201 songs for holidays, everyday, and just for fun. Includes the song "Kum
> Bachur Atzeyl."*

On the Web

Hai-Meshek
http://www.hai-meshek.co.il/
> *The Web site of Hai-Meshek, The Israel Society for the Prevention of Cruelty to
> Farm Animals. Click on the Enter-English button.*

World Animal Net
http://worldanimalnet.org/new.asp?co=ISRAEL&geo=as&prov=&cat=
> *A Web site that lists dozens of organizations in Israel dedicated to the care and
> protection of animals of all kinds.*

14. What's Jewish about Frogs and Toads?

Frogs and toads are often grouped together as being green and slimy and having strong back legs to leap and hop across ponds, bogs or fields. Toads, however, are more often warty, brown and dry skinned. Both have long tongues for eating and use their skin for breathing. But what is Jewish about frogs and toads?

The Big Idea

The world, created by God, is a wondrous place. Somehow, in a master plan, God created a time and place for a myriad of living beings. Some creatures thrive during the dark of night, others in daylight. Some animals require water and others need dry, hot spaces. Frogs and toads are quite versatile. Together they can be found in most areas of the world, although you would never find a frog in the cold weather of Antarctica, or a toad in the damp air of Madagascar. Frogs and toads are present in great forces both night and day. Best of all, they eat insects that bring disease and discomfort to people and they fill the night air with their unique song. When we think about frogs and toads, we think about the diversity of God's creations.

Jewish Values

Sometimes, the activities we are involved in with children are Jewish moments, even if it's not readily apparent. Jewish values lead to Jewish behaviors. Frogs and toads are filled with Jewish values, including:

Hoda'ah	Appreciation	הוֹדָאָה
Kavod	Respect, Honor	כָּבוֹד
Ma'aseh B'reishit	Miracle of Creation	מַעֲשֵׂה בְּרֵאשִׁית
Tza'ar Ba'alei Chayim	Kindness to Animals	צַעַר בַּעֲלֵי חַיִּים

When children explore frogs and toads, they are literally embodying Jewish values. Children's explorations are richest when the children are partners in their own learning. To engage children in these Jewish values and to deepen their learning, take time to observe children's play and analyze their comments. Seek out the children's questions and interests. Based on the children's questions, you might:

➤ Purchase a frog or toad, or kit of eggs for your classroom (see "Resources" section). Have children and parents observe the tadpoles grow into frogs, then draw and record their observations. (Ma'aseh Bereishit, Hoda'ah)

➤ Teach children how to care for the classroom frog or toad. (Tza'ar Ba'alei Chayim, Kavod)

➤ Visit a zoo, pet store or, if you can, a pond, field, bog or marshland to observe some of the variety of frogs and toads that exist in the world and their habitats. To extend this activity, bring in an assortment of books with large, clear pictures for the children to look through. (Ma'aseh Bereishit, Hoda'ah)

➤ Study in class the similarities and differences between frogs and toads. (Ma'aseh Bereishit)

➤ Discuss with children why God might have created two creatures so similar, yet with important differences. (Ma'aseh Bereishit, Hoda'ah)

Israel Connection

Behind the Seven Star Mall in Herziliyya, Israel, there is a swamp full of frogs and salamanders. A young conservationist by the name of Itai Roffman is often found splashing through this swamp looking for these creatures. Itai is concerned about endangered species and the effects pollution has on his small green friends. Using a crooked stretched umbrella, rubber boots, and something looking like a butterfly net, Itai hops from rock to rock looking for the Syrian Cat-Eyed Spade-Foot, an endangered species of frog that he hopes to save. You can read more about Itai and his frog friends at http://www.janegoodall.ca/rs/rs_success1.html. By the way, do you know Israeli frogs and toads speak Hebrew? In Israeli, frogs and toads say, "Kwa, kwa."

Hebrew Vocabulary

Here are some Hebrew words and phrases you can use as you talk about frogs and toads:

Frog	Tz'far-**dei**-ah	צְפַרְדֵעַ
Toad	Kar'pa-**dah**	קַרְפָּדָה
Lily pad	Sho-sha-**nat** Ma-yim	שׁוֹשַׁנַת מַיִם
I jump (m/f) like a frog.	A-**ni** ko-**fetz**/ko-**fe**-tzet k'mo tz'far-**dei**-ah.	אֲנִי קוֹפֵץ/קוֹפֶצֶת כְּמוֹ צְפַרְדֵעַ
Toads eat flies.	Kar-fa-**dot** och-**lim** z'vu-**vim**.	קַרְפָּדוֹת אוֹכְלִים זְבוּבִים
Frogs live in water.	Tz'far-**dim** ga-**rim** b'**ma**-yim.	צְפַרְדֵעִים גָּרִים בְּמַיִם.

Songs and Poems

Kwa, Kwa, Went the Little Green Frog
Author unknown.

Kwa, kwa
Went the little green frog
One day
Kwa, kwa
Went the little green frog
Kwa, kwa
Went the little green frog
One day
And his eyes went
A –a-goong

Boker Echad Hit-o-rair Pa-roh (One Morning when Pharaoh Awoke in His Bed)
Author unknown.

Bo-ker e-chad hit-o-rair Pa-roh
Ma-tza tz'far-dei-ah b'mi-ta-to
Tz'far-dei-ah al guf-o
Tz'far-dei-ah al rosh-o
Tz'far-dim sham
Tz'far-dim poh
Tz'far-dim m'kar-kai-rot
L'chen ko-va-cho
Kwa, kwa, kwa, kwa,
Kwa, kwa, kwa, kwa, kwa, kwa, kwa!

One morning when Pharaoh awoke
He found frogs in his bed
A frog on his body
A frog on his head
Frogs there
Frogs here
Frogs were everywhere!
This is how they jumped about:
Kwa, kwa, kwa......

Blessings

When we see a frog or toad hidden by the camouflage of its color, we can say this blessing:

בָּרוּךְ אַתָּה יְיָ אֱלֹהֵינוּ מֶלֶךְ הָעוֹלָם עֹשֶׂה מַעֲשֵׂה בְרֵאשִׁית.

*Ba-**ruch** A-**tah** A-do-**nai** E-lo-**hei**-nu **Me**-lech Ha-O-**lam** O-**seh** Ma'a-**seh** V'rei-**shit**.*
We praise you, our God, Creator of the universe, Who made the miracle of creation.

Story: Frog and Toad Get Ready for Pesach

By Deborah Schein. Inspired by the "Frog and Toad" stories of Arnold Lobel.

One day in early spring, Frog went to visit Toad.
"Toad," said Frog, "Wake up! It is time to get ready for Pesach."
Toad did not want to wake up. Toad was comfortable in his bed.
Frog tried again. "Toad, get up. It is time to clean out all of our *hametz!*"

Toad opened one eye and leaned up on one arm. "It's that time already? It seems like we just finished dressing up for Purim."

"Yes," said Frog. "Time does pass quickly when you're sleeping. But you must get up now. Pesach is only a few days away and we have much work to do."

All of a sudden Toad jumped out of bed. "Oh, Frog, I will clean out all of the *hametz*, but you must hide!"

"Hide?" said Frog. "Why must I hide?"

"Oh, Frog," said Toad. "Don't you remember? Frogs are one of the ten plagues! You will frighten others if they see you."

"No Toad, you are wrong," said Frog. "Jewish people will see me. They will remember the ten plagues, but then they will celebrate their freedom. Come Toad, help me get ready for Pesach so we can celebrate our freedom, too."

Questions and suggestions:

➤ Why was Toad sleeping while Frog was not? Do you agree with Frog or Toad about Frog needing to hide? Why?

➤ What do Frog and Toad need to do in order to get ready for Pesach?

➤ Invite the children to draw pictures of the story and then to write or dictate their ideas and thoughts.

➤ Expand the story of Frog and Toad to last the entire year. What other Jewish adventures might Frog and Toad have?

➤ Several of Arnold Lobels's "Frog and Toad" books are available in Hebrew (see

"Resources" section). Have both the English and the Hebrew versions available to children, and invite them to "read" the stories in Hebrew.

Resources

Books and Music

Jordan, Sandra. *Frog Hunt.* Brookfield, CT: Roaring Brook Press, 2002.
A group of children set out on sunny day to catch a frog. Along the way they observe a muskrat, minnows, and a fish as well.

Lobel, Arnold. *Days with Frog and Toad.* New York: Harper & Row Publishers, 1979.
Lobel wrote three other books about Frog and Toad, including Frog and Toad All Year *(1976),* Frog and Toad Together *(1979), and* Frog and Toad are Friends *(1979).*

Lobel, Arnold, *Tzefarday V'Karpad Yom Yom. (Days with Frog and Toad* in Hebrew*)* Jerusalem: Adam Motzi'im L'or, 1982.
Lobel's Frog and Toad books have been translated into Hebrew by Yehudah and Molly Meltzer. You can also find Tzefarday V'Karpad Kol HaShana, Tzefarday V'Karpad B'yachad *and* Tzefarday V'Karpad Chaverim *at www.milechai.com/product2/books/children_allhebrewbooks.html.*

Materials and Supplies

abc School Supply
http://www.abcschoolsupply.com or (800) 669-4222
Grow-a-frog kit, includes aquarium, accessories, and a tadpole coupon.

On the Web

Israeli Reptiles
http://www.geocities.com/jelbaum/creatures.html
An interesting Web site about the chameleons, lizards, turtles, amphibians, and snakes of Israel. Click on "amphibians" to read about frogs.

The Jane Goodall Institute — Roots and Shoots Israel
http://www.janegoodall.ca/rs/rs_success1.html
An article about the work of Israeli conservationist Itai Roffman.

15. What's Jewish about Spiders?

For some, spiders are fascinating, for others, terrifying. Spiders catch and eat bugs that might otherwise harm or annoy humans. They weave beautiful, intricate webs. But what's Jewish about spiders?

The Big Idea

According to the Creation story in the Torah, spiders and all other creeping things ("*remes*") were created on the sixth day, the same day that humans were created. Spiders and humans have an interesting relationship. While some spiders are poisonous and can harm humans, most spiders do their best to weave their webs in out-of-the-way spaces, where they can go about their business, catching and eating insects that we humans are more than happy to be rid of. Yet too often, we are afraid of spiders and do our best to get rid of them when we see them. Studying spiders with children should teach us just the opposite — that we need to stop and appreciate the wonders of the world God created, and the preciousness and purpose of each one of God's creations.

Jewish Values

Sometimes the activities we are involved in with children are Jewish moments, even if it's not readily apparent. Jewish values lead to Jewish behaviors. Creepy crawlers, even spiders, bring Jewish values to life. These values include:

Bal Tashchit	Do not Destroy	בַּל תַּשְׁחִית
G'milut Chasadim	Acts of Loving-kindness	גְּמִילוּת חֲסָדִים
Hachnasat Orchim	Hospitality/Welcoming Guests	הַכְנָסַת אוֹרְחִים
Hiddur Mitzvah	Beautifying a *Mitzvah*	הִדּוּר מִצְוָה
Hoda'ah	Appreciation	הוֹדָאָה
Tza'ar Ba'alei Chayim	Kindness to Animals	צַעַר בַּעֲלֵי חַיִּים

When children learn about spiders, they are literally embodying Jewish values. Children's explorations are richest when the children are partners in their own learning. To engage children in these Jewish values and to deepen their learning, take time to investigate what children already know about spiders. Observe children's play and analyze their comments. Seek out the children's questions and interests. Based on the children's questions, you might:

➤ "Spin" a review of the Jewish year by reading all the Sammy Spider books by Sylvia Rouss, in "chronological" order: Rosh HaShanah, Sukkot, Chanukah, Tu B'Shevat, Purim, Passover, Israel, and Shabbat. *(Hiddur Mitzvah)*

➤ Discuss what we can do for spiders and what spiders do for people. Then do some of the things the children list as things people can do for spiders. *(G'milut Chasadim, Tza'ar Ba'alei Chayim)*

➤ Look at lots of pictures of webs made by different kinds of spiders. Draw fancy spider webs. *(Bal Tashchit, Hiddur Mitzvah, Hoda'ah)*

➤ Have a spider's tea party and invite another class (like in the book Miss Spider's Tea Party by David Kirk) *(Hachnasat Orchim)*

➤ Count a spider's legs in Hebrew: *a-**chat**, **shta**-yim, **sha**-losh, ar-**bah**, cha-**meish**, sheish, **she**-vah, **sh'mo**-neh.* *(Hoda'ah)*

➤ Search for spider webs in your school or on the playground. Instead of breaking the web, have children draw a picture of the web, or take photographs, to protect the spider and appreciate its handiwork. *(Hoda'ah, Tza'ar Ba'alei Chayim, Bal Tashchit)*

➤ If you find a spider in your classroom, don't kill it. Discuss with the children whether to keep it or remove it gently outside. *(Tza'ar Ba'alei Chayim, Bal Tashchit)*

Israel Connection

All over the world, spiders give much support to people and our endeavors, often without appropriate thanks. The Newe Ya'ar Research Center of the Israel Ministry of Agriculture and Rural Development looked at spiders as biological control agents against injurious insects. They found that in apple, citrus, and avocado orchards and cotton fields in Israel, spiders are dominant predators and have shown that they play a very important role in suppressing the populations of various injurious insects in these crops. Serve apple, oranges or avocados for snack, and give thanks not only to God for creating the fruit, but also to the spiders for keeping the bugs away while the fruit grew.

Hebrew Vocabulary

Here are some Hebrew words and phrases you can use to talk about spiders:

Spider	*A-ka-**vish***	עַכָּבִישׁ
Leg/legs	***Re**-gel/Rag-**la**-yim*	רֶגֶל/רַגְלַיִם
Spider web	*Ku-**rei** A-ka-**vish***	קוּרֵי עַכָּבִישׁ
Eight	*Sh'**mo**-neh*	שְׁמוֹנֶה

What a beautiful web!	Ei-zeh kur ya-**feh**!	אֵיזֶה קוּר יָפֶה!
Look at that big spider!	R'**u** et ha-aka-**vish**	רְאוּ אֶת הָעַכָּבִישׁ
	ha-ga-**dol**!	הַגָּדוֹל!

Songs and Poems

Ha-a-ka-vish Ka-tan K'tan-tan (The Itsy Bitsy Spider)
Hebrew adaptation by Rachel Talmor

Ha-a-ka-vish ka-tan k'tan-tan
Ti-pes lo al ha-kir
Pit-om yo-rad ha-ge-shem
V'oto hir-tiv
Az yetz-ah ha-she-mesh
V'ib-sha lo et ha-guf
V'ha-a-ka-vish ka-tan k'tan-tan
Ti-pes la-ma-la shuv.

The itsy bitsy spider
Climbed upon the wall
Suddenly the rain fell
And he became all wet.
Out came the sun
And dried off his body
And the itsy bitsy spider
Went up once more.

Little Sammy Spider
To the tune of "The Itsy Bitsy Spider." From Clap and Count! Action Rhymes for the Jewish Year *by Jacqueline Jules. Reprinted with permission.*

Little Sammy Spider
Lived in a Jewish house,
Up on the ceiling
Quiet as a mouse.
He climbed down his web
To see the Kiddush cup.
He nearly fell inside,
So he climbed back up.

Blessings

Seeing a wonder of nature, like a beautiful spider web, is an opportunity to stop for a moment and help your children notice and appreciate the awesome world that surrounds us. You can help your children connect God's handiwork to the awesome things they see by saying a *bracha sheh b'lev* (prayer of the heart) such as,

"Thank you God for this amazing spider web!"

Or, you can say this blessing:

בָּרוּךְ אַתָּה יְיָ אֱלֹהֵינוּ מֶלֶךְ הָעוֹלָם עֹשֶׂה מַעֲשֵׂה בְרֵאשִׁית.

Ba-**ruch** A-**tah** A-do-**nai** E-lo-**hei**-nu Me-lech Ha-O-**lam** O-seh Ma'a-**seh** V'rei-**shit**.
We praise You, our God, Creator of the universe, Who makes all of creation.

Story: David and the Spider

This story from the Talmud (Alphabet of Ben Sira 24b), adapted by Maxine Handelman, illustrates the mitzvah of G'milut Chasadim (acts of loving-kindness) and Ba'al Tashchit (do not destroy), as well as demonstrating the worth of every one of God's creatures.

Once, before David became King David, he was walking in the woods when he noticed a spider's web. As David was looking, a big wind came up and tore the spider's web apart. "What a waste," thought David. "Why did God bother to create the spider, which spends all its time spinning a useless web?"

Soon after that, David heard that King Saul was very angry with him. David decided to run away, until Saul was no longer angry. David ran through fields and into the hills. But King Saul and his guards were right behind him! David looked around and saw a cave. "I can hide in there!" David crawled into the cave, listening and waiting, praying that King Saul wouldn't find him. The King and his guards climbed the hill, and David could hear them right outside the cave.

"I'll search this cave," said one of the guards.

"No need," said King Saul. "There's a great big spider web covering the entrance. If David had gone into the cave, he would have broken the web."

King Saul and his guards moved on to the next hill, and David was safe!

While David was hiding, a spider had spun a web in the opening of the cave. The spider had saved David's life! David thanked God for sending the spider. "Now I understand. Every one of God's creatures — even the little spider — is precious. Every living thing has a purpose in this world!"

Questions and Suggestions:

➤ Do you think David and the spider were friends after that?

➤ Brainstorm with children: How could a spider help you? How might you help a spider?

➤ Tell this story using puppets, a plastic spider and spider web (like the kind you can find around Halloween). Or, you can make a web out of yarn.

Resources

Books and Music

Carle, Eric. *HaAkaveesh He'a-suk (The Very Busy Spider* in Hebrew). Bnei-Brak, Israel: Sifriat Poalim — Hakibbutz Hameuchat Ltd., 2003.
> *This classic was translated by Mira Meir and can be found in Hebrew at http://www.israeliproducts.com.*

Jules, Jacqueline. *Clap and Count! Action Rhymes for the Jewish Year.* Minneapolis, MN: Kar-Ben Publishing, 2001.
> *A Jewish spin on a bounty of finger plays, nursery rhymes, and clapping games, including both original poems and new takes on familiar selections.*

Kirk, David. *Miss Spider's Tea Party.* New York: Scholastic, 1994.
> *Miss Spider has to convince her friends she won't eat them before they will come to her tea party. There are several other books about Miss Spider as well.*

Rouss, Sylvia. *Sammy Spider's First Rosh Hashanah.* Rockville, MD: Kar-Ben Copies, 1996.
> *Sammy Spider learns about Rosh Hashanah by observing the Shapiro Family celebration. Other Sammy Spider books include* Sammy Spider's First Sukkot (2004), Sammy Spider's First Hanukkah (1993), Sammy Spider's First Tu B'Shevat (2000), Sammy Spider's First Purim (2000), Sammy Spider's First Passover (1995), Sammy Spider's First Trip to Israel (2002) and Sammy Spider's First Shabbat (1998).

16. What's Jewish about Teddy Bears?

Teddy Bears are some of our earliest friends. They provide us comfort, come to our tea parties, and keep us safe at night. So what's Jewish about teddy bears?

The Big Idea

When a child holds a teddy bear, he may feel a sense of comfort that no other object can provide. A child may tell secrets to her teddy bear that she tells no one else. Teddy bears never interrupt our stories to answer the phone or watch something on TV. Playing with teddy bears can help children build the courage to attempt to make friends with real children and practice strategies for including others in their play. While significant relationships with other people are crucial to healthy development, something about the sublime, secret, secure relationship a child has with his or her teddy bear reveals the presence of God. When we think about teddy bears, and the unique relationship between children and their bears, we are made aware of the presence of God, and of *Kedushah* (holiness).

Jewish Values

Sometimes, the activities we are involved in with children are Jewish moments, even if it's not readily apparent. Jewish values lead to Jewish behaviors. Playing with teddy bears sparks lots of Jewish values. These values include:

Ahavah	Love	אַהֲבָה
B'tzelem Elohim	Created in the Image of God	בְּצֶלֶם אֱלֹהִים
Dibuk Chaverim	Cleaving to Friends	דְּבוּק חֲבֵרִים
G'milut Chasadim	Acts of Loving-kindness	גְּמִילוּת חֲסָדִים
Tza'ar Ba'alei Chayim	Kindness to Animals	צַעַר בַּעֲלֵי חַיִּים

When children play with teddy bears, they are literally embodying Jewish values. Children's explorations are richest when the children are partners in their own learning. To engage children in these Jewish values and to deepen their learning, take time to investigate what children already know about teddy bears. Observe children's play and analyze their comments. Seek out the children's questions and interests. Based on the children's questions, you might:

➤ Invite children to bring in their favorite teddy bear or other stuffed animal and have a tea party. *(Dibuk Chaverim)*

➤ Build a cave or outfit for the classroom or children's teddy bears using recycled materials. *(G'milut Chasadim, Tza'ar Ba'alei Chayim)*

➤ While teddy bears are not made in the image of God *per se*, people are, and what we share with our teddy bears is that each one of us is unique. Help children really get to know their teddy bears by exploring the smells and textures of different bears. A cute book to help with this is *That's Not My Teddy...* by Fiona Watt. *(B'tzelem Elohim, Ahavah)*

➤ Identify the parts of the bear in Hebrew (see vocabulary list).

Israel Connection

From an article by Judy Siegel-Itzkovich on the Jerusalem Post Internet Edition Web site at http://www.jpost.com/Editions/2001/05/13/Health/Health.26018.html.

Teddy Bear Hospital

In April, 2000, Yuval Bloch worked with medical students at Ben-Gurion University of the Negev to set up a teddy bear hospital. Children from two *ganim* (preschools) were selected to participate. Each child invented a "disease" or "condition" from which its stuffed animal "suffered" and discussed it with the teacher. Later, the 70 five- and six-year-olds were bused to Soroka Hospital. The teddy bear hospital was equipped with tables, bandages, otoscopes, stethoscopes, flashlights, splints, and syringes. Each "concerned parent" described the symptoms to a "teddy bear doctor". Some of the children chose nonsense illnesses, such as "color disease" or "sea disease;" others said their teddy had an earache, sore throat, chicken pox, stomachache or a broken limb. Many children said their "child" needed a shot. One child even brought two teddy bears, and claimed that one was sick and had "infected" the other. The doctor then examined the furry patient and treated it, with some help from the child. The examinations were as authentic as possible. Each "parent" was given instructions for continued treatment at home and in class. They also received a certificate marked "Teddy Bear Doctor." The visit to the teddy bear hospital had a wonderful effect on reducing children's fears about visiting the doctor.

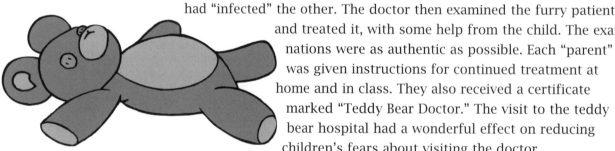

Teddy Bear Tzedakah Opportunity

With on-going terror attacks in Israel, several organizations are bringing teddy bears to children and families who are victims of terror in Israel. Teddy bears help lend emotional support to children who have been through tragedy. One such organization bringing teddy bears to Israel is Beautiful Feet Ministry, part of Liberty Ministries, Inc. (Call 704-500-6240 or e-mail belovedIwish@aol.com). Another is Caring for Children (375 Euclid Ave., #317, San Francisco, CA 94118). Some local

radio stations have been known to make such collections — search the Web for
"teddy bears Israel" for current donation opportunities.

Hebrew Vocabulary

Here are some Hebrew words and phrases you can use to talk about teddy bears:

Bear	*Dov*	דֹּב
Teddy bear	*Du-**bon***	דֻּבּוֹן
Brown	*Chum*	חוּם
Black	*Sha-**chor***	שָׁחוֹר
Honey	*D'**vash***	דְּבַשׁ
Eyes	*Ei-**na**-yim*	עֵינַיִם
Ears	*Oz-**na**-yim*	אׇזְנַיִם
Mouth	*Peh*	פֶּה
Nose	*Af*	אַף
Fur	*Par-**vah***	פַּרְוָה
Tummy	***Be**-ten*	בֶּטֶן
I love my Teddy Bear (m/f)	*A-**ni** o-**hev**/o-he-vet*	אֲנִי אוֹהֵב/אוֹהֶבֶת
	*et ha-du-**bon** she-**li**.*	אֶת הַדֻּבּוֹן שֶׁלִּי.

Songs and Poems

Doobie, Doobie (Teddy Bear, Teddy Bear)
Author unknown. Adapted by Maxine Handelman from a folk melody.

Doobie, doobie, turn around
Doobie, doobie, touch the ground
Doobie, doobie, reach up high
Doobie, doobie, touch the sky
Doobie, doobie, bend down low
Doobie, doobie, touch your toes
Doobie, doobie, find pajamas
Doobie, doobie, say Sh'ma
Doobie, doobie, turn out the light
Doobie, doobie, say Laila Tov!

Ha-Doo-bim (The Bears)

This song is on the compact disc, 100 Shirim Rishonim (100 First Songs) *by Daniela Gardosh and Talma Algayon.*

Boo-boo boo-boo boo-boo-bim!
Mi ka-mo-nu ha-doo-bim!
Kol ha-cho-ref num-num-num
U'va-ka-yitz kum-kum-kum!

Boo-boo boo-boo boo-boo-bim!
Mi ka-mo-nu ha-doo-bim!
Al eitz-im n'ta-peis,
D'vash ma-tok n'cha-peis!
Ad tza-me-ret n'ta-peis,
D'vash ka-ve-ret n'cha-peis!
Ham-ham-ham-ham-ham-ham-heem
Mi ka-mo-nu ha-doo-bim!

Boo-boo boo-boo boo-boo-bim!
Who is like the bears!
The whole winter they sleep sleep sleep
And in the summer they're up up up!

Boo-boo boo-boo boo-boo-bim!
Who is like the bears!
In the trees they climb
Sweet honey they seek!
To the treetop they climb
The beehive they seek.
Ham-ham-ham-ham-ham-ham-heem
Who is like the bears!

Blessings

There are no formal blessings for the friendship and devotion our teddy bears show us. But the blessing of this special relationship can inspire a *bracha sheh b'lev* (a prayer of the heart) such as:

Thank you, God, for helping me to find such a good friend! Please help me take good care of my teddy bear friend.

Story: The First Teddy Bear

By Maxine Handelman. This is a true story, based on information from the American Jewish Historical Society. You can tell this story using a teddy bear and puppets for President Roosevelt and Morris and Rose Michtom. When children give tzedakah, remind them that they are just like the makers of the Teddy Bear.

Teddy Roosevelt was the President of the United States about 100 years ago. One day (in 1902) he decided to take a break from being in charge of the country, and he went on a bear hunt. He tried and tried for days, but couldn't find any bears to hunt. Finally, one of Teddy Roosevelt's friends brought him a baby bear in a cage and said, "Here, you can hunt this bear." But Teddy Roosevelt said, "I will not hurt this baby bear cub." And he set the bear cub free.

Morris and Rose Michtom, a Jewish couple in New York, heard about what the President did for the bear cub. Rose sewed a stuffed bear out of velvet, and called it "Teddy's Bear." Lots of people said, "We want a Teddy's Bear!" Morris and Rose mailed the first Teddy's Bear to President Teddy Roosevelt's children, and asked if they could use his name on the bear they had made. President Teddy Roosevelt said, "I don't think my name will mean much to the bear business, but you're welcome to use it." Teddy Roosevelt was wrong – lots and lots of people wanted to buy a "Teddy Bear." Morris and Rose spent all their time making teddy bears. They became very rich. But Rose and Morris knew it was important to give to others. They gave lots of money to *tzedakah* to help people in the United Sates and the land of Israel.

The first teddy bear that Rose made of velvet was loved by Teddy Roosevelt's children and grandchildren. Today, you can see that bear if you go to the Smithsonian Museum in Washington, DC.

Questions and Suggestions:

➤ Provide children with fabric scraps and lots of different kinds of materials so that they can make their own Teddy Bears.

➤ Why did Rose and Morris Michtom think it was important to give their money away to other people? Do you have to be rich to give *tzedakah*? Discuss with the children how Judaism tells us that every person should give *tzedakah*, because there is always someone worse off than we are.

Resources

Books and Music

Gardosh, Daniela and Talma Alyagon. *100 Shirim Rishonim (100 First Songs)*. Tel Aviv, Israel: Kineret Publishing House, 1970.
> *Includes the song, "Ha-Doo-bim." Compact disc and songbook, available at http://www.israeliscent.com.*

Watt, Fiona. *That's Not My Teddy...* Tulsa, OK: EDC Publications, 2000.
> *Each page has a different teddy bear that a child can touch with different characteristics that are a sensory treat for toddlers.*

Zalben, Jane Breskin. *Beni's Family Treasury: Stories for the Jewish Holidays*. NY: Henry Holt & Company, Inc., 1998.
> *Beni, Pearl, Rosie, and other members of the Bear family celebrate and experience many holidays and Jewish life cycle events in Jane Breskin Zalben's books, which also include* Beni's First Wedding *and* Pearl's Marigolds for Grandpa.

On the Web

American Jewish Historical Society — The Jewish Teddy Bear
www.ajhs.org/publications/chapters/chapter.cfm?documentID=239
> *The full story of Rose and Morris Michtom, inventors of the Teddy Bear. The American Jewish Historical Society fosters awareness and appreciation of the American Jewish past and serves as a national scholarly resource for research through the collection, preservation and dissemination of materials relating to American Jewish history.*

The Jerusalem Post Newspaper: Online News from Israel
http://www.jpost.com/Editions/2001/05/13/Health/Health.26018.html
> *An article about the Teddy Bear Hospital at Ben Gurion University in Israel.*

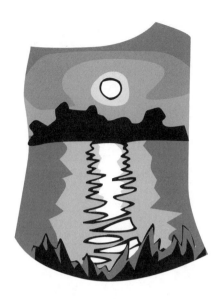

Part III: The World Around

17. What's Jewish about Colors?

Colors are magical. They are always around us wherever we look. Varying in hue and tone, they can depict mood and absorb or reflect heat. Colors can also be mixed, blended, faded, and created. Colors are magical, but what's Jewish about colors?

The Big Idea

Colors are mentioned many times in the Torah. There is the rainbow sent as a covenant between God and Noah after the flood, Joseph's coat of many colors, the cloth and materials used to create the *Mishkan* (portable sanctuary), the clothing of the High Priest and even the blue cord to be woven into the *tzitzit* (fringes of the *tallit*). The Talmud debates the exact shade of this addition to the *tzitzit* — a color known as *t'che-let*, for which the recipe is now believed to be lost. Colors came into existence with the creation of the world. When the sun shines, colors glow brighter. As the day passes, colors fade and darkness covers the earth. God gave us the ability to make colors for ourselves so we might recreate symbolically what God has created. Together people and God make the world a beautiful place. When we think about colors, we think about our partnership with God, and God as Creator.

Jewish Values

Sometimes, the activities we are involved in with children are Jewish moments, even if it's not readily apparent. Jewish values lead to Jewish behaviors. Colors are filled with Jewish values, including:

Brit	Partnership with God	בְּרִית
Hiddur Mitzvah	Beautifying a Mitzvah	הִדּוּר מִצְוָה
Ma'aseh B'reishit	Miracle of Creation	מַעֲשֵׂה בְּרֵאשִׁית

When children explore colors, they are literally embodying Jewish values. Children's explorations are richest when the children are partners in their own learning. To engage children in these Jewish values and to deepen their learning, take time to investigate what children already know about colors. Observe children's play and analyze their comments. Seek out the children's questions and interests. Based on the children's questions, you might:

➤ Go on a color hunt to see all the natural colors created by God (e.g., green leaves, blue sky) *(Ma'aseh B'reishit)*

➤ Take another walk to look for people made colors (e.g., paint, dyed fabric) *(Brit)*

➤ Use colors to beautify the world — paint a beautiful picture to decorate a wall, or plant a color garden. *(Brit, Hidur Mitzvah)*

➤ Feel the warmth or coolness of colors and discuss what part God plays in this phenomenon. *(Ma'aseh B'reishit)*

➤ Invite the children to explore with a mirror in the sun or with sunlight and water to create rainbows. *(Brit)*

➤ Explore how colors mix together, are absorbed into paper, or how primary colors can be extracted from secondary colors. *(Ma'aseh B'reishit)*

Israel Connection

The city of Jerusalem is often called *Y'rushalayim shel Zahav*, City of Gold. When the sun shines on the rose-colored Jerusalem stone used to construct much of the city, a golden glow appears. Place a few large and beautiful pictures of Jerusalem near or in your block corner. Be sure your block corner is equipped with rocks and arched blocks. Also provide the children with a variety of yellow and pink paper of various textures to fill in as walls or windows. See the "Resources" section below for a good poster source.

And don't forget blue and white, the colors of the Israeli flag. Originally the flag of the World Zionist Organization, it became the flag of Israel in the year 1948. The two blue stripes against the white rectangle represent the tallit (prayer shawl) worn in synagogue. The star in the middle is called the *Magen David* or the "Shield of King David." In English this star is better known as the "Star of David" or the "Jewish Star." The stripes and star are "dark sky-blue" as officially decreed by Israel's Provisional Council of State. Be sure an Israeli flag hangs in your classroom.

Provide blue paper, scissors, and glue and invite the children to cut blue strips and triangles. Soon you will have many blue and white Israeli flags decorating the classroom.

Hebrew Vocabulary

Here are some Hebrew words you can use as you explore colors:

Color/s	*Tze-vah/Tz'va-im*	צֶבַע/צְבָעִים
Red	*A-dom*	אָדֹם
Yellow	*Tza-hov*	צָהֹב
Blue	*Ka-chol*	כָּחֹל

White	La-**van**	לָבָן
Orange	Ka-**tom**	כָּתֹם
Green	Ya-**rok**	יָרֹק
Purple	Sa-**gol**	סָגֹל
Black	Sha-**chor**	שָׁחוֹר
Brown	Hum	חוּם
Gold	Za-**hav**	זָהָב
Pink	Va-**rod**	וָרֹד
Rainbow	**Ke**-shet	קֶשֶׁת

Songs and Poems

Hakeshet — The Rainbow

From Songs of Childhood *by Judith Kaplan Eisenstein,*
Frieda Prensky, and Ayala Gordon. Used with permission.

Hi-ney, hi-ney, ke-shet!
Ba-sha-ma-yim ke-shet
Ke-shet ba-sha-ma-yim,
Yo-fi la-ei-na-yim.

Come over here!
There's a rainbow in the sky
In the sky there is a rainbow
Pretty to the eyes.

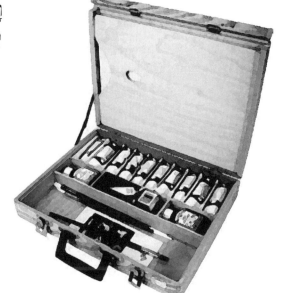

Ka-chol V'la-van (Blue and White)

This classic Israeli folksong can be found on the recording "Apples On Holidays and
Other Days" by Leah Abrams. Used with permission.

Ka-chol v'la-van (2x)
Zeh tze-va she-li (2x)
Ka-chol v'la-van (2x)
Tziv-ei ad-ma-ti (2x)
Ka-chol v'la-van (4x)

Blue and White — these are my colors, the colors of my land.

Blessings

When we see a rainbow, this is the blessing we say:

בָּרוּךְ אַתָּה יְיָ אֱלֹהֵינוּ מֶלֶךְ הָעוֹלָם זוֹכֵר הַבְּרִית
וְנֶאֱמָן בִּבְרִיתוֹ וְקַיָּם בְּמַאֲמָרוֹ.

Ba-**ruch** A-**tah** A-do-**nai** E-lo-**hei**-nu **Me**-lech Ha-O-**lam** Zo-**cheir** Ha-**brit**
V'ne-e-**man** Biv'ri-**to** V'ka-**yam** B'ma-a-ma-**ro**.
We praise You, our God, Who remembers the covenant and is faithful in keeping promises.

There are no formal blessings to say when we explore and appreciate colors that are not necessarily part of a rainbow. But seeing beautiful colors can inspire a *bracha sheh b'lev* **(a prayer of the heart) such as:**

Thank You, God, for creating a world full of beautiful colors!

Story: Rainbows on the Ceiling

by Deborah Schein

When I was four years old, I had the most wonderful teacher. Her name was *Morah* Sara and she loved everyone and everything. She could also make unbelievable things happen in our classroom. One sunny day, while I was painting a picture at the easel, I looked up on the ceiling and there I saw a rainbow of colors dancing and shimmering. We were all excited. *Morah* Sara asked us what we knew about rainbows. Where do they come from? Why was one here today? While we were talking, the rainbow suddenly disappeared. We all ran to the window to see where it had gone. Jeremy said he thought it would come back. I, on the other hand, had some doubts.

Well, Jeremy was right. That rainbow kept coming and going until one day, Eli found a fancy little mirror sitting on the windowsill of the classroom. It was a "rainbow on the ceiling" day. When Jeremy picked up the mirror, the rainbow moved to the wall and then right onto my shoulder. The rainbow was dancing on me! Jeremy could make the rainbow move by moving the mirror. It didn't last long. The sky was turning gray with clouds and our rainbow soon disappeared.

We were now all looking for rainbows, all of the time. I spotted a rainbow in the corner of the turtle's cage, just as the sun hit the water. *Morah* Sara brought in a glass prism and some prism glasses. We all agreed to call our class the rainbow class. We began making our own rainbows. We used watercolor paints on paper, food coloring dropped onto filtered paper, wet tissue paper laid on top of each other, rainbow stew with cornstarch and markered colored strips of paper sitting in water. We discovered how to mix colors and how to extract some colors from more complex colors. Finally we created an arched rainbow for our doorway so everyone would know who we were — The Rainbow Room.

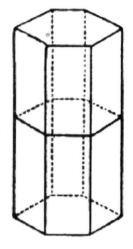

One day, after weeks of exploration with colors and after a big rain, Adam looked up to see a breathtaking rainbow reaching across the sky. He called us to the window. We were all speechless and amazed. Without a word, we quickly put on our coats and went out into the moist air. And in a hushed voice *Morah* Sara taught us the blessing for seeing a rainbow:

בָּרוּךְ אַתָּה יְיָ אֱלֹהֵינוּ מֶלֶךְ הָעוֹלָם זוֹכֵר הַבְּרִית
וְנֶאֱמָן בִּבְרִיתוֹ וְקַיָּם בְּמַאֲמָרוֹ.

*Ba-ruch A-tah A-do-nai E-lo-hei-nu Me-lech Ha-O-lam Zo-cheir Ha-brit
V'ne-e-man Biv'ri-to V'ka-yam B'ma-a-ma-ro.*
We praise You, our God, Who remembers the covenant and is faithful in keeping promises.

Questions and Suggestions:

➤ How did the rainbows come to be in the classroom? What made the rainbows disappear?

➤ What part does God play in making rainbows?

➤ Try to make your own rainbow.

Resources

Books and Music

Abrams, Leah. *Apples on Holidays and Other Days.* Cedarhurst, NY: Tara Publications, 1988.
> *Includes the song "What is Yellow, Red or Green?" and the poem "Apples." Compact disc, cassette, and book available from Tara Publications, (800) TARA-400 or www.jewishmusic.com.*

Eisenstein, Judith Kaplan, Frieda Prensky, and Ayala Gordon. *Songs of Childhood.* New York: United Synagogue Commission on Jewish Education, 1955.
> *A wonderful book filled with Hebrew songs of childhood for all occasions including everyday activities, community workers, holidays, trips, and seasons. The Hebrew words are all written in transliteration, include simple translation, and are easy to read. Out of print, may be found in libraries or resource centers.*

Grossman, Laurie. *Colors of Israel.* Minneapolis, MN: Carolrhoda Books, 2001.
What color is Israel? It is black like the mud from the Dead Sea, tan like the wild goats that roam the desert, and gold like the dome of the ancient mosque of Jerusalem.

Kassirer, Sue. *Joseph and His Coat of Many Colors.* New York: Simon & Schuster Books for Young Readers, 1977.
This book captures the courage, drama, and beauty of the story of Joseph and his coat in a poetic and artistic interpretation.

Pinkney, Sandra L. *A Rainbow All Around Me.* New York: Scholastic Inc., 2002.
"Colors are in everything I see. A piece of the rainbow — you and me."

Wildsmith, Brian. *Joseph.* United Kingdom: Oxford University Press, 1997.
The story of Joseph illustrated in bright colors.

Materials and Supplies

All Jewish Learning — (425) 385-3779 or e-mail alljewishlearning@yahoo.com
A wonderful resource of quality Judaic classroom materials, including a Kotel poster set and an Israeli Flag mini poster.

On the Web

Make a Rainbow
http://www.funology.com/laboratory/lab022.cfm
A simple recipe for making a rainbow.

About Rainbows
http://www.unidata.ucar.edu/staff/blynds/rnbw.html
An interesting technical discussion of what causes rainbows.

The Flag and the Emblem
http://www.mfa.gov.il/mfa/go.asp?MFAH0cph0
Information about the Israeli flag, with pictures.

18. What's Jewish about the Farm?

Some material adapted from the Machon L'Morim: Bereshit curriculum

So many exciting things happen on the farm: there are crops to tend to, animals to care for and play with, tractors to ride. As grown-ups we know that running a farm requires a lot of hard work. But what is Jewish about the farm?

The Big Idea

The farm is perhaps one of the best examples of the partnership between people and God. Farmers plant the crops, but depend on God for rain and sun in the proper amounts and seasons. Farmers care for the animals and reap the rewards of the animals' labors, but God created the animals in the first place. God gives people the *chochma* (wisdom) to figure out what to plant and when, and the ability to communicate with others, to increase our planting abilities even further. Even today, when a majority of the physical labor on the farm is done by machines, we still depend on God to give us the *chochma* to create these machines and use them safely and efficiently. So, when we explore the farm with our children, we are constantly reminded on the partnership between people and God.

Jewish Values

Sometimes, the activities we are involved in with children are Jewish moments, even if it's not readily apparent. Jewish values lead to Jewish behaviors. On the farm, many Jewish values are in action every day. These values include:

Brit	Partnership with God	בְּרִית
Chochma	Wisdom	חָכְמָה
G'milut Chasadim	Acts of Loving-kindness	גְּמִילוּת חֲסָדִים
L'ovda U'l'shomrah	To Work and Keep the Land	לְעָבְדָהּ וּלְשָׁמְרָהּ
Shomrei Adamah	Guardian of the Earth	שׁוֹמְרֵי אֲדָמָה
Tikkun Olam	Repair of the World	תִּקּוּן עוֹלָם
Tzedakah	Justice and Righteousness	צְדָקָה

When children act like a farmer and take care of the land and the farm animals, they are literally embodying Jewish values. Children's explorations are richest when the children are partners in their own learning. To engage children in these Jewish values and to deepen their learning, take time to investigate what children already know about the farm. Observe children's play and analyze their comments. Seek out the children's questions and interests. Based on the children's questions, you might:

➤ Have plants in the classroom or on the playground for children to care for. *(Shomrei Adamah)*

➤ Plant a vegetable garden. Share the harvest with another class or family members. *(L'ovda U'l'shomrah, G'milut Chasadim)*

➤ Play Hebrew music while pretending to plant the field. *(L'ovda U'l'shomrah)*

➤ Build a barn or a house for the farmer from popsicle sticks and other recycled materials. *(Tikkun Olam)*

➤ Ask the children what the farmer does on the farm, and how God helps the farmer. Act out their answers. *(Brit, Chochma)*

➤ The Torah tells us that when we harvest our fields, we must not harvest the corners of the fields, and if we drop anything, we must leave it so that the poor and the hungry can come and feed themselves (Leviticus 19:9-10; Deuteronomy 24:19-21). Ask the children why God might have put that rule in the Torah. How can we give *tzedakah* in similar ways today, even if we are not a farmer harvesting a field (i.e. buying an extra can of food whenever we go to the grocery store)? *(Tzedakah)*

Israel Connection

When we think of the farm and Israel, we immediately think of the *kibbutz* (a farming collective common in Israel). The *kibbutz* of the twenty-first century is very different from the *kibbutzim* that were created when Israel was becoming a new state. The *kibbutz* of today puts less focus on farming and more focus on industry, allowing more room for individual interests and living styles. Only about 2.5 percent of Israel's population lives on a *kibbutz* today. Even so, we have much to learn from studying the *kibbutz*.

➤ Create a *kibbutz* with your children. Talk about the important decisions of how to live collectively but still keep individual interests.

➤ Do the children think that everyone should eat every meal in the *chadar ochel* (dining room) together, or just one meal a day?

➤ Should every person try every job on the *kibbutz*, or should each person find what he or she is good at, and stick to that?

➤ What types of crops do the children want to grow on the *kibbutz*?

➤ What kinds of animals would they like to raise?

➤ Do they want to have a factory, or a hotel for tourists?

➤ Search online for more information about *kibbutzim* to help you make your decisions. To start, there is a very good article at http://www.us-israel.org/jsource/Society_&_Culture/kibbutz.html. After a good bit of planning, act out life on the kibbutz that you have "designed" in your classroom.

Hebrew Vocabulary

Here are some Hebrew words and phrases you can use as you pretend to be a farmer working the land:

Farm	*Cha-**vah***	חַוָּה
Farmer	*I-**kar***	אִכָּר
Barn	***Go**-ren*	גֹּרֶן
Cow shed	***Re**-fet*	רֶפֶת
Earth/ground	*A-da-**mah***	אֲדָמָה
Field	*Sa-**deh***	שָׂדֶה
Rain	***Ge**-shem*	גֶּשֶׁם
Sun	***She**-mesh*	שֶׁמֶשׁ
Let's plant a seed.	***Bo**-u niz-**ra** ze-rah.*	בֹּאוּ נִזְרַע זֶרַע.

Songs and Poems

Dod Moshe ("Uncle Moshe Had a Farm")
Folk song, the Israeli version of "Old MacDonald Had a Farm." A recorded version can be found on Zimmy Zim's Zoo and Noah's Ark Too *by Paul Zim.*

La dod Mo-she ha-yi-ta cha-va,
Eey aye eey aye oh.
Oo-va cha-va ha-yi-ta *(animal name)*,
Eey aye eey aye oh.
Eem *(animal sound)* po,
Eem *(animal sound)* sham,
(Animal sound) kol laz-man.
La dode Moshe ha-yi-ta cha-va,
Eey ay eey ay oh.

Animals: horse = *soos*, duck = *barvaz*, cow = *parah*. See Chapter 13 for more.

The Planting Song
Words and music by Jeff Klepper. From Songs for Growin' *by Kol B'Seder.*
Used with permission.

There are plants and trees that give us
Nearly everything we need
But don't forget they started out
As tiny little seeds
You can throw them in the air
Or you can hold them in your hand
     But someday those tiny seeds will grow
     And trees will fill the land

    Chorus:
     So, take a little seed
      Plant it in the ground
       And that seed will grow as the seasons flow
       With branches all around

    In the Torah it is written
     When we saw the promised land
    We planted trees at every turn
    For this was God's command

    And today in modern Israel
    Here they made the desert bloom
In such a tiny country
For a tree, there's always room

In the Talmud is a saying
Written many years ago:
Every plant has a special star
To teach it how to grow

So, if you happen to be planting
And someone comes along
Finish what you're doing
And together sing this song!

Blessings

When we eat something that grew in the ground, we can say:

בָּרוּךְ אַתָּה יְיָ אֱלֹהֵינוּ מֶלֶךְ הָעוֹלָם בּוֹרֵא פְּרִי הָאֲדָמָה.

Ba-ruch A-tah A-do-nai E-lo-hei-nu Me-lech Ha-O-lam Bo-rei P'ri Ha-A-da-mah.
We praise You, our God, Creator of the universe, Who creates the fruit of the earth.

When we eat something that grew on the tree, we can say:

בָּרוּךְ אַתָּה יְיָ אֱלֹהֵינוּ מֶלֶךְ הָעוֹלָם בּוֹרֵא פְּרִי הָעֵץ.

Ba-ruch A-tah A-do-nai E-lo-hei-nu Me-lech Ha-O-lam Bo-rei P'ri Ha-Eitz.
We praise You, our God, Creator of the universe, Who creates the fruit of the tree.

Story : Tzedakah from the Field

By Maxine Handelman. This story, based on a midrash (Tanhuma Re'eh 10), *teaches us the importance of* tzedakah, *even on the farm.*

Once there was a farmer named Simon who owned a large field. Simon worked hard, and every year he was able to reap a great harvest. To thank God for his good fortune, each year Simon set aside a generous portion of his harvest to give to *tzedakah*, to feed hungry people.

When Simon become old and could no longer work the land, he called his son, David, to him and said, "My son, I am giving the farm to you. Be careful to give a generous amount to *tzedakah* each year, because that is why the farm reaped such a good harvest."

The first year, David did as his father told him, and he gave a generous portion of the harvest to *tzedakah*. But the next year David said to himself, "I can thank God for the harvest by giving a smaller amount of the harvest to *tzedakah*. No one will know, and I will have more to eat for myself." But the following year, although he worked just as hard, the harvest David was able to reap was smaller. Each year, David gave less of the harvest to *tzedakah*, and each following year, the harvest yielded less and less food. This went on until David was quite poor.

One day his relatives came by the farm, dressed up for a *simcha*. David said to them, "How can you rejoice when I have lost almost everything I had? You should be kinder to me!"

The relatives said, "Your loss of fortune is your own fault. If you had not been so greedy, God would still be your partner on this farm, and you would still have your fortune."

David was ashamed of his greediness, and listened to what the relatives said. After the next harvest, he gave the most generous portion he could to *tzedakah*. The following year, the field reaped a much bigger harvest, as it had in the days when Simon, his father, was farming the field. From then on, David always gave the most generous portion of the harvest to *tzedakah*, and the farm always reaped a bountiful harvest.

Questions and suggestions:

➤ Why is it important for a farmer to give thanks to God?

➤ What happened when David did not listen to his father and became greedy?

➤ What happens when we become greedy?

➤ Create a *tzedakah* project in your classroom in which children can be as generous as they can possibly be.

Resources

Books and Music

Edwards, Michelle. *Chicken Man.* New York: Lothrop, Lee and Shepard Books, 1991.
    A delightful story of life with the animals on a kibbutz.

Kol B'Seder. *Songs for Growin'.* New York: Transcontinental Music Publications, 2001.
    A collection of songs about Jewish objects at home and in the synagogue, songs about prayer and blessing, songs celebrating the joys of growing Jewishly, and songs about Jewish holidays. Compact disc, available from A.R.E. Publishing, Inc., (800) 346-7779 or www.arepublish.com.

Machon L'Morim: Bereshit Curriculum Guides. Baltimore, MD: Center for Jewish Education, 1998.
    A professional development program designed to facilitate the integration of Jewish concepts and values into everyday secular themes. Available from the Center for Jewish Education, 5708 Park Heights Avenue, Baltimore, MD 21215, (410) 578-6943 or http://www.machonlmorim.org.

Sasso, Sandy Eisenberg. *Noah's Wife: The Story of Naamah.* Woodstock, VT: Jewish Lights Publishing, 2002.
    Noah's wife Naamah is called upon by God to gather the seeds of every type of plant on Earth and bring them safely onto the ark before the great flood.

Silverman, Erica. *When the Chickens Went on Strike.* New York: Dutton Children's Books, 2003.

One Rosh Hashanah, a boy overhears some chickens planning a strike. They are sick of being used for kapores, *the New Year custom in which people swing a live chicken over their heads, hoping to erase their bad deeds. In this skillful adaptation of a story by Sholom Aleichem, the boy pleads with the revolutionaries, saying he needs them to make* kapores *so that his father will be proud of him.*

Zim, Paul. *Zimmy Zim's Zoo & Noah's Ark Too.* Paul Zim Productions, 1995.
Eighteen educational and entertaining songs, including "Dod Moshe." Available from Mile Chai Jewish Books, http://www.milechai.com.

On the Web

Kids Farm
http://www.kidsfarm.com
Kids Farm is about animals and people that live and work on a ranch in Colorado. Young children can learn about farm and wild animals, animal sounds, what grows, farm equipment and a wildlife rehab center. The site also features spelling, puzzles, horses, cows, chickens, sheep, goats, elk, a kids rodeo, and guest pets.

Welcome to the Living Land — Eretz HaChaim
http://www.thelivingland.org/
Eretz HaChaim is a kosher organic farming community located near Amherst, MA. and focused on Torah learning, living, and outreach through a hands-on approach centered on the farm.

19. What's Jewish about Light and Dark?

Light greets the eye every morning. It plays hide and seek between the windows, walls, and floors, as well as with trees, clouds and buildings. It spreads around and between everything there is. At the end of the day the light disappears into darkness. But what is Jewish about light and dark?

The Big Idea

Young children do not have a strong sense of clock or calendar time. But children do have sensitivity to rhythm, sequence, and order. When we focus on the natural flow of a day and watch as light brightens and then diminishes into night, a sense of time begins to develop. Why does light and dark cycle in this way? The answer to the cycle of day and night comes from *B'reishit,* the story of creation in the Book of Genesis:

On the first day of creation, God said, "Let there be light" and there was light. God saw that the light was good, and God separated the light from the darkness. God called the light Day, and the darkness God called Night. And there was evening and there was morning, a first day.

Jewish days and holidays begin and end with the sun going down precisely because of this biblical description of each day: "and there was evening and there was morning." When we think about how the light of day moves toward the dark of night, we are made aware of the sacredness of Jewish time.

Jewish Values

Sometimes, the activities we are involved in with children are Jewish moments, even if it's not readily apparent. Jewish values lead to Jewish behaviors. Light and dark are filled with Jewish values, including:

Brit	Partnership with God	בְּרִית
Hoda'ah	Appreciation	הוֹדָאָה
"Jewish Time"	Making the Ordinary Sacred	
Ma'aseh B'reshit	Miracle of Creation	מַעֲשֵׂה בְּרֵאשִׁית
Rosh Chodesh	The New Month	רֹאשׁ חֹדֶשׁ

When children explore light and dark, they are literally embodying Jewish values. Children's explorations are richest when the children are partners in their own learning. To engage children in these Jewish values and to deepen their learning, take time to investigate what children already know about light and dark. Observe children's play and analyze their comments. Seek out the children's questions and interests. Based on the children's questions, you might:

➤ Invite children to draw pictures and dictate words to describe the sky during different parts of the day or different times of the year. Organize the children's work on a panel so that observable changes can be detected and studied by the entire learning community. This is a good way to show the parallel between the movement of the moon and Jewish holidays. *(Ma'aseh B'reishit,* "Jewish Time," *Rosh Chodesh)*

➤ Once all the children have arrived at school, take time to recite "*Modeh Ani*". This is a morning prayer signifying that each day God renews the world and each of us as well (see the "Blessings" section in this unit for the text of "*Modeh Ani*"). *(Hoda'ah,* "Jewish Time," *Ma'aseh B'reishit)*

➤ Light can offer hope in time of darkness. In the middle of winter or during a moment of sadness, light a candle and discuss how the light from the candle makes you feel. *(Brit)*

➤ Create places for shadow and light to play in the classroom. Invite the children to make observations and draw pictures of how the shadow and light change throughout the day. *(Hoda'ah, Ma'aseh B'reishit)*

➤ Play shadow games outside on a sunny day. One game is called shadow tag. Players freeze when their shadow is stepped on by another player. Invite the children to make up their own shadow games. *(Brit)*

➤ Have the children study their own shadows and draw pictures showing how the shadow attaches to their bodies. *(Ma'aseh B'reishit)*

Israel Connection

Israel's land is about one-third desert. This means much sun, little water, and the need for shade. One of Israel's largest deserts is known as the Negev. It is rocky with very little vegetation, and is crisscrossed with *wadis.* (*Wadi* is an Arabic word which describes a dry erosion that leaves a valley or a canyon across desert land.) The Hebrew word for *wadi* is *nahal,* which in translation means "dry river bed." Israel is full of *nahalim,* and in some there exist natural springs which create beautiful oases complete with shade trees. Here we have the contrast between sun and shade; light and dark.

➤ Research and discuss the deserts of Israel. Help the children feel and see the desert. For beautiful pictures go to http://www.schaik.com, then scroll down to the Negev Desert

link and click. Photos of waterfalls and oases in Israel can be seen at
http://www.geocities.com/jelbaum/Waterscape.html.

➤ Pretend you are going to visit the Negev. Discuss how people and animals deal
with so much light and which animals actually can live in such conditions.

➤ Talk about Bedouin life. Bedouins are shepherds who have lived in the Negev
desert for hundreds of years and know the ways of the desert. *Israel*, by Shirley
W. Gray, offers appropriate text and illustrations for young children on these
topics.

Hebrew Vocabulary

Here are some Hebrew words and phrases you can use as you explore light and dark:

Light	*Or*	אוֹר
Dark	**Cho**-shech	חֹשֶׁךְ
Shadow	*Tzal*	צֵל
Dawn	*Sha-char*	שַׁחַר
Sunset	*Sh'ki-**yat** ha-cha-**ma***	שְׁקִיעַת הַחַמָּה
Good morning.	**Bo**-ker Tov	בֹּקֶר טוֹב
Good night.	**Lai**-la Tov	לַיְלָה טוֹב
I am hot.	*Cham li.*	חַם לִי.
I am cold.	*Kar li.*	קַר לִי.
It is dark outside.	**Cho**-shech ba-**chutz**.	חֹשֶׁךְ בַּחוּץ.
It is light outside.	*Or ba-**chutz**.*	אוֹר בַּחוּץ.

Song and Poems

Or Zarua

Music by Jeff Klepper, text from Psalm 97:11.
Found on the recording, Snapshots: The Best of Kol
B'Seder Vol. 1. *Used with permission.*

Or za-ru-a la-tza-dik
Ul-yish-rei-lev simcha.

Light is sown for the righteous,
And joy for the upright in heart.

Light

By Deborah Schein

God makes day, beginning with one ray
Adding more light
Until the light is just right.

Then ever so slowly
And ever so holy
The sun goes down
Darkness abounds

One day, one night
Boker Tov, hello light

One day, one night
Laila Tov, good night.

Blessings

When we think about light and dark, this is the blessing we say:

בָּרוּךְ אַתָּה יְיָ אֱלֹהֵינוּ מֶלֶךְ הָעוֹלָם עֹשֶׂה מַעֲשֵׂה בְרֵאשִׁית.

*Ba-**ruch** A-**tah** A-do-**nai** E-lo-**hei**-nu Me-lech Ha-O-**lam** O-seh Ma'a-seh V'rei-**shit**.*
We praise You, our God, Creator of the universe, Who creates the miracles of creation.

A *bracha sheh b'lev* (a prayer of the heart) you might say is:

Thank You, God, for bringing light and then dark, day and then night every day.

Modeh Ani

There are numerous melodies for this blessing — one can be found on Days of Wonder, Nights of Peace *by Mah Tovu.*

מוֹדֶה אֲנִי לְפָנֶיךָ מֶלֶךְ חַי וְקַיָּם שֶׁהֶחֱזַרְתָּ בִּי נִשְׁמָתִי בְּחֶמְלָה
רַבָּה אֱמוּנָתֶךָ.

*Mo-**deh** A-**ni** L'fa-**ne**-cha Me-lech Chai V'ka-**yam** She-he-che-**zar**-ta Bi Nish-**ma**-ti B'**chem**-la Ra-**ba** E-mu-na-**te**-cha.*

I give thanks to You, living and enduring Ruler, Who has returned my soul to me in compassion. Great is Your faithfulness.

Story: When the Lights Went Out

By Deborah Schein

One day the lights went off all over the city. It was dark in the halls, dark in the bathrooms, and almost dark in our classroom. My teacher was very calm, and that kept me from being scared. She seemed to know just what to do. She asked, "Where can we go to find light on a sunny afternoon?" Naturally, we all knew the answer and in chorus responded with, "OUTSIDE!" So, outside we went to sit under the big oak tree where we often sat to hear a story.

Today, instead of telling a story, my teacher had questions for us. First she asked us, "Where does the light come from?" We knew the light inside came from electricity. Today, nobody was sure why those lights were off. But the light outside had a different source and we knew the answer.

"From the sun," said Sara.

"Yeah, the sun gives off light," said David.

"Because it is daytime," said Ari.

"Right, it is light during daytime," said Ben.

Our teacher was not quite satisfied with these answers. She pressed on, "Does anyone know why it is light during the day?" Nadav had an answer. "You know, God made the world that way." We all looked over at Nadav. We remembered learning about *B'reishit* and the first day of creation. "God said, 'Let there be light' and there was light. God saw that the light was good, and God separated the light from the darkness. God called the light Day, and the darkness God called Night. And there was evening and there was morning, a first day." Our eyes were wide and bright with new understanding. Every day God creates light and dark! Every day it is good. Every day since the beginning of creation! We looked at each other in amazement. Every day, even today when the lights went out in our classroom! All at once, first softly and then with strong voices, we began to sing *"Modeh Ani"* — thank you, God, for each new day. Thank you, God, for making light even when there are no lights on inside!

Questions and Suggestions:

➤ What would you do if the lights went off in your classroom?

➤ Why did the children in this story sing *"Modeh Ani?"*

➤ List all the different light sources you can think of. Use some of them in your classroom. (Candles, flashlights, lanterns, mirrors and water, to name a few)

➤ How do God and people create a partnership with light?

Resources

Books and Music

Abraham, Michelle Shapiro. *Good Morning, Boker Tov.* New York: UAHC Press, 2001.
A book about "Modeh Ani" for very young children.

Gray, Shirley W. *Israel.* Minneapolis, MN: Compass Point Books, 2002.
Introduces the geography, peoples, culture, religious traditions, and history of Israel using simple language and lovely pictures.

Kol B'Seder. *Snapshots: The Best of Kol B'Seder Vol. 1.* West Roxbury, MA: Kol B'Seder, 2004.
This compact disc includes the song "Or Zarua." Available from A.R.E. Publishing, Inc., (800) 346-7779 or www.arepublish.com.

Mah Tovu. *Days of Wonder, Nights of Peace: Family Prayers in Song for Morning and Bedtime.* Springfield, NJ: Behrman House, Inc., 2001.
This compact disc and booklet features two songs each for morning and bedtime, including a version of "Modeh Ani."

Sasso, Sandy Eisenberg. *Adam & Eve's First Sunset: God's New Day.* Woodstock, VT: Jewish Lights Publishing, 2003.
A story about Adam and Eve's first nightfall and the partnership they began with God.

Waldman, Sarah. *Light: The First Seven Days.* San Diego, CA: Harcourt Brace Jovanovich, 1993.
A beautiful book about creation.

On the Web

Israeli Waterscapes
http://www.geocities.com/jelbaum/Waterscape.html
Stunning photos of Israeli waterfalls and oases.

Willem's Worldwide Webpage
http://www.schaik.com
Scroll down to the "Negev Desert" link to find beautiful pictures of Israel's deserts.

20. What's Jewish about the Post Office?

Young children love using paper and pens for writing and drawing pictures. And who doesn't like to send and receive gifts and letters through the mail? Put these together and it spells "post office." But what is Jewish about the post office?

The Big Idea

When given writing tools such as pencils, crayons, markers, and paper, young children are developmentally driven to make marks. Maria Montessori described this process as an "explosion into writing." Thomas Newkirk, an educator from the University of New Hampshire, has documented how these markings and drawings develop at a very young age into recognizable symbolic drawings, letters, and numbers. Educators from Reggio Emilia speak about the arts as one of the "hundred languages" that children use for communicating and understanding. Vygotsky shares a belief that language is the tool of the mind that connects one individual to another through use of a common language. One could say that children possess an internal love for words and a driving force to communicate. This serves Jewish children especially well as they take an active role in the Jewish community, which spans the globe and transmits tradition through stories, Torah, and other uses of the written and oral word. What better way to reinforce these elements of writing, communicating, and community building then through communication with others via mail. So when we think about sending and receiving mail through the post office, we are reminded of *kehillah* (community).

Jewish Values

Sometimes, the activities we are involved in with children are Jewish moments, even if it's not readily apparent. Jewish values lead to Jewish behaviors. The post office is filled with Jewish values, including:

Derech Eretz	Proper, Decent Behavior	דֶּרֶךְ אֶרֶץ
G'milut Chasadim	Acts of Loving-kindness	גְּמִילוּת חֲסָדִים
K'lal Yisrael	All Jews are One People	כְּלַל יִשְׂרָאֵל
Kavod	Respect, Honor	כָּבוֹד
Kehillah	Community	קְהִלָּה
Simcha shel Mitzvah	Joy in Fulfilling a Commandment	שִׂמְחָה שֶׁל מִצְוָה

When children attempt to communicate with others they are acting on Jewish values. Children's explorations are richest when children are partners in their own learning. To engage children in these Jewish values and to deepen their learning, take time to investigate what the children already know about letters and the post office. Observe children's play and analyze their comments. Seek out the children's questions and interests. Based on the children's questions you might:

➤ Send letters, cards, and gifts at appropriate and opportune times such as thank-you notes, apologies, and congratulations to friends, family members, and individuals within your community. Use Hebrew words in the text such as Shalom (hello, good-bye, peace), *Todah* (thank you) and *Mazel Tov* (good luck and congratulations). *(G'milut Chasadim, Derech Eretz, Kavod)*

➤ When someone loses a close relative, send a letter of condolence. It is customary to say, "May his/her memory be a blessing." *(Kavod, Kehillah, Derech Eretz, G'milut Chasadim)*

➤ When a new baby is born to a family in your class, provide materials for the children to create cards to welcome the new baby into the Jewish community and to wish the family a *Mazel Tov* (congratulations). *(Derech Eretz, Kehillah, Kavod, Simcha shel Mitzvah)*

➤ Right before Rosh Hashana, invite the children to create and mail their own New Years cards to family and friends. This is a great time to visit the local post office, if you have not yet done so. *(Kehillah, Kavod)*

➤ Set up a pen-pal connection with a school in Israel. Contact your local Federation for help with connecting with *ganim* (preschools) in Israel. Send letters, photos and pictures drawn by your children as often as you can to maintain the strongest relationship for your children. *(Kehillah)*

Israel Connection

To reach its intended destination, every letter must have a stamp! The stamp is always "stuck" onto the top right hand corner of a card or envelope, and varies in cost depending on the weight of the letter and its destination. In 2004, an airmail letter to Israel from the USA cost $.80 and took about two weeks to arrive.

There are other interesting aspects to stamps. Stamps come in a multitude of colors, pictures and values. A website with interesting stamps from Israel depicting pictures of Israeli food, holidays, history, places, greetings, etc. can be found at http://www.jr.co.il/pictures/stamps/index.html. After looking at these stamps, invite the children to create their own Jewish stamp. To extend this activity, you might have an exchange of stamps designed by children in America with those in Israel. Also, collect stamps from Israel from families who correspond with Israeli families.

Hebrew Vocabulary

Here are some Hebrew words and phrases you can use as you explore the post office:

Letter	*Mich-**tav***	מִכְתָּב
Envelope	*Ma-a-ta-**fah***	מַעֲטָפָה
Stamp/stamps	*Bul/bu-**lim***	בּוּל/בּוּלִים
Dear Sarah	*Sa-**rah** y'ka-**rah***	שָׂרָה יְקָרָה
Dear Joseph	*Yo-**sef** ya-**kir***	יוֹסֵף יָקִיר
Love	*A-ha-**va***	אַהֲבָה
Mail (n)	***Do**-ar*	דֹּאַר
Post Office	*Mis-**rad** **Do**-ar*	מִשְׂרַד דֹּאַר
I sent a gift.	*Sha-**lach**-ti ma-ta-**nah**.*	שָׁלַחְתִּי מַתָּנָה.
I got a letter.	*Ki-**bal**-ti mich-**tav**.*	קִבַּלְתִּי מִכְתָּב.
I wrote a letter.	*Ka-**tav**-ti mich-**tav**.*	כָּתַבְתִּי מִכְתָּב.

Songs and Poems

A Letter, A Letter, A Rosh HaShanah Letter
By Deborah Schein. Sung to the tune of "A Tisket, a Tasket, A Green and Yellow Basket."

A letter, a letter,
A Rosh HaShana letter.
I made a card
And mailed it far
And soon my friend
Will get it!

Will get it, will get it
And soon my friend
Will get it.
Inside I wrote
Shana tova
And soon my friend
Will get it!

No-sey Ha-Mich-ta-vim (The Mailman)

From Songs of Childhood *by Judith Kaplan Eisenstein, Frieda Prensky, and Ayala Gordon. Used with permission. It's fun to get letters — have the children take turns delivering the mail to their classmates as everyone sings:*

Sha-lom, sha-lom, sha-lom, ye-la-dim!	Hello, Children!
A-ni no-sey ha-mich-ta-vim.	I am the mailman.
Bo-u, bo-u ye-la-dim,	Come, children.
L'ka-bel et ha-mich-ta-vim,	Get your letters.
Mich-tav le-cha, mich-tav le-cha,	A letter for you, a letter for you,
Mich-tav le-cha, mich-tav le-cha.	A letter for you, a letter for you.

Blessings

There are no formal blessings for sending or receiving letters. But such moments can inspire a *brachah sheh b'lev* (a prayer of the heart) such as:

We praise You, our God, Who gives us ways to send our words to loved ones far away.

We praise You, our God, Who brings us to special moments for mailing and receiving gifts.

Story: A Birthday Lesson

By Deborah Schein

Ben was looking forward to turning four. His birthday was just a few weeks away when he discovered a catalogue that had just arrived in the mail. He opened it up and began leafing through the pages. It was a catalogue filled with pictures of hungry children from around the world. It scared him a bit so see such sad children, so Ben took the catalogue to his mother who scooped him up and placed him on her lap. Together they continued looking at the pictures. Ben's mom explained to him that many people throughout the world do not have enough food to eat, and that this catalogue was made to tell people where they might send money to help. For the time being that satisfied Ben. He jumped off his mom's lap and went off to play. But he did not forget the faces of the hungry children.

A few days later, Ben and his mom finished addressing his birthday party invitations and went to mail them at the post office. While waiting in line, Ben noticed a picture of a sad and hungry looking child. "Mom" he asked, "Is that another ad to send money to help hungry children?"

"Yes, Ben," his Mom answered. She looked closely at him. Ben was thinking deeply about this. She could tell by his sparkling eyes. It looked like he was cooking up an idea. Ben was good at cooking up ideas. Ben's mom was curious what this idea would be, and fortunately, she didn't have to wait long to find out.

On the day of Ben's birthday their letter carrier, Charlie, brought Ben a birthday card from Grandma. Inside the card was a check. Ben took the check to his mom and said. "Here, Mom. Here is money to buy food to feed the hungry children I saw in those pictures."

"Oh," thought Ben's mom, "this is what he was cooking up." She bent down and gave her son a big hug and said, "You know Ben, you are doing *tzedakah* — justice, righteousness, and giving to others. I know Grandma would be delighted that you want to give the money she sent you to help other children. But she also sent it so you could treat yourself, as well. If you were to give a portion of this check, you will be giving quite a lot."

Ben thought this over carefully. "You mean I could give just some of my birthday money to help the hungry children, and keep some for myself, and I will be doing the *mitzvah* of *tzedakah*?

"That's exactly what I mean," said his Mom.

"Okay then," said Ben. "Let's do it."

After Ben and his mom had walked to the mailbox to mail off his *tzedakah*, Ben leaned into his mom and whispered, "I feel so good inside — like someone has just given me a big present."

His mom smiled, took his hand and said back to him, "Someone did just give you a big gift. It is called being part of the Jewish people. And, you have just added another big step toward being a thoughtful Jew. *Yasher Koach,** Ben, and happy birthday!"

*Well done! (literally, "your strength went in the right direction")

Questions and Suggestions:

➤ What would you do if you saw pictures of hungry children? Do you think Ben did the right thing?

➤ Make a list of places you might give *tzedakah*.

➤ Collect *tzedakah* every *Yom Shishi* (Friday) and together as a class decide where to send it.

Resources

Books and Music

Ahlberg, Janet & Allan. *The Jolly Postman.* Boston: Little, Brown and Company, 1986.
A fanciful book filled with a variety of letters written by imaginary but well-known friends.

Eisenstein, Judith Kaplan, Frieda Prensky, and Ayala Gordon. *Songs of Childhood.*
New York: United Synagogue Commission on Jewish Education, 1955.
A wonderful book filled with Hebrew songs of childhood for all occasions including everyday activities, community workers, holidays, trips, and seasons. The Hebrew words are all written in transliteration, include simple translation, and are easy to read. Out of print, may be found in libraries or resource centers.

Hample, Stuart. *Children's Letter's to God.* New York: Workman Publishing Company, 1991.
The appeal of Children's Letters to God *is timeless, and universal. It cuts across ages, faiths, temperaments. "Dear God: I read the Bible. What does begat mean? Nobody will tell me. — Alison."*

Kaczynski, Gloria. *Here Comes the Mail.* New York: Bradbury Press, 1992.
The inner workings of the postal system are revealed as the author traces the path of a little girl's letter from her home in New Mexico to her cousin's home in Utah. Includes tips on how to address an envelope.

On the Web

Israeli Postal Authority
http://www.postil.com/newmail.nsf/hompageEng?OpenForm
The home page of the Israeli Postal service, in English. Click on the "New Stamps" link at the top to see dozens of Israeli stamp designs.

The United States Postal Service
http://www.usps.com
The home page of the USPS has a lot of information about how the postal service works, tools for calculating postage, and pictures of stamps (click on the "Buy Stamps & Shop" link).

21. What's Jewish about Rocks?

Any child walking down a path can easily be captivated by a rock. The rock might glisten in the sun or be small enough to hold securely in one's hand. Maybe the rock is very smooth, or rough and full of holes. Rocks definitely offer wonderment to children. So what is Jewish about rocks?

The Big Idea

Many early childhood classrooms possess a beautiful collection of rocks. The rocks can be found or bought, but it is most important for children to understand that all rocks are very old and come from the earth. Rocks are beautiful and varied just like people. A pile of rocks can be sorted by color, shape, size, texture, or place of origin. There is yet a deeper significance for rocks. Rocks are enduring. They symbolize stability and strength. At times the Torah and *siddur* refer to God as *"Tzur"* — "the Rock." When we think about rocks, we can be made aware of the strength and stability of God.

Jewish Values

Sometimes, the activities we are involved in with children are Jewish moments, even if it's not readily apparent. Jewish values lead to Jewish behaviors. Rocks are filled with Jewish values including:

B'tzelem Elohim	Created in the Image of God	בְּצֶלֶם אֱלֹהִים
Bal Tashchit	Do not Destroy	בַּל תַּשְׁחִית
Brit	Partnership with God	בְּרִית
Derech Eretz	Proper, Decent Behavior	דֶּרֶךְ אֶרֶץ
Kavod	Respect, Honor	כָּבוֹד
Ma'aseh B'reishit	Miracle of Creation	מַעֲשֵׂה בְרֵאשִׁית

When children explore rocks, they are literally embodying Jewish values. Children's explorations are richest when the children are partners in their own learning. To engage children in these Jewish values and to deepen their learning, take time to investigate what children already know about rocks. Observe children's play and analyze their comments. Seek out the children's questions and interests. Based on the children's questions, you might:

➤ Go on a rock hunt to discover where rocks come from. Note their beauty, variety and properties. *(Ma'aseh B'reishit)*

➤ Discuss the many uses of rocks in building roads, streets, walls, and structures. Put rocks in the block area so children can explore and represent what they see. Emphasize the use of rocks for building and not throwing. *(Brit, Derech Eretz)*

➤ Place a basket of beautiful rocks in the classroom for independent exploration by the children. These rocks can be counted, compared, sorted, patterned, washed, etc. *(Bal Tashchit, Kavod, Derech Eretz, Ma'aseh B'reishit)*

➤ Invite children to dictate stories about how God created rocks, as well as stories about the similarities between God and rocks. *(B'tzelem Elohim)*

➤ Discuss whether rocks are alive or not. *(Ma'aseh B'reishit)*

➤ Discuss how to care for rocks so that they do not break. *(Bal Tashchit, Kavod)*

➤ Discuss ways to use rocks so they do not harm others. *(Derech Eretz)*

Israel Connection

Israel is well known for her stones, including Jerusalem Stone and Eilat Stone. Jerusalem Stone is quarried from the hills near Jerusalem, and it is mandated that all buildings in Jerusalem be faced with this stone. Jerusalem Stone, prized for its golden color, is also exported all over the world. Eilat Stone, also known as King Solomon's Stone, is the national stone of Israel. It comes from King Solomon's copper mines in the Timna Valley, in the south of Israel near the Red Sea. Eilat Stone is blue in color and is composed of a variety of minerals such as chrysocolla, azurite, and turquoise. Some people believe that Eilat Stone has healing properties.

If possible, collect stones from Israel to place in your classroom block area. Ask people who are going to Israel to bring back stones. Also, include posters and books of Israel in which stone is prominent as well as beautiful. Encourage the children to build replicas of the *Kotel*, learn about archeology, and become aware of the existence of Jerusalem Stone and turquoise from King Solomon's mines. Such pictures might also evoke the children's imagination and a desire to someday visit Israel. (See the "Resources" section below for helpful Web sites and books.)

Hebrew Vocabulary

Here are some Hebrew words and phrases you can use as you talk about rocks:

Rock	*E-ven*	אֶבֶן
Build	*Liv-**not***	לִבְנוֹת
Strength	***Ko**-ach*	כֹּחַ
Please sort the rocks.	*B'va-ka-**sha**, ma-**yen** et ha-a-va-**nim**.*	בְּבַקָשָׁה, מַיֶן אֶת הָאֲבָנִים.
Rock of Israel (a name of God)	*Tzur Yis-ra-**el***	צוּר יִשְׂרָאֵל
I built a wall!	*Ba-**ni**-ti kir!*	בָּנִיתִי קִיר!

Songs and Poems

I Had a Little Stone
By Deborah Schein

I had a little stone
I held it in my hand
It came to me from Israel
Once buried in the sand.
It saw the prophet Deborah
It sat upon the land
Until my mother found it
And put it in my hand.

It's very old, she told me,
A crumbled part of land
It might have seen creation
And been held in God's own hand.
So treat it very carefully
She warned me with a smile
"I will", I said and put the stone
On top of my treasure pile.

Ma'oz Tzur (Rock of Ages)

"Tzur" is another name for God, meaning Rock. This very well known song, by an unknown poet from thirteenth century Germany, is sung at Chanukah.

Ma'oz tzur y'shuati
Lecha na'eh l'shabeiach
Tikon beit t'filati
V'sham todah n'zabeiach
L'eit tachin matbeiach
Mitzar ham'nabeiach
Az egmor b'shir mizmor
Chanukat hamizbeiach.

Rock of Ages let our song
Praise Your saving power;
You amid the raging foes,
Were our sheltering tower
Furious they assailed us,
But Your arm availed us,
And Your word broke their sword,
When our own strength failed us.
And Your word broke their sword,
When our own strength failed us.

Blessings

When you discover a beautiful rock you might say this blessing:

בָּרוּךְ אַתָּה יְיָ אֱלֹהֵינוּ מֶלֶךְ הָעוֹלָם עֹשֶׂה מַעֲשֵׂה בְרֵאשִׁית.

*Ba-**ruch** A-**tah** A-do-**nai** E-lo-**hei**-nu **Me**-lech Ha-O-**lam** O-**seh** Ma-a-**seh** V'rei-**shit**.*
We praise You, our God, Creator of the universe, Who makes all of creation.

Story: Deborah's Rock

By Deborah Schein

Deborah could not believe that she was finally in the land of Israel! She had been waiting all her life for this trip. When she and her family arrived at the spot, between Ramah and Bethel in the hills of Ephraim, Deborah looked out on the land and tried to imagine herself as the Deborah of long ago. The Deborah of the Torah was known for her wisdom, power, and passion. Here she would sit under a palm tree as people came to her for advice.

It was then that young Deborah's eyes fell upon the rock. It was pink and rugged.

She bent down and picked it up. Holding it in her hand she felt something new — she felt connected to the land, and she felt the presence of other Jews past, present, and future. Even more importantly, she felt the strength and power of God's presence.

Deborah brought the rock home. She found a special place for it to sit. Every time Deborah wanted to feel close to God, close to Israel and other Jewish people, she held the rock. The special feelings always returned. I am sure she would be glad to share her rock with you, if you were to meet her. So keep an eye open for every Deborah you meet.

Questions and suggestions:

➤ Why was this rock so special to Deborah? Share something that is special to you.

➤ Why is the land of Israel so special to Jewish people all over the world?

➤ Hold a rock in your hand and share the story that the rock tells you.

Resources

Books and Music

Baylor, Byrd. *Everybody Needs A Rock.* New York: Aladdin Paperbacks, 1974.
Describes the qualities to consider when selecting the perfect rock for play and pleasure.

Cohen, David. *A Day in the Life of Israel.* San Francisco, CA: Collins Publishers, 1994.
A coffee table book filled with beautiful pictures of Israel, including places and faces.

On the Web

BiblePlaces.com — Photos of Israel from the Pictorial Library of Bible Lands
http://www.bibleplaces.com
Beautiful pictures of Biblical structures.

22. What's Jewish about Space?

With contributions from Susan Remick Topek. Some material adapted from the Machon L'Morim: B'reishit curriculum.

Children are captivated by the moon, stars, sun, and planets. Space travel is also a favored topic with children. So what's Jewish about space?

The Big Idea

Children are fascinated with discovering all that they can about the sun, moon, stars, and planets. Even the youngest child can observe the moon and how it changes. The moon is our Jewish timekeeper. Older children can connect to the cycle of the Jewish year by watching the moon, which tells us when many Jewish holidays are coming. We learn from the Torah that the sun, moon, and stars were created on the fourth day of creation. Even one of the names of God — *Avinu sheh baShamayim* (Our Father Who is in Heaven) — connects God and the Jewish people through space. While many Jewish concepts arise during a study of space — Jewish time, Jewish people, Torah — the biggest idea of all is that God created everything that is in space.

Jewish Values

Sometimes, the activities we are involved in with children are Jewish moments, even if it's not readily apparent. Jewish values lead to Jewish behaviors. Studying space sparks lots of Jewish values. These values include:

Derech Eretz	Proper, Decent Behavior	דֶּרֶךְ אֶרֶץ
"Jewish Time"	Making the Ordinary Sacred	
Ma'aseh B'reishit	Miracle of Creation	מַעֲשֵׂה בְּרֵאשִׁית
Rosh Chodesh	The New Month	רֹאשׁ חֹדֶשׁ
T'filat Haderech	Traveler's Prayer	תְּפִלַּת הַדֶּרֶךְ

When children pretend to fly to the moon or imagine what life might be like on Mars, they are literally embodying Jewish values. Children's explorations are richest when the children are partners in their own learning. To engage children in these Jewish values and to deepen their learning, take time to investigate what children already know about space. Observe children's play and analyze their comments. Seek out the children's questions and interests. Based on the children's questions, you might:

➤ Tell the creation story, and focus especially on the creation of the sun, moon and stars. (Ma'aseh B'reishit)

➤ Celebrate Rosh Chodesh every month. Watch the moon change shape throughout the month. As you study the phases of the moon, make connections between the various phases and Jewish time — i.e., a crescent moon tells us it is Rosh Chodesh, or even Rosh Hashanah. The full moon can tell us that it is Sukkot, Tu B'Shevat or the first night of Pesach. A waning quarter moon might mean that it is Chanukah. (Rosh Chodesh, "Jewish Time")

➤ Discuss God's wisdom and ingenuity in creating the solar system. Why might God have made the moon, sun, and Earth the way they are? Create the moon or planets out of papier mâché and let every child experience the power of creation. (Ma'aseh B'reishit)

➤ Take a trip to the moon or other planet. Be sure to say a prayer for a safe trip! (T'filat HaDerech)

➤ Discuss the proper behavior necessary for a long trip to space in a rocket ship. (Derech Eretz)

➤ Have a Shabbat celebration in space! You can do the same thing for Havdalah or another Jewish holiday. Imagine watching the stars from space while saying "Shalom" (hello and good-bye!) to Shabbat. ("Jewish Time")

Israel Connection

On January 16, 2003, Ilan Ramon, the first Israeli astronaut, set off with six American astronauts on the space shuttle *Columbia*. The child of Holocaust survivors, Ilan brought with him into space several notable Jewish objects, including a small pencil drawing made by a 14-year-old boy who was killed in Auschwitz, a microfiche of the Bible the size of a credit card, a miniature Torah that a young teenager managed to keep hidden in a Nazi concentration camp, and kosher food. Ilan also went to great effort to figure out how he could properly count the days and celebrate Shabbat in space, since he would be traveling in a low orbit where the sun would rise and set every 90 minutes. (He ultimately decided to follow Cape Canaveral time.) Before the mission, Ilan said, "There is no better place to emphasize the unity of people in the world than flying in space. We are all the same people, we are all human beings, and I believe that most of us, almost all of us, are good people." Tragically, the mission ended abruptly on February 1, 2003 when space shuttle *Columbia* and her crew disintegrated during reentry into the earth's atmosphere, sixteen minutes before scheduled landing. Ilan Ramon will forever be a hero to Israel and the Jewish people.

When discussing Ilan Ramon and his flight with your children, focus on the tremendous things he accomplished rather than on his tragic end. Ask them what Jewish objects they would take into space with them. Have them bring their objects in space suitcases or traveling bags (or make them from shopping bags!). Display their objects in a "Space Museum" with their explanations of the objects and why they want to take them.

Other ideas:

➤ Make Jewish rocket ships with Israeli flags attached to them. Elicit from children suggestions for materials they might use to make rocket ships. One suggestion for making easy rocket ships: attach a small bathroom cup to one end of a paper towel tube. Cover the entire roll with foil. Cut two slits the size of index cards on the end of the tube opposite the cup end. Cover index cards with foil and slide them into the slits. Attach an Israeli flag insignia and whatever else to decorate — perhaps even each child's photograph on his or her rocket ship.)

➤ Learn the Hebrew expression for "3, 2, 1 Blastoff" (see the "Hebrew Vocabulary" section below).

➤ Make posters that say "*N'siyah Tovah*" ("Good Journey") and "*B'ruchim Habaim*" ("Welcome Back") for take off and return.

➤ Look at a map of Israel as if you are looking at it from space.

Hebrew Vocabulary

Here are some Hebrew words and phrases you can use to talk about space:

Moon	*Ya-**rei**-ach*	יָרֵחַ
Moon (another term)	*L'va-**nah***	לְבָנָה
Sun	***She**-mesh*	שֶׁמֶשׁ
Astronaut	*As-tro-na-**ut***	אַסְטְרוֹנָאוּט
Star/stars	*Ko-**chav**/Ko-cha-**vim***	כּוֹכָב/כּוֹכָבִים
Earth	*A-da-**mah***	אֲדָמָה
Space	*Cha-**lal***	חָלָל
Spaceship	*Cha-la-**lit***	חָלָלִית
Sky/Heaven	*Sha-**ma**-yim*	שָׁמַיִם
We're flying to the moon!	*A-**nach**-nu tas-**im** l'ya-**rei**-ach!*	אֲנַחְנוּ טָסִים לְיָרֵחַ!

3, 2, 1, Blastoff!	Sha-**losh**, **Shta**-yim,	שָׁלֹשׁ, שְׁתַּיִם,
	A-**chat**, Shi-**gur** Mutz-**lach**!	אַחַת, שִׁגּוּר מֻצְלָח!
Have a good trip!	N'si-**ah** To-**vah**!	נְסִיעָה טוֹבָה!
Welcome Home!	B'ru-**chim** Ha-ba-**im**!	בְּרוּכִים הַבָּאִים!

Songs and Poems

Nitz-nutz, Nitz-nutz Ko-cha-vim (Twinkle, Twinkle Little Star)
Hebrew adaptation by Rachel Talmor

Nitz-nutz, nitz-nutz ko-cha-vim
Shuv atem me-hav-hei-vim.
Sham la-ma-la ba-marom
No-tz'zim k'ya-ha-lom.
Nitz-nutz, nitz-nutz ko-cha-vim
Shuv atem me-hav-hei-vim.

Twinkle Twinkle Little Stars
Again you are flashing
Up above in the sky
Sparkling like a diamond.
Twinkle Twinkle Little Stars
Again you are flashing.

You can sing this song on Rosh Chodesh:

Twinkle, Twinkle Little Moon
By Jeremy Levin

Twinkle twinkle little moon
I wonder if I'll see you soon.
Up above the world so high.
Like a crescent in the sky.
Twinkle twinkle little moon
I wonder if I'll see you soon.

Blessings

This blessing is an excerpt from the *Kiddush L'vanah*, the Sanctification of the Moon. This blessing in its entirety is recited while looking at the moon, about seventy-two hours after the new moon.

בָּרוּךְ אַתָּה יְיָ מְחַדֵּשׁ חֳדָשִׁים.

Ba-ruch A-tah A-do-nai M'cha-deish Cho-da-shim.
We praise You, our God, for renewing the months.

T'filat HaDerech is the prayer one traditionally says when embarking on a long journey. Here is an abridged version:

May it be Your will, our God, to lead us in peace, guide us in peace, and bring us to our destination in life, joy, and peace. Keep us safe on our journey. We praise You, God, who hears everyone's prayers.

Story: Heavy Challah (A Jewish Space Story)

By Susan Remick Topek, used with permission.

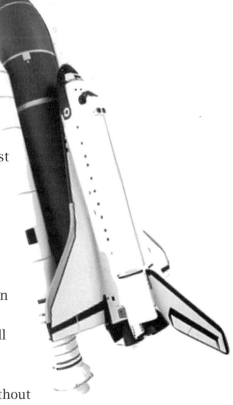

Dalia was so proud. Her son, Ilan, was the first Israeli astronaut and was going into space for the first time! She told everyone and they were proud to know Dalia and Ilan.

But Dalia was worried, like any mother would be.

Was she worried about Ilan's safety? Of course! But she knew that the space program had taken great care to make sure that Ilan would go and return safely.

Was she worried about his clothing? Of course! But she knew that the space program had designed the best space suit, from the best materials, for Ilan to wear.

Was she worried that he would be lonely? Of course! But she knew that the space program was sending other astronauts in the space shuttle with him.

Was she worried about what he would eat? Of course! And this was Dalia's biggest worry, because even though the space program was providing special kosher space meals, Dalia didn't think that Ilan would have a proper Shabbat meal in space.

"Don't worry *Ima*," he told Dalia. "I have freeze-dried matzah ball soup, noodle kugel, and roasted chicken. I even have grape juice to make kiddush in space!"

"But what about challah for Shabbat?" asked Dalia. And then, without telling Ilan, she called up the space program and arranged for Ilan to take her very own homemade challah into space!

Dalia's challah was sweet and golden brown and sometimes it had sesame seeds, or poppy seeds, or even raisins in it. But she made the heaviest challah that ever was! It took Ilan and two others to carry it to the Shabbat table. Every Shabbat, Ilan and the rest of the family and friends pretended to enjoy Dalia's challah because they did not want to hurt her feelings. But after a taste for "*HaMotzi*" they would put the rest of their challah in their napkins and bury them in the yard after Havdalah the next night.

On the day of the lift off the space shuttle weighed more than expected. Everyone wondered where the extra weight came from, but not Ilan. He guessed that his mother's challah was on board and ready for take off.

"Shalosh, Shtayim, Echad — Shigur Mutzlach!" and Ilan was traveling into space.

The next evening, before Shabbat began, Ilan took out his freeze-dried Shabbat meal. He slowly reached for Dalia's challah. And then an amazing thing happened. The challah slipped out of Ilan's fingers and began to float around the cabin.

IT WAS FLOATING! IT WAS SO LIGHT THAT IT FLOATED!

"Gravity!" shouted Ilan. "There is no gravity in space and so the challah is as light as can be!" He had never been so happy. Quickly, before Shabbat began, he took a photograph of Dalia's challah floating weightlessly so he could show everyone when he returned home.

It was a wonderful Shabbat meal. Ilan shared it with the other astronauts and they agreed that Dalia's challah was "out of this world."

Questions and suggestions:

➤ Why do mothers worry about their children, even grown-up children?

➤ Why was so important to Ilan Ramon and his mother that he celebrate Shabbat in space?

➤ Make "Heavy Challah" (see recipe below) with one group of children, and challah with yeast (see Chapter 3, Flour and Baking, p. 15) with another group. Compare the two kinds of challah.

Heavy Challah

The fastest possible recipe, when there is no time for the yeast dough to rise. Susan Remick Topek, author of the story above, says: "My children call this 'Heavy Challah' because it does not use yeast and is very dense bread. So, this recipe inspired me to think about a 'heavy challah' that would become light when there is no gravity to weigh it down!"

Ingredients:

2 eggs	2 tbsp baking powder
1/3 cup margarine, melted	1/2 tsp salt
1/3 cup sugar	raisins (optional)
1-1/2 cups water	1 egg yolk, beaten with 1 tbsp water
5 cups flour	sesame or poppy seeds

Blend eggs, margarine, sugar, and water together with an egg beater or mixer. Sift together dry ingredients. Add to moist ingredients one cup at a time, stirring well. Add raisins if desired. Remove a small piece of dough for the ritual "challah," and burn or discard. Divide the dough in two. Braid or fashion round *challot*. Place on a greased baking pan. Brush with egg-yolk wash and sprinkle with sesame or poppy seeds. Bake at 350° for 1 hour.

Resources

Books and Music

Brown, Margaret Wise. *Laila Tov, Yareach (Good Night, Moon* in Hebrew*)*. Jerusalem: Adam Motzi'im L'or, 1983.
> *This classic can be found in Hebrew at*
> www.milechai.com/product2/books/children_allhebrewbooks.html

Fowler, Allan. *So That's How the Moon Changes Shape!* Chicago, IL: Children's Press, 1991.
> *A simple explanation of the moon and why it changes shape throughout the month.*

Lehman-Wilzig, Tami. *Keeping the Promise: A Torah's Journey*. Minneapolis, MN: Kar Ben Publishing, 2003.
> *Follow the true story of the mini Torah scroll as it passes from a Dutch rabbi to a Bar Mitzvah boy during the Holocaust and finally to Ilan Ramon on his tragic mission in space. For ages 6-10, but can be adapted for preschool.*

Recht, Rick. *Free to Be the Jew in Me*. St. Louis, MO: Vibe Room Records, 2002.
> *A great recording for kids which includes the short story of why the moon is smaller than the sun. Compact disc, available from A.R.E. Publishing, Inc., (800) 346-7779 or www.arepublish.com.*

Rosenfeld, Dina. *Why the Moon Only Glows*. New York: Hachai, 1992.
> *Recounts the midrash about why the moon is smaller than the sun.*

Sofer, Barbara. *Ilan Ramon: Israel's Space Hero.* Minneapolis, MN: Kar-Ben Publishing, 2003.

Discover Ilan Ramon's extraordinary life from his childhood in Israel through his tragic death aboard space shuttle Columbia. For ages 8-11, but can be adapted for preschool.

On the Web

NASA — Home
http://www.nasa.gov

The home page of the National Aeronautics and Space Administration includes lots of information about space and space travel. The "For Kids" section features terrific games, art, stories, and activities.

HubbleSite
http://hubblesite.org/

The home of the Hubble Space Telescope includes incredible pictures, news and stories, and a kid's section with games and activities.

23. What's Jewish about Transportation?

Cars, boats, trains, planes, buses — kids are fascinated with vehicles. Adults are overwhelmed getting from place to place all day. Our lives are, to a large extent, shaped by the modes of transportation we have available to us or choose to use. So what's Jewish about transportation?

The Big Idea

We spend much of our daily energy getting from place to place. We drive to school, we take the train downtown, we walk to a friend's house. Our missions may be frivolous — taking the car to the video store to pick up a movie — or we may go with a higher purpose — driving to see a sick friend in the hospital. God gives us the intelligence to build a car or a bike path, and the wisdom to spend at least some of our time sharing the task of perfecting this world by using our cars or bikes to help others. The fact that we have the ability to go almost anywhere we want to (even to the moon), and that we can choose to travel for a whim or for a *mitzvah*, demonstrates a true partnership with God.

Jewish Values

Sometimes, the activities we are involved in with children are Jewish moments, even if it's not readily apparent. Jewish values lead to Jewish behaviors. Building cars and flying to the moon are moments filled with Jewish values, including:

Brit	Partnership with God	בְּרִית
Kehillah	Community	קְהִלָּה
Mitzvot	Commandments	מִצְוֹת
Shmirat HaGuf	Caring for the Body	שְׁמִירַת הַגּוּף
Tikkun Olam	Repair of the World	תִּקּוּן עוֹלָם

When children play with vehicles and the concepts of transportation, they are literally embodying Jewish values. Children's explorations are richest when the children are partners in their own learning. To engage children in these Jewish values and to deepen their learning, take time to investigate what children already know about transportation. Observe children's play and analyze their comments. Seek out the children's questions and interests. Based on the children's questions, you might:

➤ Talk about how too many cars (and planes and boats . . .) hurt our environment. Children can perform the *mitzvah* of repairing the world by walking or riding their bike instead of driving. Work with families to help them find opportunities to carpool or avoid using the car whenever possible. *(Tikkun Olam)*

➤ Choose to use modes of transportation to do *mitzvot* (commandments). Brainstorm with children various *mitzvot* they can go and do. Do a *mitzvah* as a class by walking to a park to pick up trash, or to the mailbox to mail cards to a sick friend, or carpool to a nursing home to sing songs and bring joy. *(Mitzvot, Kehillah)*

➤ Encourage families to perform a *mitzvah* by keeping granola bars, McDonalds gift certificates, or even bags with non-perishable meals (easy-open cans of tuna, juice boxes, snack-size fruit cocktail cans, etc.) in the car, to hand to people asking for money. *(Mitzvot)*

➤ Where do we go? List with children all the places they go: school, the store, synagogue, a friend's house, the doctor, and so on. These people and places make up the *kehillah* (community). Build a model of your community with your class, using recycled materials. Older children can even draw maps, to help everyone get around the community. *(Kehillah, Tikkun Olam)*

➤ Make a graph with your children of the family *simchas* (joyous occasions) they have gone to recently — birthday parties, *bar mitzvahs*, *brises*, etc.) and the mode of transportation they used to get there. *(Kehillah)*

➤ When we're on the go, we must take extra care to go safely and watch out for the safety of others as well. Be sure to provide helmets in the dramatic play area, materials to create seat belts in cars and planes that children build, and even traffic signs for the bicycles on the playground. When you discuss safety with children, tell them that following the rules of the road helps keep us and others safe, and that this is a Jewish value! *(Shmirat HaGuf)*

Israel Connection

The Israeli Airline is El Al. You can spot an El Al plane because it has the Israeli flag painted on its tail. El Al flies all over the world, including the United States. It takes almost 14 hours to fly directly from Los Angeles to Tel Aviv!

El Al Airlines was founded shortly after Israel became a State. On their inaugural flight in September, 1948, El Al brought the country's first president, Chaim Weizman, home from Geneva. On May 24, 1991, an El Al Boeing 747 airlifted a record-breaking 1,087 passengers, Ethiopian Jews flying from Addis Ababa to Israel, as part of Operation Solomon.

Within Israel, you will see lots and lots of cars on the road. There are also plenty of taxis in every city, as well as buses. The main bus company of Israel is Egged, which runs most of Israel's 6,000 buses. Egged's buses transport a vast number of people around Israel — about 1.1 million Israelis every day!

While trains currently represent only a tiny portion of the transportation options around Israel, rail lines do stretch the length of the country, and it is possible to take a train from Haifa in the north to Be'er Sheva in the Negev Desert in the south.

In your classroom, you can discuss and act out:

➤ How can we get to Israel?

➤ Build an El Al plane with your children.

➤ Perhaps some children will rather take their time and travel to Israel by boat.

Once in Israel, how can we get around?

➤ Display maps of Israeli cities.

➤ Draw a large map of Israel and let children drive around on it with cars dipped in paint.

➤ Be sure to make an Egged bus and encourage children to role-play being the *nahag* (driver) and the passengers.

➤ Teach your children proper bus etiquette: always give up your seat for an elderly person or a pregnant woman!

Hebrew Vocabulary

Here are some Hebrew words and phrases you can use as you travel through your day:

Car	M'cho-**nit**	מְכוֹנִית
Bus	Auto-**bus**	אוֹטוֹבּוּס
Taxi	Mo-**nit**	מוֹנִית
Train	Ra-**ke**-vet	רַכֶּבֶת
Jet Plane	Ma-**tos**	מָטוֹס
Airplane	Avi-**ron**	אֲוִירוֹן
Driver	Na-**hag**	נֶהָג
Drive safely.	Sa Biz-hi-**rut.**	סַע בִּזְהִירוּת.
Stop, please!	A-**tzor**, b'va-ka-**sha**!	עֲצוֹר בְּבַקָּשָׁה!
Excuse me!	Sli-**chah**!	סְלִיחָה!

Songs and Poems

Hinei Rakevet

An old Israeli folk tune. There is a very fun version of this song on the CD Aleph Bet Boogie *by Rabbi Joe Black.*

Hinei Rakevet
Sheh Mi-sto-ve-vet
Al gal-ga-lim, al gal-ga-lim, al gal-ga-lim.

Here is the train
That goes around
   On wheels, on wheels, on wheels.

Aviron

Israeli folksong. Can be found in The New Children's Songbook: 110 Hebrew Songs for the Young *by Velvel Pasternak.*

Aviron, aviron	(Fly hand through the air)
Yesh l'cha k'na-fa-yim	(Hold arms out like a plane's wings)
K'mo Tzi-por, K'mo Tzi-por,	(Flap arms like a bird)
Oof oof la-sha-ma-yim!	(Fly hand through the air)

Plane, plane
You have wings
Like a bird, like a bird
Flying in the sky.

Blessings

"*T'filat HaDerech*" is the prayer one traditionally says when embarking on a long journey. Here is an abridged version:

May it be Your will, our God, to lead us in peace, guide us in peace, and bring us to our destination in life, joy, and peace. Keep us safe on our journey. We praise You, God, who hears everyone's prayers.

Story: The Car that Ran from Mitzvahs

Adapted by Maxine Handelman from the story of the same name by Hanna Bandes in Chosen Tales: Stories told by Jewish Storytellers *edited by Peninnah Schram. This story provides a wonderful lesson about community and doing mitzvot — giving and accepting help with a full heart. Used with permission of the author.*

Chaya was on her way to bring a meal to a friend who was sick. Chaya was grumbling to herself, "I really didn't have time to do this today. I'll have to drop off the food and run if I'm going to make it to my meeting in time." Just then she heard a loud "Knock! Knock! Ka-bang!" and the car ground to a halt. "Oh no, not again!" Chaya had been having a lot of trouble with her car lately. She called the tow truck and waited a long time for it to come. As she watched her car being towed away, Chaya ran for the bus so she could bring the food — now cold — to her friend. She missed her meeting completely.

A few days later, Chaya got her car back from the repair shop, and was on her way to a *bris*. The day before the *bris*, Evelyn, a woman that Chaya didn't know very well, had called to ask if Chaya could give her a ride, and Chaya had agreed, reluctantly. Chaya knew it was a *mitzvah* to help someone else out, but giving Evelyn a ride meant that Chaya would have to leave much earlier, and lately Chaya had been feeling barely able to take care of herself, let alone help other people. Now, Chaya and Evelyn were on their way to the *bris*. Suddenly the car went "Put-put-put, sputter sputter spud" and stopped. Chaya apologized, "I'm so sorry. I've been having a lot of car trouble lately. I'm afraid this might make us miss the *bris*!" Evelyn said quietly, "We don't know why this happened, but clearly it's God's will." Evelyn wasn't angry at all, and her calmness helped Chaya calm down too as they waited for the tow truck.

Once again Chaya waited a few days before getting her car back from the repair shop. One night, after she got the car back, she drove it to her exercise class, even though it was starting to make scary noises again. Sure enough, after class, the car wouldn't start. Chaya was really mad, and as she walked home, she got more and more angry. Why did bad things keep happening to her? Chaya was so mad, and she wanted someone to help her figure things out. So she went to see the rabbi. He wasn't home, but the rabbi's wife, Devorah, was home. Chaya told her the whole story.

Devorah said, "Why didn't you call me? I would have picked you up from your exercise class?"

"This isn't about a ride, it's about all the bad things that keep happening to me." said Chaya.

"You should have called," repeated Devorah. "If you didn't want to call me, you could have called a bunch of other people."

"I didn't want to bother anyone. That's not the point," said Chaya.

Devorah interrupted her. "It's not a bother. That's what we're here for. We're here to help each other. That's what community is all about."

Chaya protested, "But I don't like to ask for help. I know it's a *mitzvah* to help others, and I try, but I barely have the energy to take care of myself. Besides, I just want to know why all these things keep happening to me."

Devorah shook her head and said, "Ask for help, Chaya. That's all I can say."

Chaya went home, still angry. It took many days for her car to be fixed, and during the long hours on the bus, Chaya had time to think. She thought about all the times her car had broken down: dead battery on the way to work the synagogue rummage sale. Broken fan belt on the way to bring a meal to a new mother. Stalling while driving friends to an engagement party, which meant that she hadn't been able to run the errands she had planned on running on the way to the party. Each time the car had broken down, Chaya had been on her way to do a *mitzvah* reluctantly, because she thought she **should**, not because she really wanted to. Maybe Devorah had been right. Maybe Chaya disliked doing *mitzvot* because she never let anyone help her in return.

That night Chaya got on the phone to find a friend who could help her get her car fixed right. The second friend she called knew all about cars, and spent a long time talking with Chaya. He gave Chaya the phone number of a repair shop she could trust. Chaya called them in the morning, and the repairman said he could help. The car would be ready in a few days. Chaya called another friend to drive her to get her car when it was ready. The friend said, "I'm so glad you called. I never would have gotten my new job without your help, and I've been trying to think of a way to thank you."

Chaya got her car back, and it's run fine ever since. Its troubles are over, and perhaps, Chaya's troubles are over too. Now she asks people to help her, and makes herself available to help them too. Chaya's phone rings a lot, people asking for help, people offering to do things for her, and people just calling to say hello. And somehow, everything else has been going better too.

Questions and Suggestions:

➤ Why did Chaya's car run better at the end of the story?

➤ Why is it important to ask for help, as well as help other people?

➤ In the classroom, keep a *mitzvah* graph of each time someone helps someone else, as well as each time someone asks for help from another person.

Resources

Books and Music

Bandes, Hanna. "The Car That Ran from Mitzvahs" in *Chosen Tales: Stories told by Jewish Storytellers* edited by Peninnah Schram. Northvale, NJ: Jason Aronson, Inc., 1995.
   A wonderful story about community and doing mitzvot — giving and accepting help with a full heart, in a fabulous collection of stories.

Black, Rabbi Joe. *Aleph Bet Boogie.* Albuquerque, NM: Lanitunes Music, 1991.
   This recording contains a very fun version of "Hinei Rakevet." Compact disc, available from A.R.E. Publishing, Inc., (800) 346-7779 or www.arepublish.com.

Friedman, Debbie. *Shirim Al Galgalim.* San Diego, CA: Sounds Write Productions, Inc., 1995.
   The title song of this recording represents the way we go through the Jewish year "al Galgalim," on wheels. Compact disc, available from A.R.E. Publishing, Inc., (800) 346-7779 or www.arepublish.com.

Levinson, Riki. *I Go With My Family to Grandmas.* New York: Dutton Books, 1992.
   Five little girls of roughly the same age describe the different ways their large and boisterous families travel to Grandma's house.

Paley, Cindy. *Eizeh Yom Sameach! What a Happy Day!*
   On this recording, Cindy has three fun songs about transportation: "Aviron" (Airplane — a different song than the one printed above), "Bein Harim" (Through the Mountains) and "Ha-Auto Shelanu" (Our Car). Compact disc, available from www.cindypaley.com.

Pamelnsky, Robin. *Avi's Adventures in the Mitzvah Car.* New York: Gefen Publishing House, 1997.
   Avi's magical Mitzvah Car teaches him that we can all do mitzvot if we just open our eyes.

Pasternak, Velvel. *The New Children's Songbook: 110 Hebrew Songs for the Young.* Cedarhurst, NY: Tara Publications, 1981.
   A wonderful collection of classic Hebrew songs in Hebrew, transliteration and singable English translations, complete with sheet music.

Tarbescu, Edith. *Annushka's Voyage.* New York: Clarion Books, 1998.
   Two Russian girls who leave their native home and their beloved grandparents to begin a new life in New York with their father.

24. What's Jewish about Trees?

Trees are central to Jewish life. Our Torah is called the "Tree of Life," Jewish texts are filled with stories and references to trees, and we even have a New Year of the trees, Tu B'Shevat. So in a nutshell, what's Jewish about trees?

The Big Idea

Trees are a wonder. Every tree is different. Even if you stand in the midst of a forest of oak trees, you soon notice that each tree has its own personality, its own unique characteristics. There are different kinds of trees all over the world, each suited to its particular climate and conditions. The vastness of the miracle of trees leads one to wonder about how trees were created. Our Torah tells us that God created trees on the third day of creation, even before the sun, moon, and stars were created. As we learn about trees, we are also learning about the miracle of creation.

Jewish Values

Sometimes, the activities we are involved in with children are Jewish moments, even if it's not readily apparent. Jewish values lead to Jewish behaviors. Explorations of trees, leaves and how we live with trees are full of Jewish values, including:

Brit	Partnership with God	בְּרִית
Kehillah	Community	קְהִלָּה
L'dor Vador	From Generation to Generation	לְדוֹר וָדוֹר
L'ovda U'l'shomrah	To Work and Keep the Land	לְעָבְדָהּ וּלְשָׁמְרָהּ
Ma'aseh B'reishit	Miracle of Creation	מַעֲשֵׂה בְרֵאשִׁית
Shomrei Adamah	Guardian of the Earth	שׁוֹמְרֵי אֲדָמָה
Tikkun Olam	Repair of the World	תִּקּוּן עוֹלָם

As trees "grow" in your classroom, so do Jewish values. Children's explorations are richest when the children are partners in their own learning. To engage children in these Jewish values and to deepen their learning, take time to investigate what children already know about trees. Observe children's play and analyze their comments. Seek out the children's questions and interests. Based on the children's questions, you might:

➤ Ask your children, "How does God create trees?" Then list all the ways we help God take care of trees (i.e., provide water, prune, pick fruit, guard saplings). Be sure you and your class engage in some of these ways of being a partner with God. *(Brit, Shomrei Adamah, Tikkun Olam)*

➤ Sit under a tree with your class, and try to identify all the things the tree does for the world around it (i.e., creates oxygen, provides a home to birds and insects, provides shade and food for people, keeps the soil from being washed away by rain). Then try to identify all the things that help the tree (i.e., sun, rain, people). The tree is a vital part of its community. How are each one of us a vital part of our community? *(Kehilla, Ma'aseh B'reishit)*

➤ Study the rainforest and find ways that your class can help repair the disappearing trees, i.e., use *tzedakah* money, write letters, etc. For more info, click on http://www.therainforestsite.com. *(Shomrei Adamah, Tikkun Olam)*

➤ Recycle! Encourage other classes in your school (and especially the office) to recycle paper and other materials. *(Tikkun Olam)*

➤ "Adopt" a tree near your classroom and watch it change and grow over the year. As a class, take responsibility for caring for the tree so that others will be able to enjoy it in the future. *(Brit, L'dor Vador, Shomrei Adamah, Tikkun Olam)*

➤ Make recycled paper from paper scraps and items from nature. For a good recycled paper recipe, see http://www.environmentalprinting.com/Makingpaper/handmadepaper.htm. *(Tikkun Olam)*

Israel Connection

In 1901, the Jewish National Fund was formed and began purchasing land in what is now the State of Israel. In 1905, the JNF embarked on a mission of planting trees in Israel. By 2001, JNF had planted over 220 million trees in Israel! Trees are crucial to Israel's survival. Here are several ways you can connect your class to the trees of Israel:

➤ Your class can plant a tree in Israel for any occasion. Contact the Jewish National Fund at (800) 542-TREE or http://www.jnf.org.

➤ Ask someone who's going to Israel to take pictures of the entire planting process and share the story and pictures with your class.

➤ Israel is home to many kinds of trees: almond, fig, date palm, olive, etrog, pomegranate, carob, and Jaffa orange trees. Hang posters showing the trees of Israel and talk about them with your children. See the "Resources" section at the end of this unit.

➤ Eat of the fruits of Israel, and also plant the seeds of Israeli fruits in your classroom.

Hebrew Vocabulary

Here are some Hebrew words and phrases you can use as you study trees:

Tree	*Eitz*	עֵץ
Sun	*She*-mesh	שֶׁמֶשׁ
Rain	*Ge*-shem	גֶּשֶׁם
Green	*Ya*-**rok**	יָרֹק
Leaf/leaves	A-**leh**/A-**lim**	עָלֶה/עָלִים
Branch/branches	A-**naf**/A-na-**fim**	עָנָף/עֲנָפִים
Roots	Sho-ra-**shim**	שָׁרָשִׁים
Trunk	*Ge*-zah	גֶּזַע

Songs and Poems

There are many simple Hebrew songs about trees. Here are two classics:

Atzey Zeytim Omdim
Traditional Israeli folk song. A recorded version can be found on Shalom Yeladim/Hello, Children *by Judy Caplan Ginsburgh. The following hand movements were suggested by Julie Jaslow Auerbach.*

Atzey Zeytim Omdim (4x)	(tap thighs 2x, arms up 2x, then down and begin again)
La la la…..	(wave arms gently in air; more quickly as music gets faster)

Olive trees are standing.

Tzadik Katamar
Traditional Israeli folk song, words from Psalm 92. A recorded version can be found on Taste of Eternity: A Musical Shabbat *by The Western Wind Vocal Ensemble.*

Tzadik katamar yifrach, yifrach
Tzadik katamar yifrach.
} 2x

K'erez bal-vanon yisgeh, k'erez bal-vanon yisgeh
K'erez bal-vanon yisgeh, yisgeh
} 2x

*The righteous shall flourish like the palm tree,
And grow mighty like a cedar in Lebanon.*

Blessings

There is a special blessing for the first time we see a tree in bloom:

בָּרוּךְ אַתָּה יְיָ אֱלֹהֵינוּ מֶלֶךְ הָעוֹלָם שֶׁלֹּא חִסַּר בְּעוֹלָמוֹ דָּבָר
וּבָרָא בּוֹ בְּרִיּוֹת טוֹבוֹת וְאִילָנוֹת טוֹבִים לְהַנּוֹת בָּהֶם בְּנֵי אָדָם.

Ba-ruch A-tah A-do-nai E-lo-hei-nu Me-lech ha-O-lam She-lo Hi-sar B'o-la-mo Da-var
U-va-rah Vo Bri-yot To-vot V'i-la-not To-vim L'ha-not Ba-hem B'nai A-dam.
We praise You, our God, Creator of the universe, You left nothing lacking in Your world, and created in it goodly creatures and beautiful trees to delight people's hearts.

This is the blessing for eating the fruit from the tree:

בָּרוּךְ אַתָּה יְיָ אֱלֹהֵינוּ מֶלֶךְ הָעוֹלָם בּוֹרֵא פְּרִי הָעֵץ.

Ba-ruch A-tah A-do-nai E-lo-hei-nu Me-lech ha-O-lam Bo-rei P'ri Ha-Eitz.
We praise You, our God, Creator of the universe, Who created the fruit of the tree.

You and your children might also be moved to say a *bracha sheh b'lev* (blessing of the heart) in order to simply praise God for creating such wonderful things as trees, such as:

Oh God, You have created such beautiful trees! Thank You for their shade and the colorful leaves!

Story: Honi and the Carob Tree

Adapted by Maxine Handelman from Talmud Ta'anit 23a. This is a midrash about trees, and the Jewish responsibility of one generation for another (L'dor Vador). A version of this story can also be found in the children's book, Honi's Circle of Trees *by Phillis Gershator.*

Honi the Circle Maker was well known because when the earth was dry and the people needed rain, Honi had asked God for rain from within his magic circle, and God had listened to Honi and sent rain. One day, as Honi was walking along the road, he saw an old man planting a carob tree. Honi asked the old man, "How long will it take this tree to grow carob that is good to eat?" The old man replied, "Seventy years." Honi exclaimed, "Why are you working so hard to plant this tree? You will not be alive in seventy years to eat its fruit!" The old man looked Honi straight in the eyes and said, "When I was little, I found carob trees with good fruit to eat, which my grandparents had planted for me. Now I am planting trees which will make fruit for my grandchildren." Honi walked on, thinking about what the old man had said. Soon he grew tired, and found a soft place to take a nap. As Honi slept, a very magical thing happened. The rocks around Honi began to grow until they hid him from view. Honi slept on and on, until he had slept for seventy years! When Honi awoke, he stretched and began to walk back along the road he had come. He saw an old man picking fruit from the same carob tree, which had grown much bigger and stronger. Honi asked, "Are you the man who planted this tree?" The man replied, "No. My grandfather planted this tree seventy years ago." "Oh my! I must have been sleeping for seventy years!" cried Honi. He watched the man pick the sweet carob, and he watched the man's children eating the carob with big smiles on their faces. "How wise that old man was," Honi thought. From then on, Honi always remembered to do things not for himself, but for the people to come after him.

Questions and suggestions:

➤ A *midrash* is a story about a story in the Torah, or about the sages who lived in post-biblical times. The *midrash* above helps us understand our responsibility to the earth and to future generations. Send home this story and encourage parents to talk with their children about what their grandparents did for them (i.e., move to America, save money for their education) and what the children might do for future generations.

➤ Act out this *midrash* with your children. Encourage them to think about how much effort it takes to plant and nurture a tree, and give children chances to try on different roles, even the rocks that grew around Honi as he slept.

➤ What might you do for your own children and grandchildren?

Resources

Books and Music

Alexander, Sue. *Behold the Trees.* New York: Arthur A. Levine, 2001.
> *The story of the long, slow devastation of the trees that once sheltered and protected the land in what is now Israel. Ultimately, Alexander writes of present-day efforts by Jewish people of all ages to replant the trees.*

Biers-Ariel, Matt. *Solomon and the Trees.* New York: Union of American Hebrew Congregations, 2001.
> *Solomon preferred peaceful trees to rancorous humans and was taught to speak their language by the animals who lived in the forest. When Solomon became king,*

he found himself too busy to visit the forests and his animal friends. Eventually Solomon came to understand the price that must be paid when people don't take proper care of the earth and its blessings.

Gershator, Phillis. *Honi's Circle of Trees*. Philadelphia, PA: Jewish Publication Society, 1995.
Honi, a character from Talmudic legend, is known for the planting of carob trees across ancient Israel — he plants not for himself, but for the generations to come.

Ginsburgh, Judy Caplan. *Shalom Yeladim/Hello, Children*. Alexandria, LA: Judy Caplan Ginsburgh, 1993.
Includes the song "Atzey Zeytim Omdim." Compact disc, available from A.R.E. Publishing, Inc., (800) 346-7779 or www.arepublish.com.

Rouss, Sylvia. *Sammy Spider's First Tu B'Shevat*. Minneapolis, MN: Kar-Ben Publishing, 2000.
Sammy watches the Shapiros plant a tree in early spring. The year passes as the tree grows, and Sammy learns about the seasons as it flowers in the summer and its leaves turn in the fall.

The Western Wind Vocal Ensemble. *Taste of Eternity: A Musical Shabbat.*
Includes the song "Tzadik Katamar." Compact disc, available from Sounds Write Productions, www.soundswrite.com.

Materials and Supplies

Benny's Educational Toys
Benny's has a wonderful "Trees of Israel" poster — visit http://www.jewisheducationalmaterials.com

On the Web

Jewish National Fund
http://www.jnf.org
The Jewish National Fund is the caretaker of the land of Israel, on behalf of its owners — Jewish people everywhere. From this site you can purchase trees to be planted in Israel.

The Rainforest Site: Help Save Our Rainforests!
http://www.therainforestsite.com
By visiting this site and clicking on the link, you can help preserve endangered rainforests.

Part IV: All about Me

25. What's Jewish about Babies?

Every living being is capable of reproducing something in the image of itself. An acorn grows into a big oak tree, a small kitten into an elegant cat, and a human baby grows into a mature man or woman. But what is Jewish about babies?

The Big Idea

Judaism has many famous sayings about children and babies. In the book of Proverbs we read, "From the mouth of babes comes wisdom." There is a *midrash* which states that "the world is sustained by the breath of children." There is also the blessing of children, "*Birkat Banim*," recited by parents to their children at the Shabbat table. Most importantly, Jews throughout the ages have been aware that there would be no future, no continuation for Judaism without the concept of *L'dor Vador*, from generation to generation. Babies are the link that connects one generation to another, sustaining Jews and Jewish beliefs.

Jewish Values

Sometimes, the activities we are involved in with children are Jewish moments, even if it's not readily apparent. Jewish values lead to Jewish behaviors. Thinking about babies is filled with Jewish values, including:

Ahavah	Love	אַהֲבָה
B'tzelem Elohim	Created in the Image of God	בְּצֶלֶם אֱלֹהִים
Hoda'ah	Appreciation	הוֹדָאָה
K'lal Yisrael	All Jews are One People	כְּלַל יִשְׂרָאֵל
Kehillah	Community	קְהִלָּה
L'dor Vador	From Generation to Generation	לְדוֹר וָדוֹר
Masoret	Tradition	מַסֹרֶת

When children think about babies, they are literally embodying Jewish values. Children's explorations are richest when the children are partners in their own learning. To engage children in these Jewish values and to deepen their learning, take time to investigate what children already know about babies. Observe children's play and analyze their comments. Seek out the children's questions and interests. Based on the children's questions, you might:

➤ Encourage students and their families to attend either the *brit milah* (baby naming ceremony and circumcision for a male baby), or *simchat bat* (baby naming for a female baby) when a new baby is born into your classroom community. Provide information as to the time and location of the *simcha* (celebration) welcoming the newborn child into Judaism. *(Masoret, L'dor Vador, Kehillah, K'lal Yisrael)*

➤ Guide the class in creating a gift for the new baby. A quilt with a Jewish theme is a nice idea and is packed with lots of learning for all the students, including what babies need and more specifically, what Jewish babies need. In the process of making such a gift, students can become more aware of the meaning and feeling of giving and have opportunity to reflect back on their own growth and relationships to family and Judaism. *(L'dor Vador, Hoda'ah)*

➤ Invite a new baby (and parents) to visit the classroom. (If the class has made a gift, this is a perfect time to give it!) Take time to prepare for this visit so that the children know how to behave, have questions to ask, and so that your guest feels comfortable and welcomed. *(Ahavah, Hoda'ah)*

➤ Place a new baby doll into your dramatic play area and invite the children to have a *brit milah* or *simchat bat* for the doll. Invite the doll to its first Shabbat, first Chanukah, etc. *(Masoret, Kehillah)*

➤ Invite parents to send a short baby story of their child along with a baby picture. Place both the story and the picture next to a recently drawn self-portraits of each child. This could be in book form, a wall panel (documentation) or simply displayed on a bulletin board. Ask the children to reflect back on their earliest memories (Jewish, family, or other). The miracle of growth will be quite apparent to all! *(B'tzelem Elohim, Ahavah, Hoda'ah)*

Israel Connection

It is customary to plant a tree in Israel in honor of the birth of a Jewish baby. During Talmudic times, a cedar tree was planted for a boy and a cyprus or evergreen tree for a girl. When it was time to marry, branches from both trees were cut to provide poles for the wedding *chupah*. When a baby is born to your classroom community, you might consider planting the appropriate tree, or using classroom *tzedakah* money to plant a tree in Israel. Visit http://www.jnf.org for information on planting trees in Israel.

Hebrew Vocabulary

Here are some Hebrew words and phrases to use as you learn about babies:

Baby (m/f)	*Ti-**nok**/Ti-no-**ket***	תִּינוֹק/תִּינוֹקֶת
Bottle	*Bak-**buk***	בַּקְבּוּק
Diaper	*Chi-**tul***	חִתּוּל
Pacifier	*Mo-**tzetz***	מוֹצֵץ
I see (m/f) a baby.	*A-**ni** ro-**eh**/ro-**ah** ti-**nok***	אֲנִי רוֹאֶה/רוֹאָה תִּינוֹק.
I am not a baby.	*A-**ni** lo ti-**nok**.*	אֲנִי לֹא תִּינוֹק.
I am growing!	*A-**ni** ga-**deil**!*	אֲנִי גָּדֵל!

Songs and Poems

In God's Image
By Deborah Schein

The rabbi says we look like God,
But I just can't believe
That God can look like all of us —
My baby, Gramps, and me.

Mommy says it's not our hair,
Or bones, or teeth, or thighs,
But something more important,
In our hearts and in our eyes.

She says I'll understand this,
As I grow from young to old.
But that's another problem,
'Cuz I'm already five you know!

Laila, Laila
A traditional Hebrew lullaby to sing to your babies. A recorded version can be found on the recording From Generation to Generation: A Legacy of Lullabies *by Tanja Solnik.*

Laila, laila, ha-ru'ach goveret,
Laila, laila
Ho-ma ha-tza-me-ret

Laila, laila
Kochav m'zamer
Numi numi kabi et ha-ner (2x)
Laila, laila
Numi numi kabi et ha-ner

Night, night, the breeze is blowing
Night, night the tree tops rustle
Night, night, a star is singing,
Rest, rest, extinguish the light.

Blessings

When we think about babies, there are two blessings we can say:

The "*Shehecheyanu*" is a blessing about gratitude for the gift of life, said when something is done for the first time, in this case, upon meeting a new baby.

בָּרוּךְ אַתָּה יְיָ אֱלֹהֵינוּ מֶלֶךְ הָעוֹלָם שֶׁהֶחֱיָנוּ וְקִיְּמָנוּ וְהִגִּיעָנוּ לַזְּמַן הַזֶּה.

Ba-ruch A-tah A-do-nai E-lo-hei-nu Me-lech ha-O-lam She-he-che-ya-nu V'ki-y'ma-nu,
V'hi-gi-ya-nu La-Z'man Ha-Zeh.
We praise You, our God, Creator of the universe, for giving us life, sustaining us, and helping us to reach this moment.

"*Birkat Banim*" is said by parents over their children *Erev* Shabbat (Friday night). Parents who come to class to share Shabbat with their children can be encouraged to bless their children (or all the children in the class):

To a son:

יְשִׂמְךָ אֱלֹהִים כְּאֶפְרַיִם וְכִמְנַשֶּׁה.

Y'sim-cha E-lo-him k'Ef-ra-yim v'chi-M'na-sheh.
May God make you like Ephraim and Menasheh.

To a daughter:

יְשִׂמֵךְ אֱלֹהִים כְּשָׂרָה רִבְקָה רָחֵל וְלֵאָה.

Y'si-meich E-lo-him k'Sa-rah Riv-kah Ra-chel v'Le-ah.
May God make you like Sarah, Rebecca, Rachel and Leah.

And to all children:
May God bless you and keep you.
May God's face shine on you and may God be gracious to you,
May God's face be lifted up to you and give you peace.

Story: A Baby's Wisdom

Retold by Maxine Handelman, based on a midrash (Bereshit Rabbah 8:1).

One afternoon, Lily was taking a walk with her mom and dad through the neighborhood. Her dad was pushing a stroller in which Lily's new baby brother, Lev, lay sleeping. Lily liked to ask questions. "Mom," she said, "why does that house have this box in the front?"

"That's the mailbox, Lily," answered her mother. Lily's mom was used to answering Lily's questions. "The box is there so the mail carrier can leave mail for this family."

Lily looked around some more. She looked toward the sky, and asked, "What are the clouds for, Mom?"

"The clouds hold the rain so when it gets too dry on the ground, the rain can fall."

Lily looked around as they walked. She was trying to decide what to ask next, and as she thought, she placed one finger to her lips. Her finger brushed a spot under her nose, a small indentation. "Hey mom!" said Lily. "What's this spot for, here under my nose?"

"Ah," smiled her mother. "For that I will tell you a story. When a baby is growing inside his mommy's tummy, he's not just growing. He's learning. The angels come to teach the baby everything there is to know in the whole world. The angels teach the baby Torah, and *Talmud* and *Midrash*. The angels teach the baby how God created the world, and all the songs that have ever been sung. The angels tell the baby all the laws the Jewish people received at Mt. Sinai. The angels teach the baby the best recipes for challah and chicken soup and chocolate toffee squares that are kosher for Pesach. And through the long months that the baby is growing inside the mommy, the angels tell the baby all of the Jewish stories that have ever been told."

"But," continued Lily's mommy, "if a baby was born knowing all that, he wouldn't have anything to learn his whole life. So, right at the moment that a baby is being born, an angel comes and — tap! — touches right under the baby's nose. Everything the baby learned over the last nine months goes flying out of the baby's head, and the angel's touch leaves a little indentation, just like the one under your nose. Some people believe that that is the reason babies cry when they are born, because they know they will have to spend their entire lives relearning all the stories and searching for that perfect chocolate toffee recipe for Pesach."

Lily touched the spot under her nose thoughtfully. She made her mother stop walking so she could look closely, and her mom had a spot like that too. Lily looked in the stroller, and sure enough, baby Lev had an indentation under his nose too.

"Mom," asked Lily, after some time. "Did you ever find that perfect chocolate toffee recipe for Pesach that the angels taught you?"

"Well, your Aunt Frannie did share her recipe with me, and it's pretty tasty. Maybe it's the one the angels taught her."

"Maybe the angels take all the learning away from the babies so we can learn from each other our whole lives," said Lily, her finger still rubbing the spot under her nose.

Lily's mom smiled and gave her a big hug. "I think you're pretty smart. Maybe the angels didn't tap *everything* out of your head when you were born."

Questions and suggestions:

➤ What do you imagine the angels taught you before you were born?

➤ Share this story with parents. Then ask parents to share with their child a story from their family that the angels might have told the child before he or she was born.

➤ Invite children to draw self-portraits. Allow them to look at their faces closely in a mirror and encourage them to include the indentation under their nose in their portrait. (By the way, the medical term for that little indentation is "filtrum.")

Resources

Books and Music

Silverman, Judy. *Rosie & the Mole: The Story of a Bris.* New York: Pitspopany Press, 1999.
> *Rosie is jealous of all the fuss everyone is making over her new baby brother. He is getting a naming ceremony and a bris — while all she received as a baby was a naming ceremony.*

Solnik, Tanja. *From Generation to Generation: A Legacy of Lullabies.*
> *Includes the song "Laila, Laila." Compact disc, available from http://www.tanjasolnik.com.*

Wilkowski, Susan. *Baby's Bris.* Rockville, MD: Kar-Ben Copies, 1999.
> *Sophie becomes a big sister and, during the first eight days of her brother's life, learns about the customs of a bris (circumcision) and celebrates the event with her family and new brother Ben.*

26. What's Jewish about Classroom Jobs?

It is quite common to see children in early childhood classrooms washing off tables, putting away toys, or throwing away napkins and cups from snack. Classroom jobs have become part of helping children learn how to be self-sufficient, independent, and capable. So, what is Jewish about classroom jobs?

The Big Idea

One common Hebrew translation for the word "job" is *avodah*. But, as with many ancient Hebrew words, the meaning has changed according to the context in which the word is used. In ancient times, the word *avodah* was the name given to the Temple service where sacrifices were offered up to God. After the destruction of the Temple, the word *avodah* became *avodah sheh b'lev*, "service of the heart". At this point *avodah*, or prayer, became the primary means of worshiping God. Later still, the word *avodah* became the word associated with work, specifically to those working to build the land of Israel.

Here, the word "job" reflects responsibilities given to children in a classroom context in which the children work together as a *kehillah*, a community. Classroom jobs can serve as a model for the *mitzvot* (commandments) that form the structure of Jewish life and guide us in being members of the Jewish community. Maria Montessori, an innovative Italian 19th century early childhood educator, believed that young children actually build who they become by using their hands, heart, and will — doing a job, wanting to do it, and wanting to do it well. She believed that such work helps children reach their full potential and allows them to grow in understanding of what it means to be part of a community. As young Jewish children learn to be responsible by choosing to participate in classroom jobs, they are learning about being part of a *kehillah* (community) and learning to live a life of *mitzvot*.

Jewish Values

Sometimes, the activities we are involved in with children are Jewish moments, even if it's not readily apparent. Jewish values lead to Jewish behaviors. Performing classroom jobs is filled with Jewish values, including:

Kavanah	Intention	כַּוָּנָה
Kavod	Respect, Honor	כָּבוֹד
Kehillah	Community	קְהִלָּה
Mikdash M'at	A Mini-sanctuary	מִקְדָּשׁ מְעַט

When children explore classroom jobs, they are literally embodying Jewish values. Children's explorations are richest when the children are partners in their own learning. To engage children in these Jewish values and to deepen their learning, take time to investigate what children already know about classroom jobs. Observe children's play and analyze their comments. Seek out the children's questions and interests. Based on the children's questions, you might:

➤ Invite children and parents to help prepare the classroom or make needed changes so that everyone feels responsible for the environment. *(Kehillah, Mikdash M'at)*

➤ Expect and show the children how to clean up after themselves. Tell the children that it is important to leave materials and activities ready for the next person. Ask children why this is important. *(Kavod, Kavanah)*

➤ Praise positive behavior and teach the children how to help each other to make positive choices during the day. It is a child's job to make good choices during the day and this is made easier if parents, teachers, and friends are there to help and model. When a child grows in his/her abilities to help, the classroom can become a *Mikdash M'at. (Kehillah, Kavod, Kavanah, Mikdash M'at)*

➤ Create a list of classroom jobs with the children. Do some research first, by looking at what jobs might be needed. This way, children will clearly understand what each job entails and how to perform the job. *(Kehillah, Kavod, Kavanah)*

Israel Connection

If you were to visit Israel, you would see people doing similar jobs as you see people doing in North America — there are grocery clerks, bank tellers, business people, bus drivers, police, and even the president of the country. One big difference is that most of the people doing these jobs in Israel are Jewish. Not everybody in Israel is Jewish, but the majority of the population is and Israel is the only place in the world where this is true.

Many stores in Israel are closed on Shabbat and other Jewish holidays. On Fridays, busy shoppers and storekeepers take time to wish each other "Shabbat Shalom." You will find a *mezzuzah* on the doors of most stores in Israel, even at the gas station. Stores are decorated for holidays like Purim.

This is certainly not the case in North America. To emphasis this, pretend that you are all in Israel and help the children recreate the house-keeping corner into an Israeli restaurant, store, or *kibbutz*. Where does the *mezzuzah* go on the store doorframe? What decorations would the children hang in an Israeli gas station before Pesach? Can you find all the Hebrew terms you would need in your Israeli restaurant (such as waiter, menu, and "Check, please")? Check a dictionary or ask a Hebrew speaker to help you out.

Hebrew Vocabulary

Here are some Hebrew words and phrases you can use as you explore classroom jobs:

This is my job.	*Zo ha-a-vo-**dah** she-**li**.*	.זוֹ הָעֲבוֹדָה שֶׁלִּי
Time to clean up.	*Z'**man** l'na-**kot**.*	.זְמַן לְנַקּוֹת
Can I help clean up?	*Ef-**shar** la-a-**zor** l'na-**kot**?*	?אֶפְשָׁר לַעֲזוֹר לְנַקּוֹת
Please:	*B'va-ka-**sha**:*	:בְּבַקָּשָׁה
Wash the tables.	*L'na-**kot** et hashul-cha-**not***	.לְנַקּוֹת אֶת הַשֻּׁלְחָנוֹת
Hold the door.	*L'ha-cha-**zik** et ha-**de**-let.*	.לְהַחֲזִיק אֶת הַדֶּלֶת
Straighten the shelves.	*L'sa-**der** et ha-ma-da-**fim**.*	.לְסַדֵּר אֶת הַמַּדָּפִים
Blocks	*Ku-bi-**yot***	קֻבִּיּוֹת
Papers	*N'ya-**rot***	נְיָרוֹת

Songs and Poems

Al Sh'losha Devarim
Music by Chaim Tzur, text from Pirkei Avot 1:2. The music to this song can be found in The Complete Jewish Songbook for Children: Manginot, *edited by Stephen Richards.*

Al sh'loshah d'varim (2x)
Al sh'losha, shlosha d'varim
Ha'Olam ha'Olam omed.
Al haTorah, v'al ha-avodah v'al g'milut chasadim (2x)

On three things the world stands:
On Torah, on worship, and on caring deeds

Avodah — Work
By Deborah Schein

Pick up your toys
Hold the door
Clean up for snack
Then clean up some more.

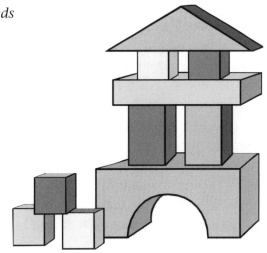

Work together
Or do it alone
Jobs at school
Jobs at home

Do it with purpose
Do it with care
Do it right
Not to do it again.
Do your job
Using all your heart
Create Shalom —
Mikdash m'at.

Blessings

When we think about classroom jobs, this is a blessing we can say:

בָּרוּךְ אַתָּה יְיָ אֱלֹהֵינוּ מֶלֶךְ הָעוֹלָם שֶׁעָשַׂנִי בֵּן (בַּת) חוֹרִין.

Ba-ruch A-tah A-do-nai E-lo-hei-nu Me-lech Ha-O-lam She-a-sa-ni Ben (Bat) Cho-rin.
We praise You, our God, Creator of the universe, Who made me (m/f) a free person.

Story: The Day the Puzzles Fell

A story about classroom jobs, by Deborah Schein.

Morah Sara felt it in her bones. It was time for this class of four-year-olds to create a list of jobs in order to keep the classroom clean and workable, in order for the environment to feel like a *Mikdash M'at,* a mini-sanctuary for learning. Every child was now comfortable playing in the room. Many friends had been made, many conflicts had been resolved, and *Morah* Sara had a pretty good sense as to who would get along with whom. She came to school determined to have a discussion about *avodah* (work) during group time. But before she had a chance to gather the classroom of children together, Steven had already created a mess bigger than any group of children could possible tackle by dumping all the puzzle pieces out in a big pile. What was to be done? *Morah* Sara did the only thing she knew would work. She gathered the children together and posed the problem: "Class, we are a *kehillah*, a community, and for some reason, all the puzzles have been dumped in the middle of the room. What should we do?"

The children thought for a moment. Michael volunteered, "We could pick up all the pieces?" *Morah* Sara asked, "How will you organize yourselves?" Emily suggested, "We could give each puzzle frame a spot on the floor and then sort the colors." Rachel, her twin said, "We really know these puzzles. We can do it!"

And so the children got to work. They laid out the puzzle frames and began sorting. Soon small groups of children were working diligently on each puzzle. Only Steven was sitting in a beanbag chair, pouting. *Morah* Sara went over to him. "Steven, why don't you take each puzzle as it is finished and place it carefully on the puzzle rack?" Steven's face lit up as he got up to follow the teacher's suggestion. At this point *Morah* Sara whispered to him, "Isn't it nice to have friends to help out when you need them?" Steven gave his teacher a sly smile and went off to help his classmates.

After the puzzles were put away, the class sat down for the much-needed discussion on jobs. The outcome was a set of jobs to be done in small groups. During activity time, some of the children in the class drew pictures of the jobs. *Morah* Sarah said that they would finish the chart tomorrow and classroom jobs would begin. The children could barely wait!

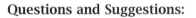

Questions and Suggestions:

➤ What jobs do you think the children in the story picked for their job chart? How do they compare to the jobs in your classroom?

➤ It often works best to group children to do jobs. This way a more competent child might teach a child who is just learning to do a job, and problems are avoided when someone is absent. A teacher needs to spend some time thinking about which children can and cannot work together.

➤ Rotate jobs after a week. Daily changing is too frequent. A week on the job gives children an opportunity for mastery.

➤ Keep a job chart, using clothes pins or Velcro backed cards labeled with the children's names that can be moved in a circular fashion from job to job. This offers children the opportunity to predict and then know what job will soon be theirs.

Resources

Books and Music

Cohen, David Elliot and Lee Liberman. *A Day in the Life of Israel.* San Francisco, CA: Collins Publishers, 1994.

> *In a single day, fifty of the world's finest photojournalists captured extraordinary images of everyday events, yielding these 200 remarkable photographs of Israel's history, culture, and geography. Included are photos of people doing a variety of jobs.*

Edwards, Michelle. *Chicken Man.* New York: Lothrop, Lee and Shepard Books, 1991.
A delightful story of life with the animals on a kibbutz, and how a positive attitude about doing any job can make all the difference.

Eisenberg, Ann. *Bible Heroes I Can Be.* Rockville, MD. Kar-Ben Copies, Inc., 1990.
Introduces such biblical figures as Noah, Rebecca, and King David and shows how their accomplishments and attributes can be emulated in modern life.

Richards, Stephen, ed. *The Complete Jewish Songbook for Children: Manginot.* New York: Transcontinental Music Publications, 2002.
201 Jewish songs for holidays, everyday, or just for fun.

27. What's Jewish about Classroom Rules?

At the beginning of each school year, children and teachers are grouped together into new learning communities called classes. These classes, like all groups, work best if rules exist to guide and regulate behavior. But what is Jewish about classroom rules?

The Big Idea

In true Jewish form, creating rules for a Jewish early childhood classroom is a Jewish process in itself. It is a process of reflection, dialogue, repetition, and testing (checking out hypotheses/predictions). In the beginning, a new group of children and teachers come together near to the time of the celebration of Rosh HaShanah, the birthday of the world, a new Jewish year. The fall holidays come to an end with the celebration of Simchat Torah, a holiday which focuses on the ending and beginning of the reading of the Torah. The Torah holds our Jewish history and offers rules to live by, such as those found within the Ten Commandments. These rules help Jews to live "good" Jewish lives. And so, between the time of Rosh HaShanah and Simchat Torah, children and teachers should be thinking about the rules that will help them, as a new class of learners, to achieve shalom, peace, in their classroom. Having good rules that are understood and followed by all will bring shalom so that learning can be achieved by all — parents and teachers as well as the children. When we make rules for our classrooms, we are made aware of the *mitzvot* performed *bein adam l'chaveiro* — between people and people — so that shalom can be achieved in the world.

Jewish Values

Sometimes, the activities we are involved in with children are Jewish moments, even if it's not readily apparent. Jewish values lead to Jewish behaviors. Having rules and following rules is filled with Jewish values, including:

Derech Eretz	Proper, Decent Behavior	דֶּרֶךְ אֶרֶץ
G'milut Chasadim	Acts of Loving-kindness	גְּמִילוּת חֲסָדִים
Kavod	Respect, Honor	כָּבוֹד
Kehillah	Community	קְהִלָּה
Sayver Panim Yafot	Cheerfulness, a Pleasant Demeanor	סֵבֶר פָּנִים יָפוֹת

Sh'lom Bayit	Peace Within the Home	שְׁלוֹם בַּיִת
Shalom	Peace, Completeness	שָׁלוֹם
Teshuvah	Repentance	תְּשׁוּבָה

As members of the community grow more comfortable with each other, classroom rules are shaped by Jewish values. When children create and live by rules, they are literally embodying Jewish values. Children's explorations are richest when the children are partners in their own learning. To engage children in these Jewish values and to deepen their learning, take time to investigate what children already know about rules. Observe children's play and analyze their comments. Seek out the children's questions and interests. Based on the children's questions, you might:

➤ Have a classroom meeting at the beginning of the school year, but after the children have had some opportunity to play together and get to know each other. At this meeting, ask the children, "What kind of a classroom do you want? What rules do we need to create such a community?" Then list the children's ideas and thoughts and discuss with them how to best write each rule. *(G'milut Chasadim, Kehillah, Sh'lom Bayit, Kavod)*

➤ Invite the children to create a rules chart for the classroom. The children can use inventive spelling or dictations for the words and they can draw pictures that will help to remind them of the rules. This chart should be placed in a prominent place in the classroom for all to see. *(Kehillah, Kavod, Shalom)*

➤ Encourage the children to be kind to one another. This means to help each other, speak kindly, to share, and to respect each other. When you witness such actions, call attention to the deed and identify it by name as a Jewish value. For example, when Jonathan lets Sarah take a turn at the water fountain before him, you can say, "Jonathan, you really showed *Derech Eretz* by helping Sarah. You're helping create *Shalom* in our classroom." *(G'milut Chasadim, Derech Eretz, Kavod)*

➤ Give children the words to use when a problem arises. If, for example, Joseph is tugging a toy out of Hannah's hand, you might say to Joseph, "Joseph, ask Hannah, 'Can I have that toy when you're finished?'" Then help Joseph find something else to play with. Remind Hannah to give the toy to Joseph when she's finished. See books by Becky Bailey for more information on this type of social building. *(Kavod, Kehillah, Shalom)*

➤ Problem-solve with the children what should be done if a rule is continually broken. Is there something in the classroom environment that needs to change to help children follow the rule more easily? *(Kavod, Kehillah, Shalom, Teshuvah)*

➤ Help children see the consequences of their actions. If one child helps another child put on his coat, that child might then hold the door for the first child as they go outside. If a child hits, he or she may be hit by others. *(Sh'lom Bayit)*

Israel Connection

Rules for Jewish Israeli children mean something different than they do for Jewish North American children. There are places in Israel that are unsafe. There are people living nearby that may hurt Israeli children for being Jewish. Soldiers with guns are a common sight, and guards sit at many public doors checking bags and guarding the people. Living in this way gives even the youngest child a deeper understanding of the importance and necessity of rules.

Within the classroom, the rules for North American and Israeli children are quite similar. Children learn to share, talk nicely, listen to one another, use materials properly, and walk while indoors. North American Jewish children and Israeli Jewish children both learn about the Ten Commandments and are continuously learning about *mitzvot.* Growing up to be good people who make good decisions, give *tzedakah,* and are *mensches* are common goals for Jews all over the world. Following rules is but one step toward achieving these goals. With the help of the children in your classroom, make a list of rules that all Jewish children might use in a classroom whether in North America or Israel.

תּוֹדָה רַבָּה!

Hebrew Vocabulary

Here are some Hebrew words and phrases (and one Yiddish word) you can use as you talk about classroom rules:

Rules	*Mish-pa-**tim***	מִשְׁפָּטִים
Good Person	*Mensch* (a Yiddish word)	מענטש
Can I help?	*Ef-**shar** la'a-**zor**?*	אֶפְשָׁר לַעֲזוֹר?
Thank you	*To-**dah** Ra-**bah**.*	תּוֹדָה רַבָּה.
You're welcome.	*B'va-ka-**shah**.*	בְּבַקָשָׁה.
Please	*B'va-ka-**shah***	בְּבַקָשָׁה
Use your words.	*L'hish-ta-**mesh** ba-**lim** sheh-la-**chem**.*	לְהִשְׁתַּמֵשׁ בַּלִּים שֶׁלָכֶם

Songs and Poems

Hillel's Song
Lyrics by Mah Tovu (Steve Brodsky and Josh Zweiback), music by Mah Tovu with Sam Glaser. Hebrew text from Pirkei Avot 2:6. From the compact disc Only This *by Mah Tovu. Used with permission.*

A long time ago there lived a great teacher, Hillel was his name
People would ask him all kinds of questions, his wise answers brought him fame
Someone once asked, "In a place that is evil, how are we supposed to behave?"
Hillel thought for a moment, he pondered the question
And this is the answer he gave:

Chorus:
B'makom sh'eyn anashim (3x)
Hillel omer hishtadel l'hiyot ish

Every person has two inclinations, for evil and for good
  Hillel knew that it's not always easy to act the way we should
  So we look to our parents, our teachers, our children, and we search for the answer inside
  And in the struggle between what's right and what's wrong
  We let this lesson be our guide

Chorus

"Where people are acting inhuman,"
Hillel said, "We must strive to be human.
Make peace with your sister and brother,
What is hateful to you do not do to another."

So many questions, not enough answers as we travel along the road
But if we remember the words of wise Hillel we will always know which way to go
When we find ourselves in a place that is evil and we don't know how to behave
If we stop for a moment, and ponder the question
We'll remember the answer he gave

Chorus

"In a place where there are no human beings," Hillel said, "strive to be a human being."

What are Rules For?
By Deborah Schein

What are rules for?
Please tell me now!
I want to be good,
But I don't know how.

My Ima says
To use Kavod
I will try right now
By feeding my toad.

My Abba says
Derech Eretz is the way
To stay out of trouble
Both night and day.

I think I have it,
I must be kind,
Not for a moment,
But all of the time.

Blessings

There are no formal blessings for following the rules of a community. But the blessing of being a creator of *shalom* can inspire *brachot sheh b'lev* (prayers of the heart) such as:

Dear God, thank You for giving me the knowledge to know the right thing to do and the ability to do it. Thank You for giving me words to share my thoughts and feelings.

Story: Hillel's Essential Rule

By Maxine Handelman, based on Talmud Shabbat 31a.

There once was a man who knew nothing about the Torah, but he was interested in learning. He was also the kind of man who liked to challenge other people. He came to a great rabbi named Hillel. The man said to Hillel, "I want you to teach me the whole Torah, but not in the usual way. I want you to teach me the whole Torah while you stand on one foot." Hillel was always up for a good challenge. He carefully balanced himself on one foot, and said to the man, "What is hateful to you, do not do to your fellow man. This is the entire Torah, all of it. The rest is commentary. Now go and study it." As Hillel put his foot down slowly, the man thought, "How could this one 'Golden Rule' be all of Torah?" Deep in thought, he began to walk away from Hillel, and suddenly realized that he had not said thank you. "I would hate if someone did not thank me for teaching them and giving them some of my time," he thought. He rushed back to Hillel and thanked him for the lesson in Torah.

The man walked through the market on his way home. As he strolled past the fruit seller, he absent-mindedly popped some grapes into his mouth. All of a sudden, he noticed the angry face of the fruit seller, and said to himself, "I would hate it if someone stole grapes from me." He rushed back to pay the fruit seller for the grapes he had eaten. All day long, the man noticed how he hurt people when he did something to them that he would hate them doing to him.

Towards evening, the man passed by a schoolhouse. Through the open windows, he could hear the school children chanting the words of Torah, the words dancing into the air. The man listened to the children and decided, "Perhaps Hillel was right, and this essential rule is what the Torah is all about. But I would hate if I presented someone with a big challenge and they didn't wrestle with me." The man went into the schoolhouse and joined the children in studying Torah.

Questions and Suggestions:

➤ What might the "Essential Rule" in your classroom be?

➤ If Hillel told the man the most important thing in the Torah, why should the man go and study the rest of the Torah?

➤ Practice this essential rule in your classroom. What happens when everyone treats everyone else according to this rule?

Resources

Books and Music

Bailey, Becky. *Easy To Love, Difficult to Discipline.* New York: Harper Collins Publishing Inc., 2000.
   Seven basic skills for turning conflict into cooperation.

Cone, Molly, *Who Knows Ten: Children's Tales of the Ten Commandments.* Union of American Hebrew Congregations, 1999.
   Presents each of the Ten Commandments with stories illustrating their meanings.

Mah Tovu. *Only This.* Denver, CO: Mah Tovu, 1996.
This compact disc includes "Hillel's Song." Available from A.R.E. Publishing, Inc., (800) 246-7779 or www.arepublish.com.

Nerlove, Miriam, *The Ten Commandments for Jewish Children.* Albert Whitman & Co., 1999.
Delicate watercolors paint the drama of Moses delivering the Ten Commandments to the Israelites as each of the commandments is displayed on tablet-shaped pages. Includes a contemporary application of the commandments as they apply to the lives of children.

Topeck, Susan Remick, *Ten Good Rules.* Minneapolis, MN: Kar-Ben Publishing. 1992.
Introduces the Ten Commandments from a Jewish perspective, in language appropriate for very young children.

Video

Kids for Character. Los Angeles, CA: The Josephson Institute of Ethics, 1996.
Thirty beloved children's characters, including Barney, Thomas the Tank Engine, and Lamb Chop team up to introduce their young admirers to the Six Pillars of Character in this sixty minute video. Learning right from wrong has never been so much fun! Available at http://www.charactercounts.org.

On the Web

Character Counts! Character Education Resources
http://www.charactercounts.org
CHARACTER COUNTS! is a nonprofit, nonpartisan, nonsectarian character education framework that teaches the Six Pillars of Character: trustworthiness, respect, responsibility, fairness, caring, and citizenship.

28. What's Jewish about Faces?

One of many important things a teacher must remember is that each student is special and like no one else. Each child brings something distinctive of him/herself to be shared with the entire classroom community. Recognizing this uniqueness begins when we look at each child's face. But what is Jewish about faces?

The Big Idea

Faces can and do tell a lot about a person. First there are its parts — a nose for smelling, a mouth for eating and speaking, two ears for listening and hearing, and two eyes for seeing. Eyes are also the "windows to the soul" and an indicator of the uniqueness of each individual. And there are expressions — smiles, frowns, and grimaces — for others to read. The face is an amazing body part. No wonder it is one of the first things a baby notices.

What else does the face tell us? There is a Jewish saying from Kohelet (Ecclesiastes) which says that wisdom lights up a person's face. One only needs to look into the face of a child as he or she learns something new to see the glow and know that wisdom is there. Each child has his/her own way of processing information and his/her own way of sharing it with others. As we think about faces, we are made aware of God's ability to make us all different, even as we are all created in God's image.

Jewish Values

Sometimes, the activities we are involved in with children are Jewish moments, even if it's not readily apparent. Jewish values lead to Jewish behaviors. Studying faces is filled with Jewish values, including:

B'tzelem Elohim	Created in the Image of God	בְּצֶלֶם אֱלֹהִים
Chochma	Wisdom	חָכְמָה
Hiddur Mitzvah	Beautifying a Mitzvah	הִדּוּר מִצְוָה
Kavod	Respect, Honor	כָּבוֹד
Kehillah	Community	קְהִלָּה
Sayver Panim Yafot	Cheerfulness, A Pleasant Demeanor	סֵבֶר פָּנִים יָפוֹת

When children explore faces, they are literally embodying Jewish values. Children's explorations are richest when the children are partners in their own learning. To engage children in these Jewish values and to deepen their learning, take time to investigate what children already know about faces. Observe children's play and analyze their comments. Seek out the children's questions and interests. Based on the children's questions, you might:

➤ Invite the children to see their own uniqueness as they draw detailed self-portraits. Provide mirrors for close scrutiny of faces and add dictation, or invite the children to write something about their uniqueness. *(Kavod, B'tzelem Elohim)*

➤ Take the original self-portraits and create many copies so that each child can recreate their own image using a variety of art media (pastels, crayon, black and white, etc.) Display these portraits so that each of the children's uniqueness is felt in the classroom, whether the children are present or not. *(Kavod, Kehillah)*

➤ Play a game where one child is blindfolded. Have this child gently feel the hair, face, and hands of another child while trying to recognize who it might be. A variation to this game is to play it with disguised voices. *(Chochma, Kehilla)*

➤ Help the children to see the uniqueness in others. You might say to the children, "Now that Sara can tie her shoes, if your shoe becomes untied, you might ask Sara to tie it for you." *(Hiddur Mitzvah, Kehillah)*

➤ Role play the value of *Sayver Panim Yafot* with children. Let them respond to an encounter with a cheerful face or a grouchy face.

Israel Connection

Israel is a Jewish country, but not all her inhabitants look alike or have the same cultural heritage. Today the Jews that inhabit Israel include Ethiopian Jews with dark skin, Orthodox Jews with beards and *payes* (side-curls), brown-faced Jews from India, and colorfully dressed Jews from Yemen. There are also Jews in Israel who come from America, France, the United States, South America, the Soviet Union, and many other places. Israel also has non-Jews living within her borders — there are Arab Muslims, Arab Christians, Palestinians, Bedouins, Armenians and Christians. All of these people try to coexist in an area smaller than most of the states in the United States. To help children understand the many faces of Israel, place a few books and posters of Israel in the dramatic play area that show some of Israel's different faces. Be sure to include a variety of fabrics and props. Don't forget scarves and other items that represent some of the different cultures that exist in Israel. Full-length mirrors will help children see themselves in some of the different roles.

Hebrew Vocabulary

Here are some Hebrew words and phrases you can use as you explore faces:

Face	Pa-**nim**	פָּנִים
Eye/eyes	Ein/ei-**na**-yim	עַיִן/עֵינַיִם
Ear/ears	**O**-zen/oz-**na**-yim	אֹזֶן/אׇזְנַיִם
Mouth	Peh	פֶּה
Nose	Af	אַף
Smile	Chi-**yuch**	חִיּוּךְ
Frown	Za-**af**	זַעַף
I have two eyes.	Yesh li shtei ei-**na**-yim.	יֵשׁ לִי שְׁתֵּי עֵינַיִם.
My face is not clean.	Pa-**nai** lo n''ki-**yot**.	פָּנַי לֹא נְקִיּוֹת.
My face is clean.	Pa-**nai** n'ki-**yot**.	פָּנַי נְקִיּוֹת.

Songs and Poems

A Sense of Uniqueness
By Deborah Schein

Listen to our voices,
Hear the bells,
Fragrances around
For us to smell.
Taste a kiss,
Water on hand,
Touch and see
All that we can.
Hear, smell, taste and touch
See the uniqueness
In each of us.
Bless our senses
Learn through them
Thank you God
For all five of them!

Mi Ani? (Who Am I?)

From Songs of Childhood *by Judith Kaplan Eisenstein, Frieda Prensky, and Ayala Gordon. Used with permission.*

The Boy's Song:
Mi ani, Mi ani	I am me, I am me.
Yeled ani.	I am a boy.
*Uri shemi!	*I am Uri!

*Have the boys in the class sing this song using their own name.

The Girl's Song:
Mi ani, Mi ani	I am me, I am me.
Yaldah ani.	I am a girl.
*Nechamah shemi!	*I am Nechamah!

*Have the girls in the class sing this song using their own name.

Blessings

This is the blessing said upon seeing a person who is very wise.

בָּרוּךְ אַתָּה יְיָ אֱלֹהֵינוּ מֶלֶךְ הָעוֹלָם שֶׁנָּתַן מֵחָכְמָתוֹ לְבָשָׂר וָדָם.

Ba-ruch A-tah A-do-nai E-lo-hei-nu Me-lech Ha-O-lam She-na-tan Mei-choch-ma-to L'va-sar Va-dam.
Praised are You, Adonai our God, who has given wisdom to human beings.

Story: The Power of the Tongue

This classic story has roots in Torah and Midrash. Retold here by Maxine Handelman, based on a version in The Classic Tales *by Ellen Frankel.*

Once the king of Persia was very ill. His doctors announced that his only hope to get better would be to drink the milk of a lioness. But who could get the milk of a lioness? Even the king's most courageous hunters were too afraid to try and milk a lioness.

So the king of Persia went to his friend, King Solomon, to ask for help. King Solomon turned to his most faithful helper, Benaiah ben Yehoyada, and asked him to go and collect milk from a lioness. Benaiah said, "For you, King Solomon, I will do it!"

Benaiah took ten goats with him into the mountains. He soon came upon a cave where a lioness was nursing her cubs. On the first day, Benaiah threw a goat to the lioness, but stayed far outside the cave. The next day, he threw her another goat, and moved a little bit closer. Each day, Benaiah threw a goat to the lioness and moved a little bit closer. By the tenth day, the lioness was so used to him, and so well fed, that she let Benaiah come and play with her cubs. She even let him take some of her milk, which he stored carefully in a glass jar.

Benaiah took the jar full of milk and rushed back to King Solomon. King Solomon was very pleased. He sent Benaiah and the jar of milk on to see the king of Persia. It was a journey of several days, and one night while Benaiah slept, all the parts of his body began to argue about who was most important.

The legs said, "We are the most important, for if we had not walked up the mountain to the lioness's den, Benaiah would not have been able to get the milk."

The hands said, "But if we hadn't milked the lioness, Benaiah would have no milk to bring to the king of Persia."

The eyes argued, "If we had not shown Benaiah the way, he never would have found the lioness's den in the first place."

The mind said, "If I had not shown Benaiah how to befriend the lioness, he never would have been able to get close enough to get the milk."

Then the tongue spoke up, "No, you are all wrong! I am more important than all of you put together, for without speech, nothing is possible."

All the other parts of the body laughed at the tongue and said, "Who do you think you are? You are not important at all!"

The tongue replied, "Soon you will all agree that I have more power than any of you."

The parts of the body were still arguing over who was the most important the next morning as Benaiah went to give the milk to the king of Persia. The legs walked proudly, the hands carried the jar securely, the eyes made sure Benaiah did not trip. As Benaiah approached the king, the tongue suddenly took over and said, "Here is the dog's milk you wanted."

"What?" said the king. "Dog's milk! Are you making fun of me?" And he had Benaiah thrown in jail.

All the parts of the body quivered with fear. "Now do you see," said the tongue, "that I am the most important part of the body?"

"Yes, yes!" cried all the other parts of the body. "You are the most important."

The tongue spoke up to the guards in the jail. "Excuse me, but I made a mistake before. I have in my jar the milk of a lioness." The guards brought Benaiah to the king, Benaiah explained the mistake, and the king drank the milk of the lioness. In a few days his sickness was gone and he was cured.

Benaiah returned to King Solomon and told him the entire story. Solomon wrote in his book of Proverbs, "Death and life are in the power of the tongue" (Proverbs 18:21).

Questions and suggestions:

➤ Would Benaiah have been able to get the milk with only his tongue, or did he need the partnership of all his body parts?

➤ Why is the tongue, and what we say, so important?

➤ The rabbis provide many guidelines for how we should speak to each other, including warnings against *lashon hara* (bad or harmful speech). Try to go for an hour in your class without anyone saying anything hurtful to anyone else. If you can do an hour, try a whole day!

Resources

Cohen, David Elliot and Lee Liberman. *A Day in the Life of Israel*. San Francisco, CA: Collins Publishers, 1994.

In a single day, fifty of the world's finest photojournalists captured extraordinary images of everyday events which yielded the 200 remarkable photographs of Israel's history, culture, and geography — including many faces.

Eisenberg, Ann. *Bible Heroes I Can Be*. Rockville, MD: Kar-Ben Copies, Inc., 1990.

Introduces such biblical figures as Noah, Rebecca, and King David and shows how their accomplishments and attributes can be emulated in modern life.

Eisenstein, Judith Kaplan, Frieda Prensky, and Ayala Gordon. *Songs of Childhood*. New York: United Synagogue Commission on Jewish Education, 1955.

A wonderful book filled with Hebrew songs of childhood for all occasions including everyday activities, community workers, holidays, trips, and seasons. The Hebrew words are all written in transliteration, include simple translation and are easy to read. Out of print, may be found in libraries or resource centers.

Frankel, Ellen. *The Classic Tales: 4,000 Years of Jewish Lore*. Northvale, NJ: Jason Aronson Inc., 1989.

An amazing anthology of classic Jewish stories, including sources for each.

29. What's Jewish about Family?

Some material adapted from the Machon L'Morim: Bereshit curriculum

We are who we are because of our families. Each of our families is different, with its good points and its bad. From our earliest memories to our strongest alliances, it's all about family. So what's Jewish about family?

The Big Idea

A family can be many different things. A family might include one parent, two parents of opposite genders, two parents of the same gender, or some combination of aunts, uncles and grandparents. Children may come into a family the traditional biological way, through adoption, or some combination thereof. We may look like our immediate family members, or share no physical similarities at all. Additionally, we are each a part of many families: our "family of origin," our extended family, possibly our family by marriage, a created family of friends, and the family of the Jewish people. Every family has its own stories, traditions, and rituals. The entire first book of the Torah is an epic tale of the first Jewish family, from Abraham to Joseph. No matter what the make-up of a family, every family depends on the strength of the relationships between its members. God is found in significant relationships between people. When we think about all of the different relationships found in a family, we are made aware of the presence of God, and of *Kedushah* (holiness).

Jewish Values

Sometimes, the activities we are involved in with children are Jewish moments, even if it's not readily apparent. Jewish values lead to Jewish behaviors. Families are filled with Jewish values, including:

B'tzelem Elohim	Created in the Image of God	בְּצֶלֶם אֱלֹהִים
K'lal Yisrael	All Jews are One People	כְּלַל יִשְׂרָאֵל
Kedushah	Holiness	קְדֻשָׁה
Kibud Av v'Eim	Honor your Father and Mother	כִּבּוּד אָב וְאֵם
L'dor Vador	From Generation to Generation	לְדוֹר וָדוֹר
Mishpacha	Family	מִשְׁפָּחָה
Sh'lom Bayit	Peace Within the Home	שְׁלוֹם בַּיִת
Masoret	Tradition	מַסֹרֶת

When children explore family, they are literally embodying Jewish values. Children's explorations are richest when the children are partners in their own learning. To engage children in these Jewish values and to deepen their learning, take time to investigate what children already know about family. Observe children's play and analyze their comments. Seek out the children's questions and interests. Based on the children's questions, you might:

➤ Invite children to draw a picture of their family. Create a family gallery in your classroom. (*L'dor Vador, Mishpacha*)

➤ Work with the class families to create family trees with their children. Be sensitive with "non-traditional" families. As much as possible, ask the families to include photographs on their family trees to make the concepts and memories more concrete for children. (*L'dor Vador, Mishpacha*)

➤ Create a class photo album with pictures of each child's family. You can also hang these photos on the wall for children to look at all the time. (*K'lal Yisrael, Mishpacha*)

➤ Have children create a mural with magazine pictures of different kinds of families (*L'dor Vador, K'lal Yisrael, B'tzelem Elohim, Mishpacha*)

➤ Role play different family relationships, and problem solve different strategies for creating peace in the home. (*Sh'lom Bayit, Mishpacha*)

➤ Invite grandparents and parents to come in and tell stories of their parents (*L'dor Vador, Kibud Av v'Eim, Masoret, Mishpacha*)

➤ Work with families to collect stories about the people for whom each child was named. Explore children's English and Hebrew namesakes. (*L'dor Vador, Masoret, Mishpacha*)

➤ Examine family photos (from the class or from a magazine) for similarities and differences between family members. Talk about how we are each different, but still created in the image of God. This can also lead to a discussion on the different kinds of families. (*B'tzelem Elohim, Mishpacha*)

➤ Have each child dictate a story about why and how his relationships with each member of his family are special or holy. (*Kibud Av v'Eim, Kedushah, Mishpacha*)

Israel Connection

Beit Hatefutsot, the Nahum Goldmann Museum of the Jewish Diaspora, is an incredible museum in Tel Aviv. It conveys the story of the Jewish people from the time of their expulsion from the Land of Israel 2,500 years ago to the present. At the museum, you can learn about generations of Jewish families and communities from all over the world. You can trace your own genealogy, discover lost branches of your own family tree, and find stories of the places from where your family came. The museum has a Web site — http://www.bh.org.il — where you can learn about family names and Jewish communities around the world. Visit the Web site to view virtual exhibitions of Jewish families all over the world.

Hebrew Vocabulary

Here are some Hebrew words and phrases you can use as you explore families:

House	*Ba*-yit	בַּיִת
Family	*Mish-pa-**cha***	מִשְׁפָּחָה
Mother	*I-ma*	אִמָּא
Father	*A-ba*	אַבָּא
Sister	*A-**chot***	אָחוֹת
Brother	*Ach*	אָח
Baby (m/f)	*Ti-**nok**/Ti-**no**-ket*	תִּינוֹק/תִּינֹקֶת
Grandma	*Saf-ta*	סַבְתָּא
Grandpa	*Sa-ba*	סַבָּא
I love you. (m to m)	*A-**ni** o-hev ot-**cha***.	אֲנִי אוֹהֵב אוֹתְךָ.
I love you. (m to f)	*A-**ni** o-hev o-**tach***.	אֲנִי אוֹהֵב אוֹתָךְ.
I love you. (f to f)	*A-**ni** o-he-vet o-**tach***.	אֲנִי אוֹהֶבֶת אוֹתָךְ.
I love you. (f to m)	*A-**ni** o-he-vet ot-**chah***.	אֲנִי אוֹהֶבֶת אוֹתְךָ.

Songs and Poems

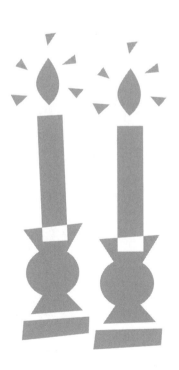

With My Family
Music by Jeff Klepper, words by Jeff Klepper and Daniel Freelander.
From the compact disc Songs for Growin' *by Kol B'Seder.*
Used with permission.

Chorus:
    It makes me glad and happy as can be
    Doing Jewish things together with my family

On Friday night together we celebrate Shabbat
With blessings for the candles and the wine
Ha-mo-tzi le-chem min ha-a-retz,
We give thanks to God for bread
We make Shabbat a very special time
Shabbat is family time.

Chorus

On Chanukah together around the shining lights
With games and songs and presents every night
Ma-oz tzur y'shu-a-ti l'cha na-eh l'sha-bei-ach
Chanukah is a very special time
Chanukah is a family time.

Chorus

And at our Pesach Seder we gather every year
Waiting for Elijah to appear
Dai dai-ei-nu, dai dai-ei-nu, dai dai-ei-nu, dai-ei-nu, dai-ei-nu
Pesach is a very special time
Pesach is a family time.

Chorus

Blessings

On Friday nights, at the Shabbat table, we have the opportunity to honor the members of our families with special blessings. Here are abbreviated forms:

Parents can say the Priestly Blessing over their children:

יְבָרֶכְךָ יְיָ וְיִשְׁמְרֶךָ.

יָאֵר יְיָ פָּנָיו אֵלֶיךָ וִיחֻנֶּךָ.

יִשָּׂא יְיָ פָּנָיו אֵלֶיךָ וְיָשֵׂם לְךָ שָׁלוֹם.

Y'va-**re**-ch'cha A-do-**nai** v'yish-m're-cha.
Ya-**er** A-do-**nai** pa-**nav** ei-**le**-cha vi-chu-**ne**-ka.
Yi-**sa** A-do-**nai** pa-**nav** ei-**le**-cha v'ya-**seim** l'cha sha-**lom**.
May God bless you and keep you.
May God's face shine on you and may God be gracious to you.
May God's face be lifted upon you and give you peace.

The husband traditionally sings *"Eishet Chayil"* (Woman of Valor), from Proverbs 31:10-31, to his wife:

אֵשֶׁת-חַיִל מִי יִמְצָא וְרָחֹק מִפְּנִינִים מִכְרָהּ.
בָּטַח בָּהּ לֵב בַּעְלָהּ וְשָׁלָל לֹא יֶחְסָר.

*Ei-shet **cha**-yil mi yim-**tza** v'ra-**chok** mip'ni-**nim** mich-**rah**.*
*Ba-**tach** bah leiv ba'a-**lah** v'sha-**lal** lo yech'**sar**.*
Who can find a woman of worth? For her price is far above rubies.
The heart of her husband safely trusts in her, and he shall have no lack of gain.

The wife can bless her husband with *"Ashrei Ish"* (Happy is the Man) from Psalm 112:

אַשְׁרֵי-אִישׁ יָרֵא אֶת-יְיָ בְּמִצְוֹתָיו חָפֵץ מְאֹד.
גִּבּוֹר בָּאָרֶץ יִהְיֶה זַרְעוֹ דּוֹר יְשָׁרִים יְבֹרָךְ.
הוֹן-וָעֹשֶׁר בְּבֵיתוֹ וְצִדְקָתוֹ עֹמֶדֶת לָעַד.

*Ash-**rei** ish ya-**rei** et A-do-**nai** b'mitz'vo-**tav** cha-**fetz** m'od.*
*Gi-**bor** ba-a-retz yi-**yeh** zar'**o** dor y'sha-**rim** y'vo-**rach**.*
*Hon va-**o**-sher b'vei-**to** v'tzid'ka-**to** o-**me**-det la-**ad**.*
Happy is the man who fears the Lord, Who delights greatly in God's Commandments.
His seed will be mighty in the land. The generation of the upright will be blessed.
Wealth and riches are in his house. His righteousness endures forever.

Being blessed with special family members can also simply inspire a *bracha sheh b'lev* (a prayer of the heart) which can be said any time in the classroom, such as:

Thank you, God, for giving me such a wonderful mommy (or daddy, aunt, sister...)!

Story: The Two Brothers

A traditional Jewish midrash (Vayikra Rabbah 13) retold by Maxine Handelman. This story highlights the values of Sh'lom Bayit and the holiness of family relationships. This story is also a picture book: The Two Brothers: A Legend of Jerusalem *by Neil Waldman.*

Ephraim and Menasha were two brothers who lived on opposite sides of a very tall hill. Both brothers were farmers. Ephraim was married and had seven children. Menasha was not married and lived alone on his farm. At harvest time, Ephraim sat at his table and watched his busy family. He thought to himself, "I am so blessed to have a wonderful wife and seven children to help me on my farm. When I get old, I know my children will help to take care of me. My brother is all alone, and has no one to help him on his farm or take care of him when he gets old. I'd like to help my brother." Ephraim sat and thought until he came up with a great plan.

That very evening, Menasha was thinking too. "My brother has so many children, so many mouths to feed. I've had a good harvest, but I only have to take care of myself. I'd like to help my brother." Menasha sat and thought until he came up with a great plan.

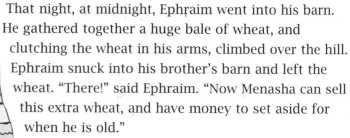

That night, at midnight, Ephraim went into his barn. He gathered together a huge bale of wheat, and clutching the wheat in his arms, climbed over the hill. Ephraim snuck into his brother's barn and left the wheat. "There!" said Ephraim. "Now Menasha can sell this extra wheat, and have money to set aside for when he is old."

That very same night, at half past midnight, Menasha went into his barn. He gathered together a huge bale of wheat, and clutching the wheat in his arms, climbed over the hill. Menasha snuck into his brother's barn, and left the wheat. "There!" said Menasha. "Now Ephraim will have plenty of food to feed his family."

In the morning, each brother had exactly the same amount of wheat as he'd had the day before. The brothers were puzzled, but could not figure out why. That night, the same thing happened. Ephraim set out with a bundle of wheat to put into Menasha's barn at midnight, and Menasha brought a bundle of wheat to Ephraim's barn at half past midnight. In the morning, they each had the same amount of wheat in their barns.

The brothers brought each other wheat for several days.

Finally, one night, Ephraim and Menasha both set out for the other's barn, each with a bundle of wheat in his hands, at the same time. The brothers reached the top of the hill and saw each other. As soon as they saw the bundles of wheat in each other's arms, they immediately understood why the amount of wheat in their barns had always been the same. The brothers dropped their bundles and ran to each other. They gave each other a long hug, each one thankful to have such a special, caring brother.

God looked down on the two brothers hugging, and was moved by how much the two brothers cared for each other. God went to King Solomon and said, "This spot, where these two brothers met and showed each other such love and caring, is where I want you to build my Holy Temple." And that is exactly what King Solomon did.

Questions and Suggestions:

➤ Why did God choose this spot for the Temple in Jerusalem?

➤ How can we show our brothers or sisters how much we care for them?

➤ Invite children to act out this story, or retell it with puppets or on the felt board.

Resources

Practically every Jewish children's book is about a family. Here are some Jewish books about special family situations:

Grode, Phylis and Shelly O. Haas. *Sophie's Name*. Rockville, MD: Kar Ben Copies, 1990.

> *Sophie Davida Finkle-Cohen is unhappy with her name. It has too many letters for a short person, she concludes, and convinces her family to call her Sue. But as "Sue" begins to learn about each of her namesakes, the name begins to fit just right.*

Karkowsky, Nancy. *Grandma's Soup*. Rockville, MD: Kar Ben Copies, 1989.

> *Grandma's soup is the highlight of the family's Sabbath dinner, until one week the soup doesn't taste so good. "Who would put cloves in chicken soup?" Grandma exclaims. A sensitive portrayal of a young girl confronting her grandmother's senility.*

Kol B'Seder. *Songs for Growin'*. New York: Transcontinental Music Publications, 2001.

> *This compact disc includes the song, "With My Family." Available from A.R.E. Publishing, Inc., (800) 346-7779 or www.arepublish.com.*

Machon L'Morim: Bereshit Curriculum Guides. Baltimore, MD: Center for Jewish Education, 1998.

> *A professional development program designed to facilitate the integration of Jewish concepts and values into everyday secular themes. Available from the Center for Jewish Education, 5708 Park Heights Avenue, Baltimore, MD 21215, (410) 578-6943 or http://www.machonlmorim.org.*

Silverman, Judy. *Rosie & the Mole: The Story of a Bris*. New York: Pitspopany Press, 1999.

> *Rosie is jealous of all the fuss everyone is making over her new baby brother. He is getting a naming ceremony and a bris — while all she received as a baby was a naming ceremony.*

Waldman, Neil. *The Two Brothers: A Legend of Jerusalem*. New York: Atheneum Books for Young Readers, 1997.

> *A quiet tale of sibling love that accounts for the origins of the Temple in Jerusalem.*

Wilkowski, Susan. *Baby's Bris*. Rockville, MD: Kar-Ben Copies, 1999.

> *The day Sophie becomes a big sister is the day she first learns about "happy tears." It is also the first time she hears the word "bris," the upcoming ceremony for her new brother.*

Zalben, Jane Breskin. *Beni's First Wedding.* New York: Henry Holt & Company, Inc., 1998.

Uncle Izzy's marriage plans are announced; Beni is invited to be the page boy and Sara is asked to be the flower girl in the wedding. There are many other stories by Zalben about Beni's family as well.

30. What's Jewish about Friends?

Nothing in this world makes us as strong as knowing we've got a friend or two we can truly count on. A child's first early childhood experience is largely focused on making those first tenuous friendships, and on learning how to be a friend. So what's Jewish about friends?

The Big Idea

There is nothing more wonderful than watching friendship bloom between young children. Even the delight that pre-twos sometimes take in greeting a familiar friend can sweep us away. Moments of true friendship are *kadosh* (holy); they are moments when we become aware that God is present in our classrooms. In Sandy Eisenberg Sasso's storybook, *God In Between*, the characters discover that "God is wherever we are. God is in the between. In between us." God is found in significant relationships between people. When we think about friends, and the unique relationship of friendship, we are made aware of the presence of God, and of *Kedushah* (holiness).

Jewish Values

Sometimes, the activities we are involved in with children are Jewish moments, even if it's not readily apparent. Jewish values lead to Jewish behaviors. Building and sustaining friendships are endeavors that are full of Jewish values, including:

B'tzelem Elohim	Created in the Image of God	בְּצֶלֶם אֱלֹהִים
Chesed	Kindness	חֶסֶד
Dibuk Chaverim	Cleaving to Friends	דִּבּוּק חַבֵרִים
Kedushah	Holiness	קְדֻשָׁה
Kehillah	Community	קְהִלָּה

As friendships develop in your classroom, children are literally embodying Jewish values. Children's explorations are richest when the children are partners in their own learning. To engage children in these Jewish values and to deepen their learning, take time to investigate what children already know about friends. Observe children's play and analyze their comments. Seek out the children's questions and interests. Based on the children's questions, you might:

➤ Hand each child in a small group of 3-5 children a piece of fruit (the same kind of fruit to each child. You can also use rocks, leaves or any collection of natural items.). Ask the children if they all have the same thing (they should agree that they do). Tell the children to examine their piece of fruit and get to know it very well, to become friends with it — they should examine it from all sides with their eyes, fingers, and noses. After a few minutes, collect all the fruit in a basket. Then ask the children, one by one, to find *their* piece of fruit. If the children have done a good job with the first part of the activity, they should each be able to find their own fruit, because truly, each piece is unique. Like the fruit, we are all made in the image of God, which means that although we may seem similar, we each have differences that make us special and unique. *(B'tzelem Elohim)*

➤ Help the children make fingerprints. Provide magnifying glasses so children can examine prints closely. Make two sets of each print, and see if the children can match them up. We all have fingers, but even our fingers are not exactly like anyone else's. The differences make us special and unique. (Adapted from *Roots & Wings: Affirming Culture in Early Childhood Programs* by Stacey York.) *(B'tzelem Elohim)*

➤ Look for acts of *chesed* (kindness) in the classroom. Create a *chesed* award (a bookmark, sticker, button, or poster) that children can give to classmates who perform acts of kindness. *(Chesed)*

➤ Many friends together create a *kehillah* (community). Give your children many opportunities to work collectively toward a common goal. Commend them on their strong friendships and their warm, inclusive community. *(Kehillah)*

➤ *Dibuk Chaverim* (Cleaving to Friends) isn't just making or having friends. This is the value of how we treat our friendships, and signifies a deep respect and caring for this significant relationship. Discuss with the children what friends do for each other. Do they share? invite friends to join in play? stand up for each other? write each other letters? Role play with your children ways they can respect and care for their relationships with friends. *(Dibuk Chaverim)*

➤ If a new child will be entering the class, brainstorm with the class about how they might make a new person feel welcome. What would it feel like to be new in a school? new in town? How might the children make friends with the new person? What if the new child was in a wheelchair? Would she be able to get into the classroom? into the school building? What would she be able to do on the playground? How would the children help this new classmate get around and play? *(Chesed, Kehillah)*

Israel Connection

Older preschool children can connect to friends in Israel through pen pal relationships. Contact your local Jewish Federation to help you connect with early childhood programs (*ganim*) in your sister city in Israel, or take advantage of any personal Israeli contacts you might have. You can send your pen pals photos of your class, pictures your children have drawn, or letters your class writes together. Be sure to ask some questions about life in Israel, so your children can have a dialog. Be realistic in your expectations. Sometimes there can be great delays between sending a package to your Israeli pen pals and receiving a response. When you receive something from your pen pals, be sure to answer as quickly as you can!

מקסין הנדלמן
1328 רחוב אדי
צקגו אלינוי 60657

Hebrew Vocabulary

Here are some Hebrew words and phrases you can use as you build friendships:

Friend (m/f)	*Cha-ver/Cha-ve-ra*	חָבֵר/חֲבֵרָה
Friends	*Cha-ve-rim*	חֲבֵרִים
Friendship	*Y'di-dut*	יְדִידוּת
Will you (m/f) be my friend? (m/f)	*A-tah ro-tzeh/At ro-tzah l'hi-yot cha-ver/cha-ve-ra she-li?*	אַתָּה רוֹצֶה/אַתְּ רוֹצָה לִהְיוֹת חָבֵר/חֲבֵרָה שֶׁלִי?
Do you want to play (m)?	*A-tah ro-tzeh l'sa-cheik?*	אַתָּה רוֹצֶה לְשַׂחֵק?
Do you want to play (f)?	*At ro-tzah l'sa-cheik?*	אַתְּ רוֹצָה לְשַׂחֵק?

Songs and Poems

There are many simple Hebrew songs and Israeli dances to sing about and with friends.

Hinei Mah Tov
Traditional folk tune. Several versions can be found in The Complete Shireinu: 350 Fully Notated Jewish Songs, *edited by Joel Eglash.*

Hinei mah tov u'manayim
Shevet achim gam yachad

How good and nice it is to sit and be all together.

Simi Yadeich

Traditional folk tune. Available on 100 Shirim Rishonim (100 First Songs) *by Daniela Gardosh and Talma Alyagon, and in* The Complete Shireinu: 350 Fully Notated Jewish Songs, *edited by Joel Eglash.*

Simi Yadeich b'yadi
Ani shelach v'at sheli. } 2x

Pair children up. During the first two lines, partners should take each other's hands and swing arms back and forth.

Hei hei, Gali-ya
Bat harim y'fei-fi-ah } 2x

During the last two lines, partners can go around in a circle together.

Put your hand in my hand
I am yours and you are mine.
Hey, hey, Galiyah, daughter of the hills,
You are beautiful.

Shalom Chaverim

Traditional folk tune. Available in The Complete Shireinu: 350 Fully Notated Jewish Songs, *edited by Joel Eglash.*

Shalom chaverim, shalom chaverim,
Shalom, shalom.
L'hitraot, L'hitraot,
Shalom, shalom.

Goodbye my friends, goodbye my friends,
Goodbye, goodbye.
Until we meet again, Until we meet again,
Goodbye, goodbye.

Blessings

The blessing of recognizing a true friend, or making a new friend, can inspire a *bracha sheh b'lev* **(a prayer of the heart) such as:**

Thank you, God, for helping me to find such a good friend!

It is traditional to recite the *Shehecheyanu* **when one sees a friend one hasn't seen for thirty days or more:**

בָּרוּךְ אַתָּה יְיָ אֱלֹהֵינוּ מֶלֶךְ הָעוֹלָם שֶׁהֶחֱיָנוּ וְקִיְּמָנוּ וְהִגִּיעָנוּ לַזְּמַן הַזֶּה.

*Ba-**ruch** A-**tah** A-do-**nai** E-lo-**hei**-nu Me-lech Ha-O-**lam** She-he-che-**ya**-nu V'ki'**ma**-nu V'hi-gi-**ya**-nu La-**z'man** Ha-**zeh**.*

We praise You, our God, Creator of the universe, for giving us life, sustaining us, and helping us to reach this moment.

Story: Friends in the Woods

Though brief, this Hasidic tale by an unknown author holds important lessons for us. A version of this story can be found in Touching Heaven Touching Earth — Hassidic Humor & Wit, *compiled by Rabbi Shmuel Avidor Hacohen.*

Once there was a man who was lost in the woods. He walked and wandered, but could not find the way out of the woods. One day, he came upon another man walking in the woods. Excitedly, the first man said, "I am lost! Perhaps you can help me find my way out of the woods." The second man shook his head and said, "I am lost also. But perhaps we can walk together and help each other. The way you have come from is not the way out of the woods, and the way I have come from is not the way out of the woods." So the two men walked on together in a new direction, and by the time they found their way out of the woods, they had become great friends.

Questions and suggestions:

➤ Why did the two men become friends?

➤ What might have happened if the two men had not found each other?

➤ Act out this story, and add more detail about how the two people became friends (or maybe even why they became lost in the first place).

Resources

Books and Music

Eglash, Joel, ed. *The Complete Shireinu: 350 Fully Notated Jewish Songs.* New York: Transcontinental Music Publications, 2001.

> *This comprehensive single-volume collection of Jewish songs features the best of Israeli, Jewish summer camp, traditional, contemporary, and Sephardic genres in fully notated form. Includes "Hinei Mah Tov," "Simi Yadeich," and "Shalom Chaverim."*

Ganz, Yaffa. *The Story of Mimmy and Simmy*. New York: Feldheim Publishers, 1985.
Two little girls, one rich and one poor, envy one another. After they change places, they find that they are no happier than before. This is an appealing exploration of the question asked in Pirke Avot 4:1 — "Who is rich? One who is satisfied and happy with whatever he has."

Gardosh, Daniela and Talma Alyagon. *100 Shirim Rishonim (100 First Songs)*. Tel Aviv, Israel: Kineret Publishing House, 1970.
Compact disc and songbook of classic Israeli children's songs, available at http://www.israeliscent.com. Includes a version of "Simi Yadeich."

Gellman, Ellie. *Tamar's Sukkah*. Rockville, MD: Kar-Ben Copies, 1999.
A little girl decorating her sukkah with help from friends. "Something seems to be missing" until Tamar realizes that "a sukkah full of friends is exactly what a sukkah should be."

Hacohen, Shmuel Avidor, comp. *Touching Heaven Touching Earth — Hassidic Humor & Wit*. Tel Aviv, Israel: Sadan Publishing, 1976.
A collection of Hassidic tales. Out of print, may be found online or in libraries.

Levine, Arthur. *Pearl Moskowitz's Last Stand*. New York: Tambourine Books, 1993.
A wonderful story about an elderly woman who decides she will save the last tree on her street from being cut down. She and a group of ethnically diverse friends use their wiles to divert an earnest young bureaucrat from his efforts at urban renewal.

Polacco, Patricia. *Mrs. Katz and Tush*. New York: Yearling Books, 1994.
Larnel Moore, a young African-American boy, and Mrs. Katz, an elderly Jewish woman, develop an unusual friendship through their mutual concern for an abandoned cat named Tush.

York, Stacey. *Roots & Wings: Affirming Culture in Early Childhood Programs*. St. Paul, MN: Redleaf Press, 1991.
This classic volume was published over a decade ago as the first practical guide for early childhood teachers on the new topic of multicultural education. It is an ideal resource for early childhood teachers, program directors, pre-service and in-service teacher trainers, and parents interested in anti-bias and multicultural education.

31. What's Jewish about Homes?

We all live in some sort of dwelling: a house, an apartment or condominium, a mobile home or trailer, a teepee or a tent. We depend on our dwelling place to keep us warm and safe. A house, when filled with certain people, objects, and events, becomes a home. So what's Jewish about homes?

The Big Idea

Anywhere people live constitutes a home, whether it be an actual house, an apartment, a tent, a trailer, or even a yurt (a round, nominally portable, self-supporting structure created from a wood frame and canvas walls and roof). The building of a house or apartment building requires forethought and partnership between people and God. Certain things and events make a home a Jewish home. A *mezzuzah*, Jewish artwork, Jewish books, Shabbat, holiday and lifecycle celebrations all transform a space into a Jewish space. The rabbis tell us that our home is a *Mik-dash M'at,* a mini-sanctuary. We can make our home a holy place. The words of the *Sh'ma*, found in the *mezzuzah* that marks a Jewish doorpost, remind us to keep God's commandments when we are sitting in our house and when we go on our way. Our behaviors in our home should reflect the holiness of the space, and we should remember to take this holiness with us even when we leave our home. When we talk about homes with children, we can explore how to create a Jewish space and what it means for us to live in a space that is filled with *Kedushah* (holiness).

Jewish Values

Sometimes, the activities we are involved in with children are Jewish moments, even if it's not readily apparent. Jewish values lead to Jewish behaviors. Homes are filled with Jewish values, including:

Brit	Partnership with God	בְּרִית
Hachnasat Orchim	Hospitality	הַכְנָסַת אוֹרְחִים
Hiddur Mitzvah	Beautifying a Mitzvah	הִדּוּר מִצְוָה
Hoda'ah	Appreciation	הוֹדָאָה
Kedushah	Holiness	קְדֻשָּׁה
Mik-dash M'at	Home as a Mini-sanctuary	מִקְדַּשׁ מְעַט
Sh'lom Bayit	Peace Within the Home	שְׁלוֹם בַּיִת
Tzedakah	Justice and Righteousness	צְדָקָה

When children learn about homes, they are literally embodying Jewish values. Children's explorations are richest when the children are partners in their own learning. To engage children in these Jewish values and to deepen their learning, take time to investigate what children already know about homes. Observe children's play and analyze their comments. Seek out the children's questions and interests. Based on the children's questions, you might:

➤ Invite your children to become Jewish Home Detectives. Encourage them to explore with their families what makes their home a Jewish home, and bring in some of the "evidence." (For non-Jewish children in your class, invite them to explore what makes their house or apartment a home.) Then together, search your school to discover what makes the building a home-away-from home. Read *Jewish Home Detectives* by Deborah Syme, and *Mrs. Moskowitz and the Sabbath Candlesticks* by Amy Schwartz. *(Mik-dash M'at)*

➤ A *sukkah* is a temporary Jewish home. During Sukkot, visit as many *sukkot* as you can, especially those belonging to children in your class. *(Hachnasat Orchim)*

➤ To build a house requires a partnership between people and God, and well as requiring the contributions of many different people: the architect, the electrician, the plumber, the decorator, and so on. As you explore the different roles of all these people, also discuss how God helps people build a house (God gives us strength, wisdom, wood, the ability to communicate with each other, and so on). *(Brit)*

➤ Some people are not lucky enough to have any kind of home to live in. Many children live in homeless shelters, cars, or on the street. If you have a local homeless shelter, call them to find out what items they can use the most (toiletries, toys, food) and start a collection. Talk with children about how they could make a home if they didn't have a house to live in. Also talk with children about being thankful they do have a home to live in, and the ways they can show that appreciation. *(Tzedakah, Hoda'ah)*

➤ Habitat for Humanity uses volunteers to build houses for people who can't afford to buy their own house. Check them out at http://www.habitat.org to learn more and explore how you and your children might get involved. *(Tzedakah)*

➤ A synagogue is a holy place that is sometimes called a *Beit Knesset* (House of Gathering), a *Beit Tefilah* (House of Worship), and a *Beit Sefer* (House of Study). Discuss with your children what makes a synagogue all these different kinds of houses, and why all of these are holy places. *(Kedushah)*

➤ A *mezzuzah* is the sign of a Jewish home. Study the *Sh'ma* (the text inside the *mezzuzah*) and explore with children how their behavior inside and outside of a space with a *mezzuzah* can reflect more holiness. Make sure you have a *mezzuzah* on your classroom door. If you don't have one, make one! *(Kedushah, Mikdash M'at, Sh'lom Bayit)*

➤ When a member of the class moves into a new home, create a *mezzuzah* for their new home as a gift from the class. Remember to make the *mezzuzah* as beautiful as you can. *(Hiddur Mitzvah, Mikdash M'at)*

Israel Connection

The majority of Israelis live in apartments, rather than in single family houses. All over Israel, you will find apartment complexes built so that there is a courtyard, a common area where all the residents can gather together. Archeologists have found that from the earliest times, people in the Middle East built their homes clustered around courtyards. These buildings are built this way on purpose, to extend the sense of community from a single family to a neighborhood of many families. The courtyard is a wonderful place for communal meals, a place for children to play, and a place for people to sit and chat during the day and at night.

Imagine this kind of community in your classroom. Invite children to create their family homes from boxes and other recycled materials. Place the homes around a courtyard, and dream together about what it would be like for the entire class to live in that kind of community. Be sure there are materials available for children to create *mezzuzot* for the homes they create.

Hebrew Vocabulary

House	*Ba-yit*	בַּיִת
Apartment	*Di-rah*	דִּירָה
Tent	*O-hel*	אֹהֶל
Wood	*Eitz*	עֵץ
Stone	*E-ven*	אֶבֶן
Brick	*L'vei-nah*	לְבֵנָה
Blocks	*Ku-bi-yot*	קֻבִּיּוֹת
I live in a house. (m/f)	*A-ni gar/gar-ah ba-ba-yit.*	אֲנִי גָּר/גָּרָה בְּבַיִת.
We're building a house!	*A-nach-nu bo-nim ba-yit!*	אֲנַחְנוּ בּוֹנִים בַּיִת!

Songs and Poems

Lo Alecha

*Music by Jeff Klepper and Daniel Freelander, text from Pirke Avot 2:21. From the
compact disc* In Every Generation *by Kol B'Seder, and in* The Complete Jewish
Songbook for Children: Manginot, *edited by Stephen Richards. Used with permission.*

Lo a-le-cha ham-la-cha lig-mor
Lo a-le-cha lig-mor (2x)
V'lo atah ben-chor-rin l'hi-ba-teil mi-me-nah
V'lo atah ben chorin (2x)

It is not your duty to complete the work,
But neither are you free to desist from it.

The Mezzuzah Song

*Words by Jeff Klepper and Susan Nanus, music by Jeff Klepper. From the compact
disc* Songs for Growin' *by Kol B'Seder. Used with permission.*

Some parchment in a little case
Found in every Jewish place
A mezzuzah, mezzuzah
We put one up, now all can see
Here lives a Jewish family
A mezzuzah, mezzuzah
It says teach our children,
Remind ourselves well
That the lesson of our people is Sh'ma Yisrael

So if it was not done before,
Put one up on your front door
A mezzuzah, mezzuzah
And when you're finished, say a prayer
To say you're glad to have one there
A mezzuzah, mezzuzah

Blessings

When we hang a mezzuzah, this is the blessing we say:

בָּרוּךְ אַתָּה יְיָ אֱלֹהֵינוּ מֶלֶךְ הָעוֹלָם אֲשֶׁר קִדְּשָׁנוּ בְּמִצְוֹתָיו וְצִוָּנוּ
לִקְבּוֹעַ מְזוּזָה.

*Ba-ruch A-tah A-do-nai E-lo-hei-nu Me-lech Ha'O-lam A-sher Kid'sha-nu
B'mitz-vo-tav V'tzi-va-nu Lik-bo-a Me-zu-zah.*
We praise You, our God, Creator of the universe, Who commands us to affix a
Mezzuzah.

Being blessed with a home can inspire a *bracha sheh b'lev* (a prayer of the heart)
such as:

Thank you, God, for giving me a home and a family with which to share it!

Story: Melissa's New Home

By Maxine Handelman

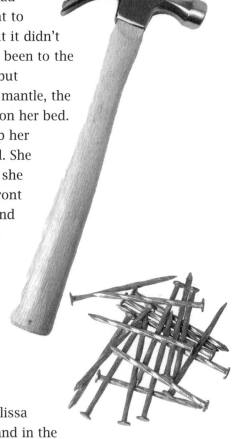

Melissa looked around her new apartment. Most of her boxes had
been unpacked, but it felt like something was missing. Melissa went to
her bookshelf and rearranged the books until they were just so. But it didn't
help. She went to the kitchen and looked in the fridge. Melissa had been to the
grocery store earlier, and all her favorite foods were in the fridge, but
something was still missing. Her Shabbat candlesticks were on the mantle, the
picture of her family was on the table, her dog Kelev was sleeping on her bed.

Suddenly a thought occurred to Melissa: she hadn't yet hung up her
mezzuzah! Melissa looked at the boxes still waiting to be unpacked. She
opened one after another, rummaging until she finally found what she
was looking for: the *mezzuzah* she had bought especially for the front
door. Melissa moved around some more things in the box, and found
two nails, just the right size for the *mezzuzah*. Now all she needed
was a hammer. She searched in the box, but there was no hammer.
Melissa looked through the open boxes — no hammer. She opened
the rest of the boxes, still no hammer! "What am I going to do?"
Melissa cried.

Just then she heard a knock at the door. *Mezzuzah* and nails
in hand, Melissa went to open the door. "Hello," she said, to the
unfamiliar woman holding a pan in her hand.

"Hi, I'm Debbie, your neighbor. I brought you a lasagna."

"Wow, that's so nice," said Melissa. "Please come in." Before Melissa
could close the door again, she heard, "Welcome to the building!" and in the

hallway was a man holding a jug of orange juice. "Thank you! Come on in," said Melissa. Just then the elevator door opened, and out stepped Melissa's Aunt Susan and Uncle Dan and their three children. "We brought you bread, salt, and a broom." "I'm so glad to see you!" said Melissa. She welcomed them all inside, and said, "Now this is starting to feel like a home. All I'm missing is . . . " Just then, the elevator door opened again, and out stepped Melissa's sister, Judy. "Hey, sis. How's the new place coming? I brought your hammer that I borrowed before you moved." "Excellent!" laughed Melissa. Now I have everything I need to make my house a home."

"Hey everyone! Come help me hang my *mezzuzah*!" Melissa's family and new neighbors gathered in her front doorway. Melissa banged in the nails and said the blessing as she hung her *mezzuzah*. "*Mazal tov!*" called everyone. "Let's eat!" said Melissa, and they all went inside Melissa's new home.

Questions and Suggestions:

➤ Why was hanging the mezuzah so important to Melissa?

➤ What would you bring to a new neighbor to make them feel welcome?

➤ Act out this story with your children. Let the children decide what they will bring to the new neighbor. They can be silly or serious.

➤ Play "Neighbor, Neighbor, where's my hammer?" (Doggie, Doggie, Where's my Bone?)

Resources

Chapman, Carol. *The Tale of Meshka the Kvetch.* New York: Unicorn Paperbacks, 1989.
   A delightful tale of how Meshka learns to appreciate what she has, including her house and her children.

Goldstein, Andrew. *My Jewish Home.* Minneapolis, MN: Kar-Ben Publishing, 2001.
   This board book follows a toddler through each room of his house as he searches for ritual objects that make it a Jewish home.

Handelman, Maxine Segal. *Jewish Every Day: The Complete Handbook for Early Childhood Teachers.* Denver, CO: A.R.E. Publishing, 2000.
   Includes a chapter of a complete mezzuzah curriculum.

Kol B'Seder. *In Every Generation.* Evanston, Il: Kol B'Seder, 1993.
   Compact disc includes the song "Lo Alecha." Available from A.R.E. Publishing, Inc., (800) 346-7779 or www.arepublish.com.

————. *Songs for Growin'*. New York: Transcontinental Music Publications, 2001. *Compact disc includes "The Mezzuzah Song." Available from A.R.E. Publishing, Inc., (800) 346-7779 or www.arepublish.com.*

Lemelman, Martin. *My Jewish Home*. New York: UAHC Press, 1998. *This board book includes captioned pictures depicting representative objects or concepts linked with the Jewish home, such as the mezzuzah, Shabbat candles, and Passover.*

Lepon, Shoshana. *Hillel Builds A House*. Minneapolis, MN: Kar-Ben Publishing, 1993. *Hillel loves to build houses. However, the dwelling he creates for each holiday is inappropriate somehow. At last Sukkot arrives!*

Richards, Stephen, ed. *The Complete Jewish Songbook for Children: Manginot*. New York: Transcontinental Music Publications, 2002. *Songbook features 201 Jewish songs for holidays, everyday, or just for fun. Includes "Lo Alecha."*

Schwartz, Amy. *Mrs. Moskowitz and the Sabbath Candlesticks*. Philadelphia, PA: Jewish Publication Society, 1991. *An older woman moves from her home to a small apartment. She is sad about leaving her home. As she unpacks she finds her Sabbath candlesticks. The candlesticks motivate her to make her new apartment feel like her home.*

Syme, Deborah Shayne. *Jewish Home Detectives*. New York: UAHC Press, 1998. *Two children search their house for what makes it a Jewish home (out of print but worth looking for).*

32. What's Jewish about Senses?

Some material adapted from the Machon L'Morim: Bereshit curriculum

Sight, smell, taste, touch and hearing — we depend on our five senses to let us know everything about our world. Our senses help us get through every minute of every day — they let us know when it's safe to cross the street, what to wear when we go outside, when the coffee is ready. The luckiest of us have full use of all of our senses. If we lose even one of our senses, our entire approach to life changes. But what's Jewish about the senses?

The Big Idea

Jewish life is designed to entice all of our senses. Something as simple as frying *latkes* involves each one of our senses: we hear them sizzling in the pan, we smell them from a block away, we see when they are just brown enough to flip over, we touch them to make sure they are not too hot, and then, the best part, we taste the delicious potato pancakes! When we stood as the Jewish People at Mt. Sinai, we saw the lightning, smelled the smoke, tasted fear and wonder, felt the pressing of our brothers and sisters all around us, and heard the booming of God's voice giving us the Ten Commandments. As early childhood educators we have long understood the importance of highlighting sensory experiences for children — hence the sensory table which we fill with sand, snow, rice, cotton balls, and a myriad of other things to stimulate our children's senses. Each of our sensory systems is "hot wired" to our brains, to provide us the necessary information for navigating our world. Every sensory experience increases our ability to appreciate the wonder of the world and God's creations all around us.

Jewish Values

Sometimes, the activities we are involved in with children are Jewish moments, even if it's not readily apparent. Jewish values lead to Jewish behaviors. Senses are filled with Jewish values, including:

Hoda'ah	Appreciation	הוֹדָאָה
Shmiat HaOzen	Attentiveness	שְׁמִיעַת הָאֹזֶן
V'achalta V'savata	To Eat and Be Satisfied	וְאָכַלְתָּ וְשָׂבָעְתָּ
V'samachta B'chagecha	Rejoicing in Our Festivals	וְשָׂמַחְתָּ בְּחַגֶּיךָ

When children explore their senses, they are literally embodying Jewish values. Children's explorations are richest when the children are partners in their own learning. To engage children in these Jewish values and to deepen their learning, take time to investigate what children already know about senses. Observe children's play and analyze their comments. Seek out the children's questions and interests. Based on the children's questions, you might:

➤ Take a nature walk around the school, taking time to appreciate all of God's creations. On the walk, highlight which senses are being used. Alternatively, you can go on a "smelling walk" or a "touching walk" and focus on appreciating God's world through one sense at a time. *(Hoda'ah, Shmiat HaOzen)*

➤ Have a tasting party, saying the appropriate blessings before tasting each food. Discuss with children why each food may have a different blessing. *(V'achalta V'savata)*

➤ Use a tape recorder to play various sounds for children to identify. Be sure to include sounds such as a shofar blowing, a grogger, familiar Hebrew music, and so on. *(Shmiat HaOzen, V'samachta B'chagecha)*

➤ During both holiday and non-holiday related cooking experiences with children, highlight the senses involved in the experience. Recite any relevant *brachot*, and be sure to connect the *bracha* to the immediate sensory experience. *(V'achalta V'savata, V'samachta B'chagecha)*

➤ Provide activities for matching scents with objects (i.e., the scent of an *etrog* with an *etrog*, spices with a spice box for Havdalah). *(V'samachta B'chagecha, Hoda'ah)*

➤ Create spice boxes with different combination of scents. Make groggers with different kinds of sounds. *(V'samachta B'chagecha, Hoda'ah)*

➤ Make a "feelie" bag or box with items for children to reach in and identify by touch. Be sure to include items such as candlesticks, a *kiddush* cup, a piece of matzah, and so on. *(V'samachta B'chagecha, Hoda'ah)*

➤ Read *A Sense of Shabbat* by Faige Kobre, and create your own classroom book of sensory experiences of other holidays or of daily Jewish activities. *(V'samachta B'chagecha, Hoda'ah)*

Israel Connection

Israel is bursting with sensory experiences. A trip to the *Kotel* (Western Wall) astounds one with the magnitude and history of the place, the diversity of the visitors, the symphony of voices joined together in prayer, celebration, and tears, and the cold, smooth feel of stones touched by a thousand-thousand fingertips. An afternoon at the *shuk* (outdoor market) yields the cry of vendors ringing in your ears, colorful Israeli spices to see and smell, dried fruit to taste, fresh fish splashing in water, and, by the end of the trip, heavy bags to carry home.

➤ In your classroom, have an Israeli tasting party with foods from Israel, such as Jaffa oranges, dates, figs, and chocolate spread.

- ► You can also have an Israeli smelling party with spices from Israel, such as *za'atar* (hyssop), paprika, cumin, hawije, turmeric, saffron, or sea salt. If you don't have a local source for such foods and spices, go to http://www.israeliproducts.com and click on "spices and seasonings" (under food and wine).
- ► Read *Sammy Spider's First Trip to Israel* by Sylvia Rouss, which explores Israel through the senses.
- ► All Jewish Learning has a Kotel Poster Set, as well as a Good Foods Poster set, with fruits and veggies found in the *shuk*. These posters can help stimulate Israeli sensory discussions.

Hebrew Vocabulary

Here are some Hebrew words and phrases you can use as you explore the senses:

Hand/hands	*Yad/Ya-da-yim*	יָד/יָדַיִם
Mouth	*Peh*	פֶּה
Eye/eyes	*Ayin/Ei-na-yim*	עַיִן/עֵינַיִם
Finger/fingers (also toe/toes)	*Etz-ba/Etz-ba-ot*	אֶצְבַּע/אֶצְבָּעוֹת
Ear/ears	*O-zen/Oz-na-yim*	אֹזֶן/אָזְנַיִם
Nose	*Af*	אַף
Tongue	*La-shon*	לָשׁוֹן
Hot	*Cham*	חַם
Cold	*Kar*	קַר
Bitter	*Mar*	מַר
Sweet	*Ma-tok*	מָתוֹק
Very tasty!	*Ta-im m'od!*	טָעִים מְאֹד!
I can hear. (m/f)	*Ani ya-chol/y'cho-la lish-mo'ah.*	אֲנִי יָכוֹל/יְכוֹלָה לִשְׁמֹעַ.
I can touch. (m/f)	*Ani ya-chol/y'cho-la la-ga-at.*	אֲנִי יָכוֹל/יְכוֹלָה לָגַעַת.
I can taste. (m/f)	*Ani ya-chol/ya-cho-la lit-om.*	אֲנִי יָכוֹל/יְכוֹלָה לִטְעוֹם.
I can smell. (m/f)	*Ani ya-chol/y'cho-la li-ha-ri-ach.*	אֲנִי יָכוֹל/יְכוֹלָה לְהָרִיחַ.
I can see. (m/f)	*Ani ya-chol/y'cho-la lir-ot.*	אֲנִי יָכוֹל/יְכוֹלָה לִרְאוֹת.

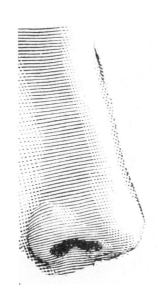

Songs and Poems

Smell a Violet

By Maxine Handelman. A song for reinforcing the parts of the body in Hebrew, adapted from the Machon L'Morim: Bereshit curriculum. Sung to the tune of the first two lines of "Twinkle, Twinkle Little Star."

To hear me tell you of my dream,
You must listen with your *oznayim*.
If you want to play on the team,
Throw the ball with your *yadayim*.
To see the cone stacked with ice cream,
You must open up your *einayim*.
To smell a violet do not cough,
You sniff the fragrance through your *af*.
When you have something to say,
You can speak it with your *peh*.

Af, Peh, Ozen

Words and music by Jeff Klepper. From Songs for Growin' *by Kol B'Seder. Used with permission.*

Af peh o-zen, a-yin, re-gel
Af peh o-zen, yad, v'rosh
Every part of my body has a Hebrew name
Let's learn a few together with
A Hebrew singing game

Shtei oz-na-yim shtei ei-na-yim,
Shtei ya-da-yim, etz-ba-ot
Shtei oz-na-yim shtei ei-na-yim,
Shtei rag-la-yim, etz-ba-ot

Nose, mouth, ear, eye, leg/foot
Nose, mouth, ear, hand and head
Two ears, two eyes, two hands, fingers,
Two ears, two eyes, two legs, toes.

Blessings

As you take a nature walk, or any time you or your children notice a wonderful thing among God's creations, you can say (from Psalms 104:24 and the morning liturgy):

מָה-רַבּוּ מַעֲשֶׂיךָ יְיָ.

Mah Ra-bu Ma'a-se-cha, A-do-nai!
How glorious are your creations, God!

We can show appreciation for the gift of sight with this blessing (also from the morning liturgy):

בָּרוּךְ אַתָּה יְיָ אֱלֹהֵינוּ מֶלֶךְ הָעוֹלָם פּוֹקֵחַ עִוְרִים.

Ba-ruch A-tah A-do-nai E-lo-hei-nu Me-lech Ha-O-lam Po-kei-ach Iv'rim.
We praise You, our God, Creator of the universe, Who helps the blind to see.

Here is a blessing for smelling flowers:

בָּרוּךְ אַתָּה יְיָ אֱלֹהֵינוּ מֶלֶךְ הָעוֹלָם בּוֹרֵא עִשְׂבוֹת בְּשָׂמִים.

Ba-ruch A-tah A-do-nai E-lo-hei-nu Me-lech Ha-O-lam Bo-rei Is-vot B'sa-mim.
We praise You, our God, Creator of the universe, Who creates scented flowers.

Story: Isaac and Jacob

In the first book of the Torah, we read the story of how Jacob is able to fool his father Isaac, due to Isaac's poor eyesight. Following is an adaptation of Genesis 27, by Maxine Handelman.

Isaac was old and his eyes were dim; he could no longer see very well at all. Isaac called his older son, Esau, to him and said, "It is time for me to give you my blessing. Please go out to fields, hunt something, and make me that stew of yours that I like so much. Bring it to me and I will give you a very special blessing." Esau went out to do as his father Isaac had told him.

Rebecca, Isaac's wife, had learned from God that Jacob was indeed the son destined to receive the blessing from Isaac. After Esau left, Rebecca called Jacob and said, "It is time for you to get the blessing instead of Esau. Go get two goats from the flock, and I will prepare your father's favorite stew so it will taste just the way Esau makes it. You can take the stew to your father, Isaac, and he will think you are Esau and he will give you the blessing."

Jacob said, "But Mother, even though Father cannot see very well, I do not think he will be so easily fooled. Esau is a hairy man and I have smooth skin. If Father touches me, he will know that I am not Esau."

Rebecca said, "Don't worry, I have thought of everything. Go and get the goats."

Jacob did as Rebecca asked, and Rebecca prepared stew for Isaac so it tasted just like Esau's stew. Then Rebecca took the skin of the goats and covered Jacob's arms and neck so if Isaac touched Jacob, he would feel like his brother, Esau. Then Rebecca dressed Jacob in Esau's best clothes, so if Isaac smelled Jacob, he would smell like his brother, Esau. Rebecca gave Jacob the stew, and sent him in to see Isaac.

Jacob said to Isaac, "Father."

Isaac said, "Yes, which of my sons are you?"

Jacob said, "I am Esau, and I have brought you your favorite stew, so you may give me your special blessing."

Isaac said, "How did you do this so quickly?"

Jacob said, "God helped me hunt and cook."

Isaac was confused. The person in front of him sounded like his son Jacob, but the stew smelled like that of his son Esau. Isaac said, "Come closer that I may feel you, my son — whether you are really my son Esau or not." Jacob stepped close to Isaac. Isaac touched Jacob's arm, and it felt like Esau. Isaac was still confused. He asked, "Are you really my son Esau?"

Jacob lied, "I am."

Isaac kissed Jacob and smelled his clothes, and he smelled like Esau. Isaac tasted the stew, and it tasted just like Esau's stew. Isaac thought to himself, "I can not be completely sure that this is my son Esau. His voice sounds like Jacob's, but he feels like Esau, and smells like Esau, and his stew tastes like Esau's, so I will give him my special blessing."

Isaac blessed Jacob with a very special blessing. Jacob thanked his father and left the room.

Questions and Suggestions:

➤ How was Jacob able to fool his father Isaac?

➤ Was it fair of Jacob to fool his father and steal his brother's blessing? How do you think Isaac and Esau felt when Esau — for real — came back to get his blessing?

➤ Blindfold one child and see if he or she can guess the identity of classmates by their voice or by feel.

Resources

Books and Music

Glazer, Devorah. *A Touch of the High Holidays: A Touch and Feel Book for Rosh Hashanah, Yom Kippur and Sukkot.* New York: Merkos L'inyonei Chinuch, 2002.
The High Holidays offer a wide variety of experiences and sensations: The bumpiness of an etrog, the soft velvet feel of a Torah scroll cover, the stickiness of honey dripping from an apple. This board book introduces the three-and-under crowd to the meaning of these special days through a series of textured holiday symbols.

Gold-Vukson, Marji. *The Sounds of My Jewish Year.* Minneapolis, MN: Kar-Ben Publishing, 2003.
Preschoolers can use this board book to explore the Jewish holidays with familiar sounds — the "sizzle, sizzle" of potato latkes on Chanukah; the "crunch, crunch" of matzah on Passover; and more.

Gold-Vukson, Marji. *The Colors of My Jewish Year.* Minneapolis, MN: Kar-Ben Publishing, 1998.
What is red? The Rosh Hashanah apple we dip in honey. That is red. Toddlers will enjoy this colorful introduction to the symbols of each of the Jewish holidays.

Grossman, Laurie. *Colors of Israel.* Minneapolis, MN: Carolrhoda Books, 2001.
What color is Israel? It is black like the mud from the Dead Sea, tan like the wild goats that roam the desert, and gold like the dome of the ancient mosque of Jerusalem.

Kobre, Faige. *A Sense of Shabbat.* Los Angeles, CA: Torah Aura Productions, 1990.
A Sense of Shabbat is a child's eye view of the Sabbath. In the sensuous photographs and simple text that make up this picture book, the taste, feel, sound, look, and touch of Shabbat come alive.

Kol B'Seder. *Songs for Growin'.* New York: Transcontinental Music Publications, 2001.
This wonderful CD includes twenty-eight songs for Jewish families about Jewish objects, prayer and blessings, and the joys of growing Jewishly. Compact disc and songbook. Available from A.R.E. Publishing, Inc., (800) 346-7779 or http://www.arepublish.com.

Machon L'Morim: Bereshit Curriculum Guides. Baltimore, MD: Center for Jewish Education, 1998.
A professional development program designed to facilitate the integration of Jewish concepts and values into everyday secular themes. Available from the

Center for Jewish Education, 5708 Park Heights Avenue, Baltimore, MD 21215, (410) 578-6943 or http://www.machonlmorim.org.

Marcus, Audrey Friedman and Raymond Zwerin. *Shabbat Can Be.* New York: UAHC Press, 1979.
   The pictures and examples give many concrete events that can help set Shabbat apart. Available from A.R.E. Publishing, Inc., (800) 346-7779 or http://www.arepublish.com.

Rosenfeld, Dina. *Five Alive.* New York: Hachai Publications, 2003.
   Young children describe the things that they see, hear, smell, taste, and touch during observances of Jewish holidays.

Rouss, Sylvia A. *Sammy Spider's First Trip to Israel: A Book About the Five Senses.* Minneapolis, MN: Kar-Ben Publishing, 2002.
   As a stowaway in a boy's model airplane, Sammy joins the family's sightseeing trip in Israel and uses his five senses to experience the country.

Materials and Supplies

All Jewish Learning — (425) 385-3779 or e-mail alljewishlearning@yahoo.com
   A wonderful resource of quality Judaic classroom materials, especially appropriate for early childhood, including a Kotel Poster Set and a Good Foods Poster set.

Part V: Popular Children's Books and Authors

33. What's Jewish about Denise Fleming?

Denise Fleming is an artist who illustrates and writes books for young children. Some of her first and most famous books are *In the Tall, Tall Grass*, *In the Small, Small Pond*, and *Barnyard Banter*. Denise Fleming writes in "terse verse" — short, crisp rhyme. She also strategically places her words right inside the pictures, which is an excellent early literacy strategy for learning to read. Her illustrations are created first from paper pulp and then color-copied into bold, bright pages that depict movement about nature. So, what is Jewish about books written and illustrated by Denise Fleming?

The Big Idea

Denise Fleming loves nature. She has a wonderful talent for using few words and simple, bright illustrations to show young children the beauty and movement that can be found in simple environments such as grass, a pond, or a barnyard. Although her books seem simple and clear, the variety and complexity of nature is not lost. Readers come away with a new understanding of what animals look like, how they live, and how they interact with a specific environment. So much of the universe and God's creations are thoughtfully brought into focus by Denise Fleming's words and illustrations. Because of this, when one reads or listens to a book created by Denise Fleming, one is offered a new opportunity to better know and understand the wondrous world created by God.

Jewish Values

Sometimes, the activities we are involved in with children are Jewish moments, even if it's not readily apparent. Jewish values lead to Jewish behaviors. Books written by Denise Fleming are filled with Jewish values, including:

Bal Tashchit	Do not Destroy	בַּל תַּשְׁחִית
Brit	Partnership with God	בְּרִית
Hoda'ah	Appreciation	הוֹדָאָה
Ma'aseh B'reishit	Miracle of Creation	מַעֲשֵׂה בְּרֵאשִׁית
Talmud Torah	Study/Love of Learning	תַּלְמוּד תּוֹרָה
Tikkun Olam	Repair of the World	תִּקּוּן עוֹלָם
Tza'ar Ba'alei Chayim	Kindness to Animals	צַעַר בַּעֲלֵי חַיִּים

When children explore stories written and illustrated by Denise Fleming, they are literally embodying Jewish values. Children's explorations are richest when the children are partners in their own learning. To engage children in these Jewish values and to deepen their learning, take time to investigate what the children know about Denise Fleming's books and illustrations. Observe children's play and analyze their comments. Seek out the children's questions and interests. Based on the children's questions, you might:

➤ Read several of Denise Fleming's books and, with the children, pick an environment to study. *(Hoda'ah, Talmud Torah, Brit)*

➤ Use Denise Fleming's books as a jumping off point for a big class project. For example, you might study ponds and actually build one in your classroom or playground. You can use paper or real water. Such decisions will depend on the children's desires and choices, and on the limitations of your own environment. Such a project will give the children a deeper understanding of a different ecosystem. *(Hoda'ah, Talmud Torah, Brit, Ma'aseh Bereishit)*

➤ Visit a real site — tall, tall grass, a barnyard, a pond. Before this visit have a discussion with the children about walking quietly and not disturbing living or nonliving things. In doing this, the children will be able to see so much more of nature. *(Brit, Hoda'ah, Tza'ar Ba'alei Chayim)*

➤ Use some of what you find outdoors to beautify your classroom. An example of this might be stones that no one could see, or beautiful grass or leaves that would have blown away. *(Bal Tashchit, Tikkun Olam, Hoda'ah, Brit)*

➤ Make something indoors that might beautify the outdoor environment you are studying. e.g., a windmill. *(Bal Tashchit, Tikkun Olam, Hoda'ah, Brit)*

➤ During winter, put out appropriate food for animals that might still be around and hungry. Do not throw trash into a pond. If you live near a dirty pond, help to clean it up. *(Bal Tashchit, Tza'ar Ba'alei Chayim, Tikkun Olam)*

Israel Connection

Denise Fleming lives in Ohio, a place of ponds and lakes, cold weather, lots of grass and fields, and home to many animals. Being a nature-loving author and illustrator, she writes about the animals and habitats that she sees and knows. If she lived in Israel, her stories would have to be quite different. She might write about warm, dry desserts, the very salty sea, or falafel for lunch. Pretend you live in Israel, and write a story using a style and form of illustration similar to Denise Fleming. You will first need to make yourself familiar with the animals and habitats in Israel. About two-thirds of Israel is desert. Use books (see the "Resources" section for some

suggestions), talk to people who have been to Israel, and visit
http://www.negev.org/About/negev_desert.htm and
http://www.schaik.com/track/israel/israel_index.html for information about and
pictures of the Negev Desert. After you have researched the Negev, create a Denise
Fleming-style classroom book about it.

Hebrew Vocabulary

Here are some Hebrew words and phrases you can use as you talk about Denise
Fleming's books and illustrations:

Grass	*De-sheh*	דֶּשֶׁא
Small pond	*B'rei-**cha** k'ta-**nah***	בְּרֵכָה קְטַנָּה
Author	*M'cha-**beir***	מְחַבֵּר
Book	*Sei-fer*	סֵפֶר
I like to read. (m/f)	*A-**ni** o-**heiv**/o-**hev**-et lik-**ro**.*	אֲנִי אוֹהֵב/אוֹהֶבֶת לִקְרֹא.
I like books. (m/f)	*A-**ni** o-**heiv**/o-**hev**-et se-far-**im**.*	אֲנִי אוֹהֵב/אוֹהֶבֶת סְפָרִים.
Please read me a story.	*B'va-ka-**sha**, tik-**ra** li si-**pur**.*	בְּבַקָּשָׁה תִּקְרָא לִי סִפּוּר.

Songs and Poems

Ode to Denise Fleming
By Deborah Schein

Thank you, Denise Fleming
For writing your books
Full of animals that twirl
And places with gook

Your paper-made pictures
Are so great to see
And the words that you write
Bring pleasure to me.

While I'm writing to you
I have one more thought
What should I do
with these bugs that I've caught?

I don't want to kill them.
That wouldn't be right
But I do want to see them
From day until night.

Let them go, said my mom,
It's more than a must!
God made them to live
In the trees and the dust.

So please tell me how
You learned all you did
From an animal-loving
And curious kid.

Blessings

There are no formal blessings that jointly acknowledge God's creations and the human ability to create story and art. But when we read books written and illustrated by Denise Fleming, we come away with a better understanding of the world created by God. This can inspire a *bracha sheh b'lev* (a prayer of the heart) such as:

Thank you, God, for giving us a world filled with different animals and habitats.

Story: In a Long, Long Year

By Deborah Schein, inspired by Denise Fleming. The Jewish Year follows the changes of nature, as one season follows another. Each season comes complete with Jewish holidays. This short story, written in the style of Denise Fleming, follows a Jewish year in season and action.

In a long, long year
What holidays appear?

Apples sweet
New Year greet.

Shofar call
Sorry, all.

Pound, pound
Sit right down.

March, lead
Torah read.

Hanukah lights
Fight for rights.

Seeds, trees
Birthdays, please!

Shake, shake
Groggers make.

Spring, clean
Freedom rings

Crunch, crunch
Matzah lunch.

Gift of Torah
Dance the Horah.

One Jewish Year ends
Tekiah again!

Questions and Suggestions:

➤ Invite children to figure out which holiday each stanza refers to.

➤ Encourage children to decorate this poem using the illustrative techniques of
Denise Fleming.

➤ Discuss other activities which might happen parallel to those activities described
in each stanza.

Resources

Books and Music

Fleming, Denise. *Barnyard Banter.* New York: Henry Holt and Company, 1994.
   *All the farm animals are where they should be, clucking and mucking, mewing
   and cooing, except for the missing goose.*

———. *In the Small, Small Pond.* New York: Henry Holt and Company, 1999.
   *A wonderful book of animated pond animals, where the illustrations move the
   reader through the seasons beginning with spring and ending with winter.*

————. *In the Tall, Tall Grass.* New York: Henry Holt and Company, 1995.
This story of an adventurous caterpillar is told with an "array of vibrant verbs and boisterous onomatopoeia". A great book for beginning readers.

————. *Lunch.* New York: Henry Holt and Company, 1998.
A hungry mouse peeks out of his hole and sniffs . . . lunch! Children can guess what fruit or vegetable comes next as the voracious rodent munches his way through yellow corn, green peas, orange carrots, and the rest of the colors vibrantly represented by Denise Fleming's unique, eye-catching style.

————. *Mama Cat has Three Kittens.* New York: Henry Holt and Company, 2002.
Mama Cat has three kittens, Fluffy, Skinny, and Boris. Where Mama Cat leads, Fluffy and Skinny follow. But what about Boris — will he ever stop napping and join the fun?

Gray, Shirley W. *Israel.* Minneapolis, MN: Compass Point Books, 2002.
Introduces the geography, peoples, culture, religious traditions, and history of Israel using simple language and lovely pictures.

On the Web

BCPL Kids Pages Denise Fleming Page
http://www.bcplonline.org/kidspage/fleming.html
Interesting information about Denise Fleming and her artistic technique.

Israel's Negev Desert
http://www.negev.org/About/negev_desert.htm
Interesting facts about the Negev, including a map.

Willem's Worldwide Webpage
http://www.schaik.com
Scroll down to the "Negev Desert" link to find beautiful pictures of Israel's deserts.

34. What's Jewish about "Goldilocks and the Three Bears"?

We are all familiar with the story of the little girl who enters the empty home of the three bears, eats their porridge, breaks baby bear's chair, and falls asleep in baby bear's bed. The earliest recorded version of the classic story of Goldilocks and the Three Bears was published in a homemade book titled, *The Story of The Three Bears metrically related, with illustrations locating it at Cecil Lodge in September 1831*, by Eleanor Mure. Based on oral tradition, Mure's version of the tale featured an old woman who intrudes into the bears' home, sampling their food and other amenities (Opie,1974). More widely known is "Story of the Three Bears," published by Robert Southey in 1837 in his collection of essays titled, *The Doctor*. This version also included an old woman, not a little girl, as the culprit. In 1849, Joseph Cundall changed the old woman into a young girl named "Silver Hair" in the version he published in his *Treasury of Pleasure Books for Young Children*. Finally, in *Old Nursery Stories and Rhymes*, illustrated by John Hassall (circa 1904), she became Goldilocks. So what's Jewish about *Goldilocks and the Three Bears?*

The Big Idea

Goldilocks is a classic example of the rude guest. She enters the house when no one is home, and presumably without an invitation. She helps herself to other people's food, breaks things, and finally takes a nap in someone else's bed. In most versions of the story, she runs away at the end without the smallest apology. We can learn a lot from Goldilocks by *not* following her example. How different the story may have been if Goldilocks had treated the bears and their home with *kavod* (respect)! She may have had a wonderful, long relationship with the bear family if she acted differently, displaying *teshuvah* (repentance) and *kedushah* (holiness) through her actions instead of rudeness. When we let God enter our relationships, we fill our relationships and our lives with *kedushah*.

Jewish Values

Often, the "secular" books and stories we read to our children every day are filled with Jewish values and moments, even if it's not readily apparent. Jewish values lead to Jewish behaviors. In "Goldilocks and the Three Bears," these values include:

Bal Tashchit	Do Not Destroy	בַּל תַּשְׁחִית
Derech Eretz	Good Manners	דֶּרֶךְ אֶרֶץ
Hachnasat Orchim	Hospitality	הַכְנָסַת אוֹרְחִים
Kavod	Respect	כָּבוֹד
Kedushah	Holiness	קְדֻשָּׁה
Teshuvah	Repentance	תְּשׁוּבָה

When children read a story like "Goldilocks and the Three Bears," they can identify Jewish values in action (and in this case they can identify some un-Jewish behaviors as well). Children's explorations are richest when the children are partners in their own learning. To engage children in these Jewish values and to deepen their learning, take time to investigate what children already know about Goldilocks. Observe children's play and analyze their comments. Seek out the children's questions and interests. Based on the children's questions, you might:

➤ Cook porridge (or instant oatmeal) with the children, so they can help Goldilocks replace what she took. *(Bal Tashchit, Kavod)*

➤ Goldilocks can help us learn how to treat our friends. During snack time, ask children what it feels like to have someone else take their food away without asking. *(Derech Eretz, Kavod)*

➤ Provide woodworking materials (older children) or puzzle or felt board pieces (younger children) of a chair so the children can "fix" the chair that Goldilocks broke. *(Bal Tashchit)*

➤ Host a breakfast or tea party and invite another class. Act out the story of Goldilocks and the Three Bears with or for your guests. *(Hachnasat Orchim)*

➤ Write part two of the story with the children, and imagine what happens when the three bears go to Goldilock's house. *(Hachnasat Orchim, Derech Eretz)*

➤ Act out the story with your children and create a new ending in which Goldilocks stays and apologizes to the three Bears for what she's done. *(Teshuvah)*

Israel Connection

At The International Festival of Puppet Theater in Jerusalem in 2003, the Goldilocks story was presented with colorful shadow puppets, as a grown-up Goldilocks returned to tell her story. This classic fairy tale has also been translated to Hebrew: *Zahavah u'Shlo-shet Ha-Du-bim* is available in book form from http://www.israeliwishes.com and on video from http://www.israeliscent.com. Invite a Hebrew speaking friend or parent to come and read the story in Hebrew to your class.

Hebrew Vocabulary

Here are some Hebrew words you can use to tell "Goldilocks and the Three Bears."

Goldilocks	*Za-***ha***-vah*	זְהָבָה
Bear/bears	*Dov/Du-***bim**	דֹּב/דֻּבִּים
Three	*Sha-***losh**	שָׁלֹשׁ
Father	*A-ba*	אַבָּא
Mother	*I-ma*	אִמָּא
Baby	*Ti-***nok**	תִּינוֹק
Bowl/bowls	*K'a-***rah***/k'a-***rot**	קְעָרָה/קְעָרוֹת
Chair/chairs	*Ki-***sei***/ki-sa-***ot**	כִּסֵּא/כִּסְאוֹת
Bed/beds	*Mi-***tah***/mi-***tot**	מִטָּה/מִטּוֹת

Songs and Poems

A Jewish Goldilocks chant
Author unknown. Adapted by Maxine Handelman.

Goldilocks went walking in the woods one day
She knocked on the door
But no one was home
No no no, no one was home.
So she walked right in
Made herself at home
She didn't care, no no no she didn't care.

Was that the right thing to do? NO!
Did Goldilocks show *kavod*? NO!

Home came the three bears.
"Somebody's been eating my porridge," said the papa bear.
"Somebody did not show *derech eretz*," said the mama bear.
"Ba-ba ba-ree-bear," said the little wee bear, "Somebody's been eating my porridge, and she ate it all up!"

"Somebody's been sitting in my chair," said the papa bear.
"Somebody did not show *derech eretz*," said the mama bear.
"Ba-ba ba-ree-bear," said the little wee bear, "Somebody's been sitting in my chair and she broke it all to bits!"

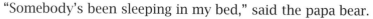

"Somebody's been sleeping in my bed," said the papa bear.

"Somebody did not show *derech eretz*," said the mama bear.

"Ba-ba ba-ree-bear," said the little wee bear, "Somebody's been sleeping in my bed, and she's still there!"

So Goldilocks woke up, and broke up the party, and ran away from there.

"Shalom, l'hitraot," said the papa bear.

"Shalom, l'hitraot," said the mama bear.

"Ba-ba ba-ree-bear," said the little wee bear, "Buzz off, kid!"

Blessings

When you sit down with your guests for a porridge breakfast, you can say this blessing:

בָּרוּךְ אַתָּה יְיָ אֱלֹהֵינוּ מֶלֶךְ הָעוֹלָם בּוֹרֵא מִינֵי מְזוֹנוֹת.

Ba-ruch A-tah A-do-nai E-lo-hei-nu Me-lech Ha-O-lam Bo-rei Mi-nei M'zo-not.
We praise You, our God, Creator of the universe, Who creates all kinds of food.

Story: Goldilocks Learns a Jewish Lesson

Adapted by Maxine Handelman from the traditional Goldilocks story. Thanks to Tzahavah Farber of Montreal for suggesting this version!

Once upon a time, there was a little girl named Goldilocks. She went for a walk in the forest. After walking quite a ways, and becoming very cold, she came upon a house. She knocked and, when no one answered, she walked right in.

At the table in the kitchen, there were three bowls of porridge. Goldilocks was hungry. She tried to wait, because she knew she shouldn't eat someone else's food. But she was so very hungry. Finally, Goldilocks could wait no more. She sat down at the table, said the blessing — *Borei Mi-nei M'zo-not* — and tasted the porridge from the first bowl.

"This porridge is too hot!" she exclaimed.

So, she tasted the porridge from the second bowl.

"This porridge is too cold," she said

So, she tasted the last bowl of porridge.

"Ahhh, this porridge is just right," she said happily and she ate it all up.

After she'd eaten the three bears' breakfasts she decided she was feeling a little tired. So, she walked into the living room where she saw three chairs. Goldilocks sat in the first chair to rest her feet.

"This chair is too hard!" she exclaimed.

So she sat in the second chair.

"This chair is too soft!" she whined.

So she tried the last and smallest chair.

"Ahhh, this chair is just right," she sighed. But just as she settled down into the chair to rest, it broke into pieces!

"Oh my!" said Goldilocks. "What can I do?" She looked around for a hammer or tape to fix the chair, but couldn't find any.

Goldilocks was very tired by this time, so she went upstairs to the bedroom. She lay down in the first bed, but it was too hard. Then she lay in the second bed, but it was too soft. Then she lay down in the third bed and it was just right. Goldilocks said the *Sh'ma* and fell asleep.

As she was sleeping, the three bears came home.

"Someone's been eating my porridge," growled Papa Bear.

"Someone's been eating my porridge," said Mama Bear.

"Someone's been eating my porridge and they ate it all up!" cried Baby Bear.

The three bears went into the living room.

"Someone's been sitting in my chair," growled Papa Bear.

"Someone's been sitting in my chair," said Mama Bear.

"Someone's been sitting in my chair and they've broken it all to pieces!" cried Baby Bear.

They decided to look around some more and when they got upstairs to the bedroom, Papa Bear growled, "Someone's been sleeping in my bed,"

"Someone's been sleeping in my bed, too" said Mama Bear.

"Someone's been sleeping in my bed and she's still there!" exclaimed Baby Bear.

Just then, Goldilocks woke up and saw the three bears. Goldilocks cried, "I'm so glad you're home! I'm sorry — I found your house when I was so cold and hungry and tired. I'm afraid I ate up your breakfast, and I broke your chair and I couldn't fix it. If you let me, I can try to make you more porridge and fix the chair." Goldilocks got out of Baby Bear's bed and straightened the covers. "That's okay," said the Three Bears. "We'd appreciate it if you could help out, and then we can take you home." Mama Bear and Goldilocks went into the kitchen to make some more porridge, and Papa Bear and Baby Bear got the hammer and fixed Baby Bear's chair. After they all ate some breakfast together, the Three Bears took Goldilocks home. After that, Goldilocks was a frequent guest in the Bear's home — always by invitation.

Questions and Suggestions:

➤ Discuss with your children how the story changes when Goldilocks shows some *kavod* (respect) and *teshuvah* (repentance).

➤ Retell the story using the flannel board or a magnetic board, but use circles for the cereal bowls, squares for the chairs and rectangles for the beds. Have children sequence the shapes in size order.

➤ Compare different versions of "Goldilocks and the Three Bears" (find different versions at your local library — there are many versions listed on amazon.com including versions from other cultures such *as Leola and the Honeybears: An African-American Retelling of Goldilocks and the Three Bears* by Melodye Benson Rosales.) Discuss how stories change over time and from place to place. Jewish stories often function this way, as well (see Chapter 35, "What's Jewish about 'I Had a Little Overcoat'").

Resources

Books and Music

Opie, Iona and Peter. *The Classic Fairy Tales.* New York: Oxford University Press, 1974.
A collection of twenty-four well-known fairy tales as they were first presented in English. Includes a summary of the history of each tale.

Rosales, Melodye Benson. *Leola and the Honeybears: An African-American Retelling of Goldilocks and The Three Bears.* New York: Cartwheel Books, 1999.
Rosales's update of a nursery staple features an adventurous African-American girl and her doll.

Vainshtein, Asi. *Zahavah u'Shlo-shet Ha-Du-bim (Goldilocks and the Three Bears).* Publisher unknown.
A Hebrew translation of the classic story. Available from http://www.israeliwishes.com.

Zahavah u'Shlo-shet Ha-Du-bim (Goldilocks and the Three Bears). Publisher unknown.
Video, available from http://www.israeliscent.com.

On the Web

Goldilocks and the Three Bears
http://www.dltk-kids.com/rhymes/goldilocks.htm
This site features a version of the story, coloring book pages, and craft ideas and templates.

SurLaLune Fairy Tales: The Annotated Goldilocks and the Three Bears
http://www.surlalunefairytales.com/goldilocks/index.html
An annotated version of the story, with fascinating (and sometimes humorous) insights into its history and development.

35. What's Jewish about "I Had a Little Overcoat"?

There is an old Yiddish folksong, "*Hob Ikh Mir A Mantl*" (I Had A Little Overcoat). The song tells the story of a tailor who, from a worn-out overcoat makes a jacket, and then a vest, and then a scarf, on and on until there's nothing left but the song which tells the story. Based on this song, there are countless versions and retellings of the story from many cultures, and at least three picture books: *Something from Nothing* by Phoebe Gilman, *Bit by Bit* by Steve Sanfield and *Joseph Had a Little Overcoat* by Simms Taback. Taback's version actually includes the song, translated into English, at the end. So what's the big deal about different versions of the same story? And what's Jewish about "I Had a Little Overcoat"?

The Big Idea

The Jewish people are "The People of the Book." We are nothing without our stories. Jewish stories travel from culture to culture, from Eastern Europe or Iran or Turkey to Israel to America and back again. Stories change from place to place, from teller to teller, from generation to generation. But kernels of wisdom travel with each story and feed us with the richness of lands and times we will never actually visit. Jewish life dictates that we never wander far from our story. On Purim, one of the four *mitzvot* (commandments) is to listen to the Megillah being read, making sure we recall the story of Esther every year. On Pesach, the entire purpose of the Seder is for us to retell the story of the Exodus, the story of how we became the Jewish People. Our most important storybook, of course, is the Torah. The Jewish calendar recognizes this. On Shavuot we celebrate receiving the Torah at Mt. Sinai, and on Simchat Torah we celebrate the moment of completing one reading and immediately beginning again. Our stories are a crucial element of just what makes us who we are, what makes us Jews. Our stories carry our traditions *L'dor Vador* — from generation to generation. Reading different versions of the same story reminds us that what makes *K'lal Yisrael*, the entirety of the Jewish People, so rich and so wonderful is the richness and the variety of the stories we tell, even as they are the same stories. Reading different versions of the same story brings us back to our most important story, the Torah.

Jewish Values

Sometimes, the activities we are involved in with children are Jewish moments, even if it's not readily apparent. Jewish values lead to Jewish behaviors. Reading stories such as those based on "I Had a Little Overcoat" are filled with Jewish values, such as:

K'lal Yisrael	All Jews are One People	כְּלַל יִשְׂרָאֵל
L'dor Vador	From Generation to Generation	לְדוֹר וָדוֹר
"Storytelling"	Passing on the Oral Tradition	
Talmud Torah	Study/Love of Learning	תַּלְמוּד תּוֹרָה
Tikkun Olam	Repair of the World	תִּקּוּן עוֹלָם

When children explore different versions of the same story, they are literally embodying Jewish values. Children's explorations are richest when the children are partners in their own learning. To engage children in these Jewish values and to deepen their learning, take time to investigate what children already know about comparing stories. Observe children's play and analyze their comments. Seek out the children's questions and interests. Based on the children's questions, you might:

➤ Read two or three versions of the "I Had a Little Overcoat" story. *Something from Nothing* by Phoebe Gilman, *Bit by Bit* by Steve Sanfield, and *Joseph Had a Little Overcoat* by Simms Taback are all good choices. Discuss with your children why the different authors and illustrators might have made the variations they made. *(K'lal Yisrael,* "Storytelling"*)*

➤ Discuss how you and your children can make "something out of nothing." Individually or in small groups, use any medium of your choice (fabric, paper, clay, bread dough) to create and recreate until all you have left is the story of what you did. (For example, you might make some bread from dough, eat some of the bread in a sandwich, make French toast with leftover bread, make croutons from the leftovers, and feed the birds the last few scraps.) Write the story with your children. *(Tikkun Olam,* "Storytelling"*)*

➤ Stories change as they get passed down. Invite two generations to come (a grandparent and a parent) to tell a family story and see if their versions are the same. Even better, invite the two generations on two different days, so they can't correct each other. *(L'dor Vador)*

➤ Listen to the song *Hob Ikh Mir A Mantl* (see the Resource section at the end of this unit) or sing the English translation from the end of Joseph Had a Little Overcoat. How does knowing the song change the story? ("Storytelling")

➤ Invite children to make up and tell stories. A day or two later, invite children to retell other children's stories. What stays the same? What changes? How do children feel about different versions of their own stories? *(L'dor Vador, K'lal Yisrael)*

➤ The "I Had a Little Overcoat" stories tell us about life in the shtetl (the small

Jewish villages of Eastern Europe), how resources were scarce so nothing was wasted. Pick some favorite stories from the Torah, and discuss with your children what these stories tell us about ourselves. *(Talmud Torah, K'lal Yisrael)*

Israel Connection

The most incredible storytelling resource exists in Israel. The Israel Folktale Archives (IFA) was established in 1955 by Prof. Dov Noy, under the auspices and framework of the Museum of Ethnology and Folklore of the Haifa Municipality. In 1983 the Archives relocated to the University of Haifa. IFA, which is the only archives of its kind in Israel, serves as a center for knowledge and information and is open to researchers, students and the general public, anyone concerned with the cultural heritage of the ethnic communities in Israel.

By the end of 1998, 21,000 folktales were preserved therein, narrated by story-tellers from various communities living in Israel, both Jewish (stemming from North Africa, Asia, Europe and America) and non-Jewish (Arabs: Moslems, Christians, Bedouin, Druze, etc.).

Create a story archive in your class. Have children collect written or tape record stories from their families (seek out extended family members as well) and create a collection of your class's favorite stories. Alternatively, ask each family to record or write their own version of a popular story (i.e. Goldilocks, Jack and the Beanstalk). Share all the versions in the class and discuss the differences.

Hebrew Vocabulary

Here is a list of Hebrew words and phrases you can use as you discuss Jewish stories:

Story	*Si-pur*	סִפּוּר
Book	*Sei-fer*	סֵפֶר
Generation	*Dor*	דוֹר
Different	*Sho-neh*	שׁוֹנֶה
Same	*O-to da-var*	אוֹתוֹ דָבָר
Similar	*Do-meh*	דוֹמֶה
Read me a story, please!	*Tik-ra li si-pur, b'va-ka-shah!*	תִּקְרָא לִי סִפּוּר בְּבַקָשָׁה!
Jacket	*M'il*	מְעִיל
Vest	*Cha-zi-yah*	חֲזִיָה
Hat	*Ko-vah*	כּוֹבַע
Pocket	*Kis*	כִּיס
Button	*Kaf-tor*	כַּפְתּוֹר

Songs and Poems

Hob Ikh Mir A Mantl (I Had A Little Overcoat)

Traditional Yiddish folksong. Yiddish words and English translation from
www.geocities.com/buddychai/Songs/Songs6.html

Hob ikh mir a mantl fun fartsaytikn shtof
Tra la la la la
Hot es nit in zikh kay gantsenem shtokh
Tra la la la la
Darum, hob ikh zikh fartrakht
Un fun dem mantl a rekl gemakht
Tra la la la

I had a little <u>overcoat</u> that I made long ago. (insert: jacket, vest, hat, pocket, button)
Tra la la la la
It had so many patches there was no place to sew
Tra la la la la
Then I thought and I prayed.
And from that <u>overcoat a little jacket I made</u> (insert: jacket a little vest I made, vest a little hat I made, hat a little pocket I made, pocket a little button I made, button nothing could be made)
Tra la la la la!
Last verse:
Now I had a little nothing that I made long ago.
It hasn't any patches, there is nothing to sew.
From that nothing this little song I made.

Blessings

When we study Torah, this is the blessing we say:

בָּרוּךְ אַתָּה יְיָ אֱלֹהֵינוּ מֶלֶךְ הָעוֹלָם אֲשֶׁר קִדְּשָׁנוּ בְּמִצְוֹתָיו וְצִוָּנוּ
לַעֲסֹק בְּדִבְרֵי תוֹרָה.

*Ba-**ruch** A-**tah** A-do-**nai** E-lo-**hei**-nu **Me**-lech Ha-O-**lam** A-**sher** Kid'**sha**-nu B'mitz-vo-**tav** V'tzi-**va**-nu La'a-**sok** B'div-**rei** To-**rah**.*
We praise you, Our God, Creator of the universe, Who made us holy with Your mitzvot, and commanded us to occupy ourselves with words of Torah.

When we are about to tell a story, we might say a *bracha sheh b'lev* (a prayer of the heart) such as this one:

God, as I tell this story, please let my voice be firm and let my story delight and teach my audience, so that they too may tell others the story.

Story: Colors Bright and Cheerful

(Another version of "I Had a Little Overcoat")
By Maxine Handelman, who wrote this version just to demonstrate that everyone can be a storyteller. You can write your own version too!

Ariana was a painter. One day she painted a canvas to be a backdrop for the town theater production of *Fiddler on the Roof.* The colors were bright and cheerful and told of happy times.

The play ran for many months, and at the end of the run, the backdrop was tattered and worn.

So Ariana took the backdrop and snipped here, cut there, until she had made a curtain for the *Aron HaKodesh* at the synagogue. The colors were bright and cheerful and told of happy times.

After several years, the curtain was tattered and worn.

So Ariana took the curtain and snipped here, cut there, until she had made a chuppah for her sister's wedding. The colors were bright and cheerful and told of happy times.

After many family weddings, the chuppah was tattered and worn.

So Ariana took the chuppah and snipped here, cut there, until she had made a dress for her daughter's bat mitzvah. The colors were bright and cheerful and told of happy times.

After several years, the dress was tattered and worn.

So Ariana took the dress and snipped here, cut there, until she had made a shawl to wear to the theater. The colors were bright and cheerful and told of happy times.

After several years, the shawl was tattered and worn.

So Ariana took the shawl and snipped here, cut there, until she had made a *kippah* for her son to wear. The colors were bright and cheerful and told of happy times.

One day, a strong wind came and blew the *kippah* away. No one could catch it — it was simply gone. Now there was nothing. So Ariana sat down and wrote a story and painted the pictures to go with it. The colors were bright and cheerful and told of happy times.

Questions and Suggestions:

➤ Write your own version of a "Something from Nothing" story with your class. Create props and act it out.

➤ Why is it valuable to be able to make something out of nothing?

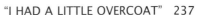

➤ How do stories help us hold on to things that might otherwise be lost or forgotten?

Resources

Books and Music

Abrams, Bonnie. *A Sudenyu of Yiddish Song.* Dynamic Records DRK 131.
   Includes a recording of the song "Hob Ikh Mir A Mantl" (I Had A Little Coat). Compact disc or cassette, available at http://www.dynrec.com/sampler/sudenyu_yiddish.html.

The Bluestein Family. *Where Does Love Come From?* Greenhays Recordings, 1986.
   This cassette by the Bluestein Family includes a recording of the song "Hob Ikh Mir A Mantl" (I Had A Little Coat). Available at http:// www.evobluestein.com/foon.html.

Gilman, Phoebe. *Something from Nothing.* New York: Scholastic, Inc. 1992.
   This version begins with a grandfather making a blanket for his grandson.

Sanfield, Steve. *Bit by Bit.* New York: Philomel Books, 1995.
   This version is told in a master storyteller's voice.

Schimmel, Nancy. *Just Enough to Make a Story: A Sourcebook for Storytelling.*
Berkeley, CA: Sisters' Choice, 3rd edition, 1992.
   Includes a version of "Hob Ikh Mir A Mantl."

Taback, Simms. *Joseph Had a Little Overcoat.* New York: Viking (a member of Penguin Putnam Books for Young Readers), 1999.
   This version, winner of the Caldecott Medal, includes music and lyrics to the song, translated into English.

Materials and Supplies

There is a storytelling doll that goes along with Simms Taback's book *Joseph Had a Little Overcoat.* It is available from Lakeshore Learning Materials at http://www.lakeshorelearning.com or call (800) 778-4456 (item # RR864).

36. What's Jewish about Leo Lionni?

Children and parents alike enjoy reading and hearing the wonderful fables created by the late Caldecott Award winner, Leo Lionni. Using torn paper, brilliant color, and an ability to make his animal characters come to life, Leo Lionni's books are visually engaging. The illustrations are also known for working together with the text to teach moral lessons to the reader. But what is Jewish about Leo Lionni's stories?

The Big Idea

Leo Lionni wrote and illustrated fables (stories in which the main characters are animals who participate in plots that teach moral lessons). But these fables are famous for more than the illustrations. According to well-known child psychologist Bruno Bettelheim, Leo Lionni's stories offer children an opportunity to experience wonderful integration of illustration with text (story). Children both see and hear each story, which helps to build a stronger understanding of the relationship between visual imagery and verbal language. This brings deeper understanding and meaning to each story.

This is what Jews have been doing for generations with Torah. The Torah is read and then each sentence, phrase, or word is interpreted based on one's own experiences. The images in reading Torah are the images already set within each person's mind, that are then stimulated by reading and discussing these ancient words. Many such thoughts have been shared, debated, written about, and chronicled in the Talmud and in Commentaries. It is no mistake that Jews are known as "The People of the Book." So when we read and discuss books written by Leo Lionni, we help young children become aware of the relationship between imagery and text — a skill used for reading and understanding Torah.

Jewish Values

Sometimes, the activities we are involved in with children are Jewish moments, even if it's not readily apparent. Jewish values lead to Jewish behaviors. Books written and illustrated by Leo Lionni are filled with Jewish values, including:

Kavod	Respect, Honor	כָּבוֹד
Shmiat HaOzen	Attentiveness	שְׁמִיעַת הָאֹזֶן
Talmud Torah	Study/Love of Learning	תַּלְמוּד תּוֹרָה

When children explore books written and illustrated by Leo Lionni, they are literally embodying Jewish values. Children's explorations are richest when the children are partners in their own learning. To engage children in these Jewish values and to deepen their learning, take time to investigate what the children already know about Leo Lionni and his books and illustrations. Observe children's play and analyze their comments. Seek out the children's questions and interests. Based on the children's questions, you might:

➤ Read several of Leo Lionni's books to a group of children. With the children, discuss, compare, and contrast these books to one another and to other books they have heard. What makes Leo Lionni's books unique to him? *(Shmiat HaOzen, Talmud Torah)*

➤ Reread with children Leo Lionni's stories that focus on showing respect and acknowledging uniqueness such as "Fish is Fish," "Cornelius," and "Frederick." Role-play the characters and then have a discussion about feelings, differences, and respect. This could also be followed up with drawings and dictation to create a class-made book. *(Kavod, Shmiat HaOzen)*

➤ Invite and encourage the children as a group or individually to write their own animal fables with a Jewish twist *(Talmud Torah)*

➤ Study some Torah together, then ask the children to illustrate the story using Leo Lionni's style and techniques of using torn paper and brilliant colors. *(Talmud Torah)*

Israel Connection

Leo Lionni might be well known for his fables, but he is not alone. According to the Torah, King Solomon was known for his wisdom and special powers. It is written that he could speak with trees, creeping things, beasts, fowl, and fishes. Because of his ability to speak with animals, King Solomon is also known for his fables. Consequently, there are many King Solomon fables written from our own Jewish heritage. Many of these fables can be found in anthologies by contemporary Jewish storytellers like Peninnah Schram and Ellen Frankel. Other such stories are written as picture books for young children, such as *King Solomon and the Bee* by Dalia Renberg, *The Wisdom Bird* by Sheldon Oberman, and *When Solomon Was King* by Sheila MacGill-Callahan. Read these stories to the children in your class and ask them to create their own interpretation of a King Solomon story, complete with text and illustrations in a style similar to Leo Lionni.

Hebrew Vocabulary

To learn/study	*Lil'mod*	לִלְמֹד
Author	*M'cha-beir*	מְחַבֵּר
Illustrator	*M'a-yeir*	מְאַיֵּר
Fable	*A-ga-dah*	אַגָּדָה
Come read a story.	*Bo-u nik-rah si-pur.*	בּוֹאוּ נִקְרָא סִפּוּר.
Come write a story.	*Bo-u nich-tov si-pur.*	בּוֹאוּ נִכְתֹּב סִפּוּר.
Please read me a story.	*B'va-ka-shah, tik-ra li si-pur.*	בְּבַקָּשָׁה תִּקְרָא לִי סִפּוּר.

Songs and Poems

A Jewish Poem for Frederick
By Deborah Schein

A Jewish Frederick, how absurd
But don't decide until you've heard
How this little mouse saved the day
With visions and a lot to say.
Just like Torah and Jewish prayer
He made life holy with hope to spare
That they'd survive the long cold days
Little mice living in Jewish ways.

An Ode to Leo Lionni
By Deborah Schein

Leo Lionni believed in peace
Shalom and respect,
Kavod if you please
And so in his fables
He helps readers see
How to be themselves,
Just as he was he.

Blessings

When we study Torah, we say:

בָּרוּךְ אַתָּה יְיָ אֱלֹהֵינוּ מֶלֶךְ הָעוֹלָם אֲשֶׁר קִדְּשָׁנוּ בְּמִצְוֹתָיו וְצִוָּנוּ לַעֲסֹק בְּדִבְרֵי תוֹרָה.

Ba-ruch A-tah A-do-nai E-lo-hei-nu Me-lech Ha-O-lam A-sher Kid'sha-nu B'mitz-vo-tav V'tzi-va-nu La'a-sok B'div-rei To-rah.

We praise You, our God, Creator of the universe, Who made us holy through Your mitzvot, and commanded us to occupy ourselves with words of Torah.

There is no formal blessing for the study of books written and illustrated by authors such as Leo Lionni. But listening to or reading a good book can inspire a *bracha sheh b'lev* **(a prayer of the heart) such as:**

Thank you, God, for giving us great books and the ability to enjoy them.

Story: Yaakov

By Deborah Schein, inspired by Leo Lionni.

In the city of Jerusalem, where Jews, Moslems, and Christians gather to pray in their respective holy places, there is an ancient wall. In Hebrew it is called the *Kotel* and it was here that a family of field mice made their home. For years and years the little mice would spend much of each week getting ready for Shabbat, collecting pieces of wax to make into candles, grapes for wine, and grains of wheat for challah. Now there was talk of war. No one knew when the war would come, how long it would last, or how they would be able to celebrate Shabbat, so they all worked even harder. All except Yaakov.

"Yaakov, why don't you work?" the others asked.

"I do work," said Yaakov. "I gather sunsets, for the coming days."

And when they saw Yaakov sitting there, staring at the hills of Jerusalem, they said, "And now, Yaakov?"

"I gather colors," answered Yaakov simply.

And once Yaakov seemed half asleep. "Are you dreaming, Yaakov?" they asked reproachfully.

But Yaakov said, "Oh no, I am gathering words. For war can be long and scary and we might need something happy and hopeful to think about."

The war came, and in the beginning, the little family of field mice had enough supplies to celebrate Shabbat at the end of each week. But little by little they had used up all of the candles, the wine was gone, and the challah was but a memory. The thought of not celebrating Shabbat made all the little mice sad and even more frightened.

Then they remembered what Yaakov had said about sunsets, colors, and words. "What about your supplies, Yaakov?" they asked.

"Close your eyes," said Yaakov as he climbed onto a large Jerusalem stone. "Now I send you the sun setting over the hills of Jerusalem." They all looked toward the sky. And as Yaakov spoke, the little mice could envision candles glowing brightly in honor of Shabbat. The little mice began to feel better.

Was it Yaakov's voice? Was it magic?

"And how about the colors, Yaakov?" they asked anxiously.

"Close your eyes," Yaakov said. And when he told them of the purple grapes growing on the vines, and of the golden brown challah freshly baked, they could just about see them and taste them.

"And the words, Yaakov?"

Yaakov cleared his throat, waited a moment, and then, as if from a real Shabbat table, he began to sing:

Sha-lom a-lei-chem, mal-a-chei ha-sha-reit, ma-la-chei El-yon, mi-me-lech ma-la-chei ham'la-chim, Ha-Ka-dosh Ba-ruch Hu.

(Peace upon you, O ministering angels, angels of the Exalted One — from the Ruler Who reigns over all rulers, the Holy One, Blessed is God.)

And ever so slowly, all the mice began to join in.

When they had finished singing the song, everyone joined together in singing all of the Shabbat *brachot* (blessings). With Yaakov's sunsets, colors, and words, the small family of mice survived the hard times until peace came to the land once again.

Questions and Suggestions:

➤ A fable is an animal story that teaches a moral. What moral lesson is found in this Jewish fable?

➤ Which Leo Lionni story does this Jewish Fable remind you of? Why?

➤ Act out the story using different animals and/or different Jewish holidays.

➤ Draw pictures of your visions of Shabbat captured by the words in this story.

➤ Sing some other songs the mice family might have sung to help them remember the feeling of Shabbat.

Resources

Books and Music

Biers-Ariel, Matt. *Solomon and the Trees.* New York: Union of American Hebrew Congregations, 2001.

> *When Solomon became king, he found himself too busy to visit the forests and his animal friends. Eventually Solomon came to understand the price that must be paid when people don't take proper care of the earth and its blessings.*

Frankel, Ellen. *The Classic Tales: 4,000 Years of Jewish Lore.* New Jersey: Jason Aronson Inc. 1989.

> *Retelling of 300 Jewish stories spanning 4000 years and three continents. Drawing from Talmudic, Midrashic, Hasidic, and folktale sources, Frankel has put together a rich anthology of Jewish tales imbued with the spiritual values of Judaism and the age-old folk wisdom of the Jewish people.*

Lionni, Leo. *Frederick's Fables — A Leo Lionni Treasury of Favorite Stories.* New York: Pantheon Books, 1985.

> *A collection of thirteen of Lionni's previously published books, presented in the same format.*

———. *Fish is Fish.* New York: Dragonfly, 1974.

> *A modern fable of a minnow who wants to follow his tadpole friend — who has become a frog — onto land.*

———. *Cornelius.* New York: Dragonfly, 1994.

> *Cornelius, a crocodile who walks upright, sees things no crocodile has ever seen before.*

———. *Frederick.* New York: Dragonfly, 1973.

> *While other mice are gathering food for the winter, Frederick seems to daydream the summer away. When dreary winter comes, it is Frederick the poet-mouse who warms his friends and cheers them with his words.*

MacGill-Callahan, Sheila. *When Solomon Was King.* New York: Dial Books for Young Readers, 1995.

> *As he grows more and more powerful, King Solomon forgets the lesson he learned from a wounded lioness.*

Oberman, Sheldon. *The Wisdom Bird: A Tale of Solomon and Sheba*. Honesdale, Pennsylvania: Boyds Mill Press, 2000.
King Solomon learns a lesson from a little bird in this story based on Jewish and African tales.

Renberg, Dalia. *King Solomon and the Bee*. New York: Harper Collin Publishers, 1994.
A retelling of the traditional tale about a bee that repays King Solomon's mercy by helping him solve the Queen of Sheba's riddle.

Schram, Peninnah. *Jewish Stories One Generation Tells Another*. New Jersey: Jason Aronson Inc., 1987.
Retelling of Jewish stories in narrative form, offering intuitive wisdom about human nature and the world.

Wiesel, Elie. *King Solomon and His Magic Ring*. New York: Greenwillow, 1999.
Vividly retold legends of King Solomon interwoven with Biblical accounts of his reign to present an exciting picture of his life.

On the Web

Kids@Random — Leo Lionni
www.randomhouse.com/kids/author/llionni.html
This web site offers an essay by Leo Lionni on how he gets his ideas, as well as a brief biography.

Appendix A
Jewish Values, Virtues, Mitzvot, and Concepts

Jewish values, virtues and *mitzvot* (commandments) are an integral part of living a Jewish life, and are also an essential element of any Jewish early childhood program. Below are explanations of all of the Jewish values, virtues, *mitzvot*, and concepts listed in this book.

Ahavah: Love   אַהֲבָה

Judaism and Jewish texts refer to many kinds of love: loving God, loving all creatures, loving charitable deeds. Even being beloved is a virtue. The Torah tells us to "Love your fellow person as yourself" (Leviticus 19:18). When we speak of *Ahavah* being a Jewish value, we can see that love and respect for other people, and a covenant of love between each one of us and God, serve as the basis for most of the *mitzvot* (commandments). To love God is to love God's creations. In our worship service, the prayer *Ahavah Rabah*, about God loving us, is followed by the *V'Ahavtah*, about us loving God. Loving relationships with God are reciprocal. With other people, we cannot always assume the same to be true. But when we strive to maintain loving feelings and act on these feelings by doing deeds of loving-kindness, we live a life of righteousness. As we love others, we become more beloved.

B'tzelem Elohim: Created in the Image of God   בְּצֶלֶם אֱלֹהִים

We are told in Genesis 1:27 that the first person was created in the "image of God." This does not mean that we resemble God in any physical way, or that God has a body or face. Rather, people are created with the ability to reason and to know good from evil. Unlike animals, we are able to make moral choices. When we speak of each person being created in the image of God, we are reminded to pay attention to what is holy about each person, and to model our behavior after that of God.

Bal Tashchit: Do Not Destroy   בַּל תַּשְׁחִית

The basis for this *mitzvah* comes from the Torah (Deuteronomy 20:19) which tells us that when, in a war, we besiege a city, we shall not destroy the trees of the city, as the trees have no way to get out of the way of the war. The rabbis explored all sorts of areas in which we must be careful not to destroy things or use them up unwisely. *Bal Tashchit* reminds us that everything ultimately belongs to God. We are merely caretakers of a world given to us on the condition that we would make wise use of it. Recycling, conserving energy, and preserving the environment all fulfill the *mitzvah* of *Bal Tashchit*.

Bikur Cholim: Visiting the Sick   בִּקּוּר חוֹלִים

This *mitzvah* is found in the Talmud (Shabbat 127a): "These are the deeds which yield immediate fruit and continue to yield fruit in time to come: honoring parents, doing deeds of kindness, attending the house of study, visiting the sick..." *Bikur Cholim* is a way to model our own behavior after God's behavior, to act *B'tzelem*

Elohim (in the image of God), because God visited Abraham when he was sick (Genesis 18:1). In the early childhood classroom, *Bikur Cholim* is an important Jewish behavior to teach when a child in the class, a teacher, or a family member is sick. You can share with children the Jewish tradition of praying for both *R'fuat HaGuf*, healing of the body, and *R'fuat HaNefesh*, healing of the spirit, by teaching them "*Mi Shebeirach*" (from Debbie Friedman's *And You Shall Be a Blessing* CD). Find ways with your children to visit or connect with those who are sick, through visits, phone trees, and sending letters, artwork, and photos.

Brit: Partnership with God   בְּרִית

The word *brit* literally means "covenant." God blessed the Jewish people with a covenant, an agreement that pledges both the Jewish people and God to work together toward the perfection of the world and full human dignity in every way for as long as it takes. Being partners with God is a concept that has far-reaching implications for how we live our lives, and what it means to be Jewish. Being partners with God means that we are always involved in taking care of the world around us, as well as the people around us. While we are not required to complete the task, we are required to keep at it to the best of our ability. From the building of a house to the making of a peanut butter and jelly sandwich, when we look around our world we discover so many things that we can do only within the context of a partnership of God. Unlike a standard contract, a *brit* is not always reciprocal. There are times when it may seem that God is not participating fully in the *brit*, and times that it may seem that we are not participating fully. Even so, we remain partners with God.

Chesed: Kindness   חֶסֶד

Chesed is encompassed in *G'milut Chasadim,* acts of loving-kindness. In the Jewish early childhood classroom, it is important for children to learn that being nice, and kind, to other people is not just a good thing to do, it's a *Jewish* thing to do. Jewish tradition expects the obligation of being kind to extend through one's whole life. Hillel taught, "What is hateful to you, do not do unto others. The rest (of Judaism) is commentary. Now go and study" (Talmud *Shabbat* 31a). This same idea, slightly rephrased, is encompassed in what some refer to as "The Golden Rule:" Treat others as you would like to be treated. Finding ways to incorporate kindness in our daily way of being is a lifelong journey. We should always be on the lookout for ways to help others. We have opportunities every day to perform both large and small acts of kindness, and Judaism tells us to take advantage of as many of these opportunities as we can.

Chochma: Wisdom   חָכְמָה

Jewish texts have much to say about *Chochma*. The Talmud asks, "Who is wise? One who foresees the future consequences of his acts" (*Tamid* 32a). *Pirke Avot* asks, "Who is wise? He who learns from all people." The rabbis understood wisdom as the ability to anticipate the implications of one's words and acts. Acting with wise forethought is part of leading a virtuous, moral, Jewish life.

Derech Eretz: Proper, Decent Behavior דֶּרֶךְ אֶרֶץ

Derech Eretz can also be translated simply as "manners." Literally, *Derech Eretz* means "the ways of the land," indicating to us that manners, or decent behavior, should be a basic, natural part of any person's daily life, even a simple person who works the land. From the Torah we learn, "Do what is right and good in the sight of the Lord" (Deuteronomy 6:18), and "Her ways [the ways of Torah] are pleasant" (Proverbs 3:17). This tells us that a certain level of fairness and courtesy is expected from us at all times. While we all have our rude moments, a constant rude or inconsiderate attitude shows that we hold our own interests and needs above anyone else's. One of Judaism's most basic concepts is that each one of us is created *B'tzelem Elohim*, in God's Image. Living a life guided by *Derech Eretz* makes evident our belief that each person is created *B'tzelem Elohim* and helps us demonstrate respect accordingly.

Dibuk Chaverim: Cleaving to Friends דְּבוּק חַבֵרִים

Pirke Avot includes *Dibuk Chaverim* among the forty-eight virtues necessary for acquiring Torah. This tells us that having and caring for friendships in a serious way is an essential element of learning and righteous living, which is what acquiring Torah is all about. Beyond merely having friends or spending time with friends, *Dibuk Chaverim* goes deeper, to represent the deep degree to which we honor and treat friends, and how we make a friendship a priority, involving love, appreciation and devotion. When we open ourselves up to trusting and mutually giving friendships, we set ourselves on the path of righteous living. Children in a classroom thrive when they have a serious friend with whom they can approach the world and make it a better place, together.

G'milut Chasadim: Acts of Loving-kindness גְּמִילוּת חֲסָדִים

In Pirke Avot 1:2 we learn: "The world stands on three things: Torah, worship, and acts of loving-kindness." The Talmud (Peah 1:1) details: "These are the things whose fruit a person enjoys in this world and whose reward is stirred up in the World-to-Come: honoring parents, doing deeds of kindness, making peace. But the study of Torah is equal to them all [because it leads to them all]." *G'milut Chasadim* is a collection of acts which detail the way we as Jews are to take care of fellow Jews, by caring for the needy, visiting the sick, comforting the mourner, and burying the dead, among others. *G'milut Chasadim* goes beyond simple kindnesses to spelling out the real life moments in which we need to take care of each other, and how to go about each of these acts with kindness and decency. In the early childhood classroom, employing *G'milut Chasadim* can instill a level of kindness into ordinary obligations. Children can learn that is it the Jewish way to help each other willingly and with care. Children can be rewarded for their acts of loving-kindness, perhaps through a "*G'milut Chasadim* Tree" which continues to bloom throughout the year.

Hachnasat Orchim: Hospitality/Welcoming Guests הַכְנָסַת אוֹרְחִים

Hachnasat Orchim literally translates as "bringing in guests" — an important act of kindness. This mitzvah is also found in the Talmud (Shabbat 127a): "Rabbi Judah said in Rab's name, 'Hospitality to strangers is greater than welcoming the presence of the *Shechinah* [the feminine aspects of God].'" It is a Jewish behavior to extend hospitality, because of the way Abraham opened his home to the three strangers who came to his tent (Genesis 18:2), and because of the lessons of the Exodus: we were strangers in the land of Egypt. In the early childhood classroom, *Hachnasat Orchim* dictates relationships the children have with each other and the wider world. *Hachnasat Orchim* provides a reason for inviting the child you did not really want to play with into the house corner with you. *Hachnasat Orchim* also brings different classrooms together, visiting each other's rooms for special occasions or simple snacks.

Hazan et HaKol: Feeding Everyone   הַזָּן אֶת הַכֹּל

In the *Birkat HaMazon*, the Grace after meals, the first blessing praises God at length for nourishing the entire world, both with mercy and compassion as well as through physical sustenance. This first blessing ends by naming God, "*Hazan et Hakol* – Who nourishes all." As we strive to model our behavior after God's, it is incumbent upon us as well to feed those that are hungry. The Talmud tells us that a person that resides in a town for even thirty days is obligated to contribute to the local soup kitchen (*Bava Batra* 8a). *Hazan et Hakol* is a *mitzvah* that even the youngest children can participate in, in very concrete ways.

Hiddur Mitzvah: Beautifying a Mitzvah   הִדּוּר מִצְוָה

It is a Rabbinic principle that when an object is required to fulfill a *mitzvah* (such as a *mezzuzah*, challah cover, *tallit*, and so on), the object should be made as beautiful as possible. This attention to detail elevates the fulfillment of the *mitzvah* itself. This is a perfect principle for young children to grasp and grapple with. When children make ritual objects, they should always strive to choose the materials with an eye for beauty, in order to uphold this value.

Hoda'ah: Appreciation   הוֹדָאָה

Hoda'ah is an attitude and an ability to look around oneself at the trees, another person's face, or a kindness such as someone holding a door open as you approach, and feel and express gratitude. We might feel *Hoda'ah* when we see the wonders of God's creations in the world, when we interact with other people, and even when we notice things about ourselves, like a day of good health or the blessing of a friendship. We can express *Hoda'ah* through blessings, both traditional blessings that begin "*Baruch Atah Adonai...*" or *brachot sheh b'lev* — blessings of the heart — which come forth spontaneously in our own words. We say the *Amidah* prayer three times a day. The first three blessings of the *Amidah* specifically focus on praising God and acknowledging God's wonders. Young children can be guided to acknowledge and express *Hoda'ah* to God and to the people around them countless times every day.

Jewish Time: Making the Ordinary Sacred

Judaism guides our use of time in so many ways: from the daily rhythm of blessings to the pause before we take a bite of food, the weekly cycle of work and Shabbat, the yearly cycle of holidays, the cycle of a Jewish life, beginning with a *Bris* or *Simchat*

Bat, through Bar and Bat Mitzvah, a wedding under a *chuppah*, and even Jewish rituals for death and mourning. All these rituals provide opportunities for sanctifying time, for making sacred what would otherwise be an ordinary moment. When we live our life according to Jewish time — checking a Jewish calendar before we schedule a meeting or field trip, balancing obligations so that we may prioritize having time to do a *mitzvah* or participate in a *simcha* — we find our lives more holy, more invested in community, and more closely connected to God.

K'lal Yisrael: All Jews are One People   כְּלַל יִשְׂרָאֵל

There are many kinds of Jews in this world: Orthodox, Conservative, Reform, Reconstructionist, Sephardic, Ashkenazic, Israeli, American, etc. Jews have different beliefs, customs, foods, and languages, yet we are bound together as One People by God, Torah, and Israel. In the early childhood classroom, the value of *K'lal Yisrael* is instrumental in instilling in children an appreciation of and tolerance for differences. Exposing children to differences among Jews, through dress, food, language, songs, and stories opens children up to the benefits of variety, and will lay the foundation for tolerance of other people in the world, Jewish and non-Jewish, who are different from them.

Kavanah: Intention   כַּוָּנָה

Kavanah can also be translated as inner disposition, and usually refers to conscious intention in the performance of a *mitzvah* or in prayer. In general, *Kavanah* is considered of great ethical importance. With regard to prayer, the rabbis tell us, "Rather little prayer with intention than much without it." Having *Kavanah* requires us to focus our thoughts and energies, clearing away distractions to the best of our ability, so that we may attend to the *mitzvah* or prayer at hand with our entire being. For young children, this translates to the development of the ability to focus, to control one's impulses, and to learn to make good choices.

Kavod: Respect, Honor   כָּבוֹד

The fifth of the Ten Commandments is *Kibbud Av v'Eim*, Honor Your Father and Mother (Exodus 20:12). Basic human relations are based on *Kavod*, on showing respect to the people with whom we interact. By honoring other people, we honor God. In the early childhood classroom, it is essential that *Kavod* be a two way street. Teachers must show their children *Kavod*, and demand, by name, *Kavod* from the children.

Kedushah: Holiness   קְדֻשָׁה

Chapter 19 of Leviticus is known as the "Holiness Code." Of all the laws given to us in the Torah, this is the collection of *mitzvot*, behaviors, and expectations that, if followed, will make the Jewish people a holy people. At the very beginning of the chapter we are told, "You shall be holy, for I, the Lord your God, am holy." The rest of the chapter is filled with laws that guide us in holy ways to treat other people, from revering our parents, to leaving the corners when we reap our fields for the poor and the stranger, to respecting the elderly. When we remember the holiness of

God, the holiness with which God has filled the world, and the concept that we are each created in the image of God, then we can remember to act in accordance with the holiness that is in each one of us.

Kehillah: Community קְהִלָּה

Pirke Avot (2:5) tells us, "Do not separate yourself from the community." As important as Jewish home and the Jewish family are, Jewish life is dependent on the community. Jewish community creates a context for so many aspects of Jewish life: prayer, holiday celebrations, life cycle events, and more. Individual Jews cannot provide for all the needs of a community. It takes the entire community to support Jewish schools, take care of the needy and elderly, to build institutions such as synagogues and *mikvahs*, and on and on. A classroom community of children, teachers, and families is just the beginning of a child's entrance into the wider Jewish community, and should serve as that entrance way — not just as an insular community unto itself.

Kibud Av v'Eim : Honor your Father and Mother כִּבּוּד אָב וָאֵם

This *mitzvah* is one of the Ten Commandments (Exodus 20:12 and Deuteronomy 5:16). By honoring one's parents, one also gives honor to God. *Kibud Av v'Eim* refers to giving parents respect, through such actions as providing them with food and drink, clothes and warmth, and caring for them when they get old.

L'dor Vador : From Generation to Generation לְדוֹר וָדוֹר

The first *mitzvah* in the Torah is the commandment to be fruitful and multiply. However, our obligation goes beyond simply having children. We are obligated to transfer to our children our Jewish tradition. Stories, laws, tradition, holidays, culture, and Jewish wisdom are all parts of the tradition that we strive to transmit *L'dor Vador*. The Talmud tells the story of Honi, who comes across an old man planting a carob tree. Honi asks, "How long will it take this tree to bear fruit?" The man answers, "Seventy years." Honi comments, "Why work so hard? You will never be here to enjoy the fruits of your labors." To which the old man replies, "My parents and grandparents planted fruit trees for me, so I am planting fruit trees for my children and my grandchildren" (*Ta'anit* 22b).

L'ovda U'l'shomra: To Work and Keep the Land לְעָבְדָהּ וּלְשָׁמְרָהּ

In the very beginning of the Torah and the creation of the world, God makes clear our responsibility to the world which has just been created. "*V'yikach Adonai Elohim et ha'adam vayanicheihu b'gan eiden l'ovda u'l'shomra* — The Lord God took the man and placed him in the Garden of Eden, to till it and tend it" (Genesis 2:15). Our job from the very beginning is to develop the world. We can live this value with young children every day in the way we care for our surroundings, from picking up garbage on the playground to using recycled materials in our art projects to tending a garden.

Lichvod Shabbat: To Honor Shabbat לִכְבוֹד שַׁבָּת

In the two versions of the Ten Commandments we are told to remember Shabbat (*zachor* - Exodus 20:8) and keep Shabbat (*shamor* - Deuteronomy 5:15). The rabbis list thirty-nine categories of work that we are not allowed to do on Shabbat, but the behaviors that we can do that help us honor Shabbat are countless: baking challah so that the house is filled with its delicious aroma as Shabbat begins, lighting candles, sharing a meal with friends, taking a leisurely walk with our family, reading a book with our child, singing at the dinner table, taking a nap, and so on. The observance of Shabbat will look different for every family. What is most important is simply that each family heeds the words of Isaiah and strives to find their own way to call Shabbat "a delight."

Ma'aseh B'reishit: Miracle of Creation מַעֲשֵׂה בְּרֵאשִׁית

The value of *Ma'aseh Bereishit* acknowledges God as one who creates something from nothing. When we speak of *Ma'aseh B'reishit*, we strive to capture the feeling of amazement we experience when we encounter the creations in God's world: the beauty of a starlit night, the wonder of a sunset, the softness of a baby's cheek. Rabbi David Wolpe speaks of becoming a "normal mystic" — one who sees the hand of God in everything. *Ma'aseh B'reishit* helps us acknowledge and appreciate the wonder and miraculous nature of each of God's creations.

Masoret: Tradition מַסֹרֶת

The root of *Masoret* comes from the word "to transmit." Our Jewish tradition is made up of stories, holidays, foods, songs, dances, family, prayers, languages, texts, and history, among other elements. Just as we come together each year at the Passover *Seder* expressly to retell the story of our Exodus from Egypt (and to see if Aunt Sarah's chicken soup will be as good as the previous year's), Jewish life cycles around the transmission of tradition. As Tevya so eloquently put it in *Fiddler on the Roof*, "Without tradition our lives would be as shaky as a Fiddler on the Roof!"

Mikdash M'at: A Mini-sanctuary מִקְדָּשׁ מְעַט

When the Second Temple in Jerusalem was destroyed, the Jewish home became the center of religious and ritual life, a mini-sanctuary, as it were. The Jewish home is the center of education and identity, a source of peace and hospitality. When we view our home - and our classroom — as a *Mikdash M'at*, we can adjust our behaviors, attitudes, and relationships to better suit a holy place.

Mishpacha: Family מִשְׁפָּחָה

Jewish life revolves around the family. The first *mitzvah* — commandment — in the Torah is to be fruitful and multiply, essentially to create a family. Jewish life cycle events are designed to honor and enrich the family. The *chuppah* under which a bride and groom stand is open on all sides to allow family to be a part of the new union. We name our children after family members, either alive or dead, as is our custom, in the hopes that memories and positive traits will remain alive in the family. At a Bar Mitzvah, the Torah is passed from grandfather to father to Bar

Mitzvah boy. An important Shabbat ritual is the blessing of each of the members of the family. Holiday celebrations are far richer when filled with family, year after year. Each Jewish family is its own universe within the larger Jewish community, and every family has something to teach the larger community.

Mitzvot: Commandments מִצְוֹת

A *mitzvah* is not simply a good deed, although many *mitzvot* are good deeds. Because a *mitzvah* is something we are obligated to do, *mitzvot* take on additional meaning. It is not just a nice thing to give *tzedakah*. Rather, we are obligated to give *tzedakah* and help the needy. Judaism does not make suggestions about how to be good people, Judaism requires us to do good things and be good people. It is this obligation that makes us distinct, makes us *kadosh* (holy). In the early childhood classroom, we must be careful not to label every good deed a *mitzvah*, for indeed, there is a long, yet specific, list of good deeds which are *mitzvot*. *Mitzvot* are "God's rules." Many of the behaviors we do engage in with children are *mitzvot*, like giving *tzedakah*, saying blessings before we eat, etc., and we should certainly point this out to children. "We give *tzedakah* because it's a *mitzvah* to help other people. It is one of God's rules to give *tzedakah*."

Ohev et HaBriyot: Loving All Creatures אוֹהֵב אֶת הַבְּרִיוֹת

Pirke Avot (6:6) lists forty-eight virtues through which Torah is acquired, in other words, which are necessary for living a righteous life. *Ohev et HaBriyot* is one of the forty-eight, along with Loving God (*Ohev et HaMakom*) and Loving Justice (*Ohev et HaTzedakot*). To love God is not enough. One must also love one's fellow human beings as well as the rest of God's creatures.

Rosh Chodesh: The New Month רֹאשׁ חֹדֶשׁ

Rosh Chodesh is the holiday which marks the beginning of each new Hebrew month. Rosh Chodesh itself is marked by the appearance of the new crescent moon in the sky. It is a *mitzvah* to celebrate Rosh Chodesh with blessings and, especially for women, by refraining from work. The moon serves as a Jewish timekeeper, announcing many of our holidays and setting the Jewish calendar. Rosh Chodesh becomes a Jewish value when we acknowledge that observing Rosh Chodesh ties us into the cycle of Jewish time and the rhythm of Jewish life.

Sayver Panim Yafot: Cheerfulness, A Pleasant Demeanor סֵבֶר פָּנִים יָפוֹת

On the surface, this value stresses "putting on a happy face." Essentially, the value *Sayver Panim Yafot* is to greet each person cheerfully, be warmhearted in the company of others, and to show friendliness. While this virtue is not telling us to never be sad or angry, or to deny these feelings, *Sayver Panim Yafot* does remind us to try and not let these negative feelings poison our interactions with others. We are encouraged to be the first to extend a smile or warm greeting, and not to wait for someone else to make welcoming overtures first. We have biblical models: Abraham, Esau and Lavan *run* to offer greetings; they don't wait for others to take the first step. Going one step deeper, this acknowledgement of the power of our face, our apparent attitude, brings to mind the concept of God's face, and the Priestly Benediction which includes the blessing, "May God's face shine upon you..." (Numbers 6:24). When a person's face shines, the light of the soul — the divine spark within each one of us — is reflected out, bringing the light of God's face into interactions with other people.

Sh'lom Bayit: Peace Within the Home   שְׁלוֹם בַּיִת

Sh'lom Bayit can also be translated as "family harmony." The Talmud speaks at length of kind and generous ways a husband must treat his wife. *Sh'lom Bayit* requires men and women, adults and children, to restrain their tempers with family members, knowing that people are often more polite with strangers and non-family members than they are with those closest to them. The value of *Sh'lom Bayit* reminds us to go out of our way to make our homes and our family relationships sources of sanctuary and well-being. (For a *Sh'lom Bayit* lesson plan, see Appendix 1 in *Teaching Jewish Virtues* by Susan Freeman, p. 347.)

Shalom: Peace, Completeness   שָׁלוֹם

"The whole Torah exists only for the sake of shalom," according to the Talmud (*Tanhuma, Shoftim* 18). Jewish prayer is filled with supplications for shalom. "Grant us Peace, your most precious gift, O Eternal Source of peace..." One of the names for God is *Oseh Shalom* — Maker of Peace. We are a people that, with a history so full of tumult and destruction, seek serenity and security, not only for ourselves, but for the whole world. "Shalom" is even the salutation we use when greeting each other or taking our leave. In the early childhood classroom, the value of Shalom takes us beyond another way to get the children quiet. Psalms 34:15 tells us "Seek peace and pursue it." Children can become *Rod'fay Shalom* — "pursuers of peace," finding ways to bring calm and community to their own classroom (one child is a *Rodef Shalom*). Peace requires action. Children can practice the *mitzvah* of *Hava'at Shalom ben Adam L'chaveiro*, bringing peace between people, by learning to mediate their own arguments. Children can learn the value of *Sh'lom Bayit,* creating peace in the home. Songs like *Oseh Shalom* and *Sim Shalom* can be regular features in the classroom song repertoire.

Shmirat HaGuf: Caring for the Body   שְׁמִירַת הַגּוּף

We are taught in Judaism that the body is a gift from God, that is does not really *belong* to us. Such a precious gift, a loan really, must be treated with respect and care. On a basic level, *Shmirat HaGuf* tells us we must care for our body by eating, bathing, sleeping, and exercising. On a deeper level, the value of *Shmirat HaGuf* reminds us of what an amazing creation the body is, one we must tend to with appreciation and responsibility. Gratitude to God and respectful, loving care of our body is all part of *Shmirat HaGuf.*

Shmiat HaOzen: Attentiveness   שְׁמִיעַת הָאֹזֶן

Shmiat HaOzen is included in Pirke Avot as one of the virtues necessary for acquiring Torah, for the way we should behave in general. The literal meaning is "a listening of the ear." *Shmiat HaOzen* goes far beyond mere listening. It includes understanding, evaluating, obeying, responding, and more. Listening to one's teachers and classmates in order to understand and absorb one's studies is all part of *Shmiat HaOzen*. But the root of "*shmiat*" is "*sh'ma*" — to listen with our whole heart, not just once but as part of an ongoing relationship. *Shmiat HaOzen* reminds us to try to be like God, a compassionate listener, to try and listen in an unbiased way to all people.

Shomrei Adamah: Guardian of the Earth שׁוֹמְרֵי אֲדָמָה

Love of nature and protection of the environment are values deeply embedded in Jewish values and texts. Jewish holidays such as Tu B'Shevat, Sukkot, Pesach and Shavuot promote conservation and/or thankfulness for the world God created. Parts of the Torah explicitly forbid wasteful practices. Respect for *Adonai*, central to Judaism, clearly translates into respect for our earth.

Simcha shel Mitzvah: Joy in Fulfilling a Commandment שִׂמְחָה שֶׁל מִצְוָה

"*Simcha*" means joy or happiness. *Simcha* might refer to a temporary state of elation, such as one might feel dancing at a wedding, or a general sense of well being, such as being able to appreciate everyday blessings. A sense of *simcha* may come from doing *mitzvot* (commandments) as well. Living a righteous and ethical life adds to a sense of our own well-being. We are likely to be happier ourselves when we treat others with dignity. When we perform a *mitzvah*, such as bringing food to a family with a new baby or visiting someone who is ill, we feel good. Performing *mitzvot* with an attitude of *simcha* helps us enjoy the highest highs of celebrations, as well as serving us with a sustaining sense of contentment and joy in our day-to-day lives.

Storytelling: Passing On the Oral Tradition

Judaism is a tradition sustained by stories. Ours is an oral tradition, from the ancient Midrash to modern tales, which twist and change through every time and every culture in which Jews have lived. In the forward to *Chosen Tales: Stories Told By Jewish Storytellers*, Rabbi Avraham Weiss describes stories as a chain, a tradition (*masoret*) which is both mutable and unbreakable. The stories we tell change with each teller who takes ownership and retells the story in his or her own voice. Yet the chain is unbreakable, as each of us passes on the meaning and intent of the stories we hear through our actions and through other stories we tell. Rabbi Weiss reminds us that "stories can help us grow in Torah." Peninnah Schram, editor of the same book, reminds us that storytelling is all about the sharing of stories so that stories can continue to be told.

T'filat HaDerech: Traveler's Prayer תְּפִלַת הַדֶּרֶךְ

T'filat HaDerech is traditionally recited by a person making a journey of some distance, as the journey is begun. While *T'filat HaDerech* is a prayer, it also represents the value of *b'techon* — security — as well as the acknowledgement that God is with us wherever we go. The prayer requests that our journey be made in *shalom* — peace — and that we reach our destination in *shalom*. We ask God to protect us from danger and enemies along the way. This prayer, written especially for a person "on the way," helps us acknowledge that God journeys with us, that we may seek protection and comfort from God at times of uncertainty. As we leave the comfort of home and set out on the road (or the airplane), God is with us all the time, wherever we may go.

Talmud Torah: Study/Love of Learning תַּלְמוּד תּוֹרָה

The Jewish People have been referred to as "The People of the Book," and indeed, so much of Judaism is centered around learning and the joy and fulfillment it brings to our lives. The Mishnah tells us that the study of Torah is equal to all the other commandments. Rabbi Akiva tells us that study is greater than practice, because it leads to practice. The ideal approach to study is *Torah Lishma* — study for its own sake. When a child begins his or her education, it is a Jewish tradition to put a drop of honey on the child's book, so that the studies should be sweet and tempting.

Teshuvah: Repentance תְּשׁוּבָה

The Talmud relates this story: Rabbi Eliezer said, "Repent one day before your death." His disciples asked him, "But one does not know on which day he will die." "All the more reason he should repent today, lest he die tomorrow" (*Shabbat* 153a). While the holiest day of the Jewish calendar is Yom Kippur, the Day of Atonement, the prayers we say on this day only apply to seeking forgiveness for sins committed against God. For offenses committed against other people, we must go directly to those people to seek forgiveness. Jewish tradition holds that *teshuvah* includes recognizing one's offense, feeling sincere remorse, undoing any damage done and appeasing the victim, and resolving never to do the offense again. And if one is a victim and the offender sincerely requests forgiveness, Jewish law requires the victim to grant forgiveness, at least by the third request.

Tikkun Olam: Repair of the World תִּקּוּן עוֹלָם

In the *Aleinu* prayer, we place our hopes in God that the world will be perfected through God's reign. Yet it is not up to God alone. We are God's partners in the completion of creation. This *mitzvah* illustrates the reciprocal relationship which God established between humans and the earth. It is our obligation to take care of the earth, and in turn, it takes care of us. Major Jewish social action efforts are based on the value of *Tikkun Olam*. *Tikkun Olam* includes the *mitzvah* of *Bal Tashchit*, preserving the earth. In the early childhood classroom, *Tikkun Olam* is embodied in efforts to not be wasteful with supplies and resources, in the way the children care for the living things (such as plants and animals) in their room, and in the way they care for their playground and other outdoor spaces. We are partners with God in the completion and repair of the world. Children will rise to opportunities to act as God's partner and take care of their world, if they are given the vocabulary of the Jewish values and *mitzvot* to go along with their actions.

Tza'ar Ba'alei Chayim: Kindness to Animals צַעַר בַּעֲלֵי חַיִּים

Tza'ar Ba'alei Chayim translates literally as preventing the pain of animals. According to Jewish law, we are allowed to use animals for our benefit, but they must be treated kindly because they too are God's creatures. Even when we kill animals for food or other uses, we must do everything within our ability to minimize the animal's pain. In the classroom, children are observing *Tza'ar Ba'alei Chayim* when they help to take care of the class pet, or when they guide a fly outside rather than swatting it. As Proverbs 12:10 teaches, "A righteous man knows the needs of his beast."

Tzedakah: Justice and Righteousness צְדָקָה

"*Tzedek, tzedek tirdof - Justice, justice shall you pursue*" (Deuteronomy 16:20). Although *tzedakah* is often translated as "charity," it has much wider connotations in the sense of giving back, or doing justice. Giving *tzedakah* is a *mitzvah*; the rabbis determined specific percentages of our income which we are obligated to give for *tzedakah*. We give because as Jews we are commanded to help, not just because it is a nice thing to do. Giving *tzedakah* is the just and right thing to do, and includes giving money, clothing, food, and time. In the early childhood classroom, *tzedakah* should take many forms, so that children are not limited to the "Penny in the *Pushke*" definition of *tzedakah*. Food drives, gently used clothing and toy drives, visiting nursing homes, all of these are and should be labeled as *tzedakah*. *Tzedakah* is another way we relate to the world around us.

V'achalta V'savata : To Eat and be Satisfied וְאָכַלְתָּ וְשָׂבָעְתָּ

The second blessing of *Birkat Hamazon*, the "blessing for food" which we say after a meal, concludes with this quote from the Torah: *V'achalta v'savata uvei'rachta et Adonai Elohecha, al ha'aretz hatova asher natan lach.* "When you have eaten your fill, give thanks to the Lord your God for the good land which He has given you" (Deuteronomy 8:10). This passage establishes a clear connection between being blessed with enough food and the land, reminding us that we depend on God for the food, and that we have a unique connection to the Land of Israel.

V'Samachta B'chagecha: Rejoicing in our Festivals וְשָׂמַחְתָּ בְּחַגֶּיךָ

Deuteronomy Chapter 16 lists the *Shalosh Regalim*, the Three Pilgrimage Festivals: Pesach, Shavuot, and Sukkot. About Sukkot, we are told: *V'Samachta b'chagecha, atah u'vin-cha . . .* "You shall rejoice in your festival, with your son and daughter . . ." (Deuteronomy 16:14). The list goes on to include numerous others in the community as well. While the passage here in the Torah is instructing us to rejoice after an intense period of self-scrutiny (Rosh Hashanah and Yom Kippur), we can extend the value of *V'samachta B'chagecha* to how we approach every holiday, especially in the early childhood classroom. *V'Samachta B'chagecha* is our reminder to approach each holiday on the Jewish calendar, even Shabbat, with a heart full of joy, reaching out to the entire community as we celebrate and rejoice.

Appendix B
Guide to Hebrew Pronunciation

The pronunciation in this book generally follows current Israeli usage. Accordingly, Hebrew words are accented on the final syllable unless otherwise noted. In the Hebrew Vocabulary and Blessings sections of each unit, the accented syllables are denoted with bold type.

The transliterated Hebrew found throughout this book generally conforms to the system widely used in most North American *siddurim*. The following guidelines for pronunciation will be helpful for the non-Hebrew speaker:

a	"ah" as in "father" (never as in "sat" or "date")
ah	"ah" as in "father" (used only at the end of a word)
e	"e" as in "bed"
eh	"e" as in "bed" (used only at the end of a word)
i	"ee" as in "visa" (never as in "sit" or "right")
o	"oh" as in "post"
u	"oo" as in "rule" (never as in "foot" or "rush")
ai	"eye" as in "aisle"
ei	"ay" as in "weigh"
oi	"oy" is in "toil"
g	as in "good" (hard 'g' — very rarely soft 'j')
ch	as in the Scottish "loch" or German "ach" (never as in "cheese")
y	as in "yellow" (always as a consonant when an initial letter)

By way of example, the phrase
   Hi-**nei** mah tov u-ma-**na**-im **she**-vet a-**chim** gam **ya**-chad
would be pronounced,
   "Hee-**nay** mah tove oo-mah-**na**-yeem **sheh**-vet ah-**cheem** gahm **yah**-chahd."

Certain words that have become accepted as standard or familiar English have not been changed — for example, Shabbat, challah, siddur, Kiddush. In these cases the doubling of the middle consonant has been kept even though the system of transliteration does not require it.

With a little practice, a non-Hebrew speaker can quickly become proficient at reading transliterated Hebrew.

Bibliography and General Resources

Jewish Values and Reference Books

Birnbaum, Philip. *A Book of Jewish Concepts.* New York: Hebrew Publishing Co., 1964.
   Definitions of some of the most important Jewish concepts and values.

Diamant, Anita with Howard Cooper. *Living a Jewish Life: Jewish Traditions, Customs and Values for Today's Families.* New York: Harper Collins Publishers, 1991.
   Describes how the customs of modern Judaism may be integrated into everyday life.

Jacobs, Louis. *The Book of Jewish Belief.* New York: Behrman House, Inc., 1984.
   What every Jewish early childhood educator should know about Jewish faith and values.

Kadden, Barbara Binder and Bruce Kadden. *Teaching Mitzvot: Concepts, Values and Activities.* Rev. ed. Denver, CO: A.R.E. Publishing, Inc., 2003.
   Overviews of forty-one mitzvot with hundreds of related activities.

Klagsbrun, Francine. *Voices of Wisdom: Jewish Ideals and Ethics for Everyday Living.* New York: Pantheon Books, 1980.
   An anthology of the Jewish tradition organized to address the concerns and controversies of Jewish life today

Leyvy, Ya'akov, ed. *Oxford English-Hebrew/Hebrew-English Dictionary.* Jerusalem: Kernerman Publishing Ltd., 1995.
   Modern dictionary with over 75,000 entries.

Frankel, Ellen and Betsy Platkin Teutsch. *The Encyclopedia of Jewish Symbols.* Northvale, New Jersey: Jason Aronson Inc., 1992.
   Jewish symbols as they help the integration of Jewish words with images within the Jewish culture.

Freeman, Susan. *Teaching Jewish Virtues: Sacred Sources and Arts Activities.* Denver, CO: A.R.E. Publishing, Inc., 1999.
   Substantive overviews of twenty-two middot (Jewish virtues), along with extensive text study material and hundreds of imaginative arts activities.

Glustrom, Simon. *The Language of Judaism.* Northvale, New Jersey: Jason Aronson Inc., 1988.
   This book gives readers translations for Hebrew as well as deeper understanding of the context behind the words.

Sivan, Dr. Reuven and Levenston, Dr. Edward A. *The New Bantam – Megiddo Hebrew & English Dictionary.* Toronto: Bantam Books, 1986.
   A comprehensive, one volume English/Hebrew, Hebrew/English Dictionary with concise explanation of the essentials of grammar in both languages.

Telushkin, Joseph. *The Book of Jewish Values: A Day-by-Day Guide to Ethical Living.* New York: Bell Tower, 2000.
> *365 nuggets of rabbinical wisdom on everything from anger to Maimonides to the telephone.*

Telushkin, Joseph. *Jewish Literacy.* New York: William Morrow and Company, Inc., 1991.
> *350 of the most important things to know about the Jewish religion, its people, and its history.*

Jewish Texts

Herford, R. Travers. *Pirke Avot - The Ethics of the Talmud: Sayings of the Fathers (Text, Complete Translation and Commentaries).* New York: Schocken Books, 1962.
> *Complete text of the Pirke Avot (Sayings of the Fathers).*

JPS Hebrew-English Tanakh. Philadelphia, PA: Jewish Publication Society, 1999.
> *Original Hebrew and contemporary English side by side.*

Kravitz, Leonard and Kerry M. Olitzky. *Pirke Avot.* New York: UAHC Press, 1993.
> *A modern commentary on Jewish ethics, edited and translated.*

Lieber, David L. *Etz Hayim Torah and Commentary.* Philadelphia, PA: The Rabbinical Assembly, 2001.
> *Torah text in Hebrew and modern English.*

Scherman, Nosson, ed. *The Complete Artscroll Siddur.* New York: Mesorah Publications, 1984.
> *Orthodox siddur with helpful commentaries.*

Teutsch, Rabbi David A., ed. *Kol Haneshamah: Limot Hol — The Daily Prayer Book.* Wyncote, Pennsylvania: The Reconstructionist Press, 1996.
> *Features liturgy for a daily minyan, ritual observances, and special readings.*

———. *Kol Haneshamah: Nashir Unevareh — Songs and Grace after Meals.* Wyncote, PA: The Reconstructionist Press, 1991.
> *A benscher with several vesions of the Birkat HaMazon (Grace after Meals), plus table songs.*

———. *Kol Haneshamah: Shabbat Vehagim — The Sabbath and Festivals.* Wyncote, PA: The Reconstructionist Press, 1996.
> *Entire liturgy for Kabbalat Shabbat, Shabbat morning and afternoon, and the pilgrimage festivals, as well as an extensive readings section.*

———. *Kol Haneshamah: Shirim Uvrahot — Songs and Blessings.* Wyncote, PA: The Reconstructionist Press, 1991.
> Shabbat and holiday table songs, blessings, prayers, and rituals for the home.

Education and Story Anthologies

Berk, Laura E. and Adam Winsler. *Scaffolding Children's Learning: Vygotsky and Early Childhood Education.* Washington, DC: National Association for the Education of Young Children, 1995.
The key concepts of Vygotsky's theories are explain and applied to early childhood education.

Frankel, Ellen. *The Classic Tales: 4,000 Years of Jewish Lore.* Northvale, NJ: Jason Aronson, Inc., 1989.
Classic stories and tales of Jewish legend; very accesible and good for reading aloud.

Handelman, Maxine Segal. *Jewish Every Day: The Complete Handbook for Early Childhood Teachers.* Denver, CO: A.R.E. Publishing, Inc., 2000.
An essential handbook for every Jewish early childhood educator.

Machon L'Morim: Bereshit Curriculum Guides. Baltimore, MD: Center for Jewish Education, 1998.
A professional development program designed to facilitate the integration of Jewish concepts and values into everyday secular themes. Available from the Center for Jewish Education, 5708 Park Heights Avenue, Baltimore, MD 21215, (410) 578-6943 or http://www.machonlmorim.org.

Moskowitz, Nachama Skolnik. *The Ultimate Jewish Teacher's Handbook.* Denver, CO: A.R.E. Publishing, Inc., 2003.
Chapter One, "Beyond Apples and Honey: The Editor's Soapbox" contains a wonderful discussion of Enduring Understandings.

Schram, Peninnah, ed. *Chosen Tales: Stories Told by Jewish Storytellers.* Northvale, NJ: Jason Aronson Inc., 1995.
Extraordinary collection of stories told by nearly seventy gifted storytellers.

Wiggins, Grant and Jay McTighe. *Understanding by Design.* Alexandria, VA: Association for Supervision and Curriculum Development, 1998.
A multifaceted approach to curriculum design, including criteria for identifying "Big Ideas" that lead to enhanced, enduring understanding.

Songbooks

Eisenstein, Judith Kaplan, Frieda Prensky, and Ayala Gordon. *Songs of Childhood.* New York: United Synagogue Commission on Jewish Education, 1955.
A wonderful book filled with Hebrew songs of childhood for all occasions including everyday activities, community workers, holidays, trips, and seasons. The Hebrew words are all written in transliteration, include simple translation, and are easy to read. Out of print, may be found in libraries or resource centers.

Gardosh, Daniela and Talma Alyagon. *100 Shirim Rishonim. (100 First Songs).* Tel Aviv, Israel: Kineret Publishing House, 1970.
Classic Israeli children's songs, available at http://www.israeliscent.com.

Jules, Jacqueline. *Clap and Count!: Action Rhymes for the Jewish Year.* Minneapolis, MN: Kar-Ben Publishing, 2001.

Jules puts a Jewish spin on a bounty of finger plays, nursery rhymes, and clapping games, including both original poems and new takes on such familiar selections.

Pasternak, Velvel. *The New Children's Songbook: 110 Hebrew Songs for the Young.* Cedarhurst, NY: Tara Publications, 1981.

110 accessible songs for Shabbat, holidays, seasons, and more. Includes melody line, chords, Hebrew texts, transliterations, and activity suggestions.

Richards, Stephen, ed. *The Complete Jewish Songbook for Children: Manginot.* New York: Transcontinental Music Publications, 2002.

Comprehensive collection of 201 Jewish songs for holidays, everyday, or just for fun. Songbook includes melody line with chords.

Rivkin, Nacha and Ella Shurin, *Come Sing With Me.* Cedarhurst, NY: Tara Publications, 1984.

Sixty-five charming songs for Shabbat and the Holidays, everyday Hebrew vocabulary, Jewish values and more! Based on four successful `Shiru Li` recordings. Melody line, chords, singable English settings, texts, transliterations, and translations.

Rouss, Sylvia A. *Fun With Jewish Holiday Rhymes.* New York: Union of American Hebrew Congregations, 1992.

Illustrated rhymes accompanied by movement activities introduce the holidays of the Jewish calendar.

General Jewish Recordings for Children

Abrams, Leah. *Apples on Holidays and Other Days.* Cedarhurst, NY: Tara Publications, 1988.

Compact disc, cassette, and book available from Tara Publications, (800) TARA-400 or http://www.jewishmusic.com.

Auerbach, Julie Jaslow. *Seasoned with Song.* Shaker Heights, OH: Julie Jaslow Auerbach, 1989.

Audiocassette, available from A.R.E. Publishing, Inc., (800) 346-7779 or http://www.arepublish.com.

Black, Rabbi Joe. *Aleph Bet Boogie.* Albuquerque, NM: Lanitunes Music, 1991.

Compact disc, available from A.R.E. Publishing, Inc., (800) 346-7779 or http://www.arepublish.com.

———. *Everybody's Got a Little Music.* Albuquerque, NM: Lanitunes Music, 1992.

Compact disc, available from A.R.E. Publishing, Inc., (800) 346-7779 or http://www.arepublish.com.

Friedman, Debbie. *Shirim Al Galgalim: Songs on Wheels.* San Diego, CA: Sounds Write Productions, 1995.

Compact disc, available from A.R.E. Publishing, Inc., (800) 346-7779 or http://www.arepublish.com.

——. *And You Shall Be A Blessing.* San Diego, CA: Sounds Write Productions, 1989.
Compact disc, available from A.R.E. Publishing, Inc., (800) 346-7779 or
http://www.arepublish.com.

Gardosh, Daniela and Talma Alyagon. *100 Shirim Rishonim (100 First Songs).* Tel
Aviv, Israel: Kineret Publishing House, 1970.
Compact disc, available at http://www.israeliscent.com.

Ginsburgh, Judy Caplan. *Amazing Songs for Amazing Jewish Kids.* Alexandria, LA:
Judy Caplan Ginsburgh, 2000.
Compact disc, available from A.R.E. Publishing, Inc., (800) 346-7779 or
http://www.arepublish.com.

——. *Boker Tov/Laila Tov.* Alexandria, LA: Judy Caplan Ginsburgh, 1989.
Compact disc, available from A.R.E. Publishing, Inc., (800) 346-7779 or
http://www.arepublish.com.

——. *My Jewish World: Kids Songs for Everyday Living.* New York: Transcontinental Music Publications, 2003.
Compact disc, available from Transcontinental Music, (800) 455-5223 or
http://www.etranscon.com.

——. *Shalom Yeladim/Hello Children.* Alexandria, LA: Judy Caplan Ginsburgh,
1993.
Compact disc, available from A.R.E. Publishing, Inc., (800) 346-7779 or
http://www.arepublish.com.

Helzner, Robyn. *I Live in the City.* Washington, DC: RAH Productions, n.d.
Compact disc, available from http://www.helzner.com.

Kol B'Seder. *Songs for Growin'.* New York: Transcontinental Music Publications,
2001.
Compact disc, available from A.R.E. Publishing, Inc., (800) 346-7779 or
http://www.arepublish.com.

Mah Tovu. *Days of Wonder, Nights of Peace: Family Prayers in Song for Morning and
Bedtime.* Springfield, NJ: Behrman House, Inc., 2001.
Booklet with compact disc, available from Behrman House, Inc., (800)221-2755 or
http://www.behrmanhouse.com.

——. *Only This.* Denver, CO: Mah Tovu, 1996.
Compact disc, available from A.R.E. Publishing, Inc., (800) 346-7779 or
http://www.arepublish.com.

Paley, Cindy. *Eizeh Yom Sameach/What a Happy Day!* Sherman Oaks, CA: Cindy
Paley Aboody.
Compact disc, available from Sounds Write Productions, Inc., (800) 9-SOUND-9 or
http://www.soundswrite.com.

Recht, Rick. *Free to be the Jew In Me.* St. Louis, MO: Vibe Room Records, 2002.
Compact disc, available from A.R.E. Publishing, Inc., (800) 346-7779 or
http://www.arepublish.com.

Sally and the Daffodils. *Tap Your Feet to a Jewish Beat.* Silver Spring, MD: Daffodil Music, 1996.
> *Compact disc, available from Tara Publications, (800) TARA-400 or http://www.jewishmusic.com.*

Shirim K'tanim (Little Songs). Jerusalem: Scopus Films, n.d.
> *Series of VHS videos, available from http://www.scopusfilms.com or Lambda Publishers Inc., (718) 972-5449. Audio CDs also available from http://www.israeliscent.com.*

Taubman, Craig. *My Jewish Discovery.* Sherman Oaks, CA: Craig 'n Co, 1995.
> *Compact disc, available from A.R.E. Publishing, Inc., (800) 346-7779 or http://www.arepublish.com.*

———. *My Newish Jewish Discovery.* Sherman Oaks, CA: Craig 'n Co., 1997.
> *Compact disc, available from A.R.E. Publishing, Inc., (800) 346-7779 or http://www.arepublish.com.*

Various Artists. *Good Morning, Good Night: Jewish Children's Songs for Daytime and Bedtime.* New York: Transcontinental Music Publications, 2001.
> *Compact disc, available from Transcontinental Music, (800) 455-5223 or http://www.etranscon.com.*

Online Hebrew Resources

Akhlah – the Jewish Children's Learning network
http://www.akhlah.com
> *Has a spoken aleph-bet so you can hear the names of each letter, as well as a dictionary and other teaching tools.*

Animated Ulpan
http://www.aish.com/literacy/judaism123/Speak_Hebrew_with_Moshe_and_Leah.asp
> *Cute vignettes with spoken Hebrew. Vocabulary lists in Hebrew and transliteration are provided as well.*

Behrman House Online Ulpan Aleph
http://www.behrmanhouse.com/ua/
> *Vocalizes words in a variety of subject areas, but does not provide transliteration. A little hard to use if you are simply searching to find out how to translate and pronounce an English word into Hebrew.*

J — Jewish Education and Entertainment
http://www.j.co.il/
> *This site has many Hebrew resources. The Language Match game pronounces the words in Hebrew.*

Jacob Richman's Hot Sites — Jewish — Hebrew Learning Sites
http://www.jr.co.il/hotsites/j-hebrew.htm
> *A listing of many Hebrew learning sites.*

My Hebrew Picture Dictionary
http://www.milon.co.il
> *Has photos and words in English, Hebrew and transliteration.*

A.R.E. Publishing, Inc.

Your source for the finest in contemporary Jewish music, included many of the recordings cited in *What's Jewish about Butterflies?*

Aleph Bet Boogie
Rabbi Joe Black

**And You Shall Be
A Blessing**
Debbie Friedman

Shirim Al Galgalim
Debbie Friedman

Shalom Yeladim
Judy Caplan Ginsburgh

In Every Generation
Kol B'Seder

**Snapshots: The Best of
Kol B'Seder Vol. 1**
Kol B'Seder

Songs for Growin'
Kol B'Seder

Only This
Mah Tovu

Free To Be the Jew In Me
Rick Recht

Available from:

A.R.E. Publishing, Inc. ◆ 6708 E. 47th Avenue Drive ◆ Denver, Colorado 80216-3409
Toll-free (800) 346-7779 ◆ In Colorado (303) 322-7400 ◆ FAX (303) 322-7407
E-mail: orders@arepublish.com ◆ On the Web at www.arepublish.com

If you like *What's Jewish about Butterflies?* you'll love

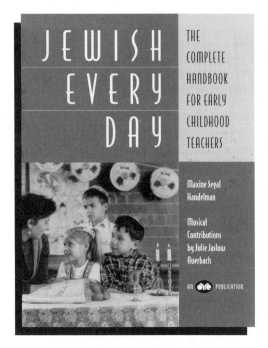

JEWISH EVERY DAY
The Complete Handbook for Early Childhood Teachers

By Maxine Segal Handelman
With musical contributions by Julie Jaslow Auerbach

A cutting-edge handbook for Jewish early childhood educators!

The field of Jewish early childhood education is constantly evolving. In recent decades, new approaches — developmentally appropriate practice, Reggio Emilia, emergent curriculum, anti-bias education, and others — have had an enormous impact on the field. Change is definitely in the wind for Jewish early childhood education, as well. At last, here is a guide to help integrate into the Jewish classroom the best that the secular field has to offer.

It is indeed a challenge to make our early childhood classrooms Jewish every day, and not just on holidays and Shabbat. This outstanding and comprehensive book will enable every teacher to create a Jewish developmentally appropriate classroom, one in which Jewish values and themes permeate every learning experience every day. God, Torah, and Israel, the cornerstones of Judaism, are fully explored. Twelve holiday chapters provide substantial background information for the teacher, as well as concepts for each age level and engaging and unque activities. Further chapters discuss storytelling, music, secular holidays, working with interfaith families, keeping kosher at school, and even how to make the summer Jewish time. An extensive bibliography accompanies each chapter, and a comprehensive list of resources, including arts and crafts, music and movement, games, science, cookbooks, and much more is provided at the end of the volume.

Written in a warm and understanding tone by an expert in Jewish early childhood education (one of the authors of *What's Jewish about Butterflies?*), *Jewish Every Day* is an invaluable contemporary resource — a must for every early childhood teacher!

Available from:

A.R.E. Publishing, Inc. ◆ 6708 E. 47th Avenue Drive ◆ Denver, Colorado 80216-3409
Toll-free (800) 346-7779 ◆ In Colorado (303) 322-7400 ◆ FAX (303) 322-7407
E-mail: orders@arepublish.com ◆ On the Web at www.arepublish.com